SOUTHERN
Home Plans

Design EE9645, p.28

Over 200 Homes From The South & Southeast

- **Southern Farmhouse & Country Styles**
- **Atlanta Classics**
- **Tennessee Traditional & Memphis Homes**

- **Texas Brick & Mansion Styles**
- **Florida, Spanish & Mediterranean Designs**
- **Coastal, Tidewater & Island Designs**

HOME PLANNERS, INC.

Published by Home Planners, Inc.
Editorial and Corporate Offices:
3275 West Ina Road, Suite 110
Tucson, Arizona 85741

Distribution Center:
29333 Lorie Lane
Wixom, Michigan 48393

Rickard D. Bailey, President and Publisher
Cindy J. Coatsworth, Publications Manager
Paulette Mulvin, Senior Editor
Amanda Shaver, Project Editor
Paul D. Fitzgerald, Book Designer

Photo Credits
Front Cover: Susan DuPlessis
Back Cover: Andrew D. Lautman

First Printing, September 1994

10 9 8 7 6 5 4 3 2 1

Printed in the United States of America.

Library of Congress Catalog Card Number: 94-076446

ISBN: 1-881955-18-4

On the front cover: Warmth radiates from this cozy Southern farmhouse,
Design EE9645. And with an ample interior, family and friends will feel
right at home. Page 28 provides a closer look.

On the back cover: In grand style, this home—Design EE2889—defines
the best of Southern Colonial design. See page 88 for all the details.

TABLE OF CONTENTS

Editor's Note

From Maryland to Tennessee, Florida to Texas, the architectural traditions of the South come together in this book to provide an excellent array of home-building opportunities. The growing home-building industry in the South, as well as an increased interest in Southern home designs nationally, underscore the popularity and significance of these regional architectural styles. In this collection, fanciful Southern Colonials capture the imagination of those interested in making new histories, while sunny Floridians satisfy the beachcomber. Punctuated with adaptations such as Jefferson's Poplar Forest home and Louisiana's Rosedown House, variety is the only constant. A turn of the page starts you on the road to your dream home, Southern style!

About The Designers

The Blue Ribbon Designer Series™ is a collection of books featuring the home plans of a diverse group of outstanding home designers and architects known as the Blue Ribbon Network of Designers. This group of companies is dedicated to creating and marketing the finest possible plans for home construction on a regional and national basis. Each of the companies exhibits superior work and integrity in all phases of the stock-plan business including modern, trendsetting floor planning, a professionally executed blueprint package and a strong sense of service and commitment to the consumer.

Design Basics, Inc.

For nearly a decade, Design Basics, a nationally recognized home design service located in Omaha, has been developing plans for custom home builders. Since 1987, the firm has consistently appeared in *Builder* magazine, the official magazine of the National Association of Home Builders, as the top-selling designer. The company's plans also regularly appear in numerous other shelter magazines such as *Better Homes and Gardens, House Beautiful* and *Home Planner*.

Design Traditions

Design Traditions was established by Stephen S. Fuller with the tenets of innovation, quality, originality and uncompromising architectural techniques in traditional and European homes. Especially popular throughout the Southeast, Design Traditions' plans are known for their extensive detail and thoughtful design. They are widely published in such shelter magazines as *Southern Living* magazine and *Better Homes and Gardens*.

Larry E. Belk Designs

Through the years, Larry E. Belk has worked with individuals and builders alike to provide a quality product. After listening to over 4,000 dreams and watching them become reality all across America, Larry's design philosophy today combines traditional exteriors with upscale interiors designed for contemporary lifestyles. Flowing, open spaces and interesting angles define his interiors. Great emphasis is placed on providing views that showcase the natural environment. Dynamic exteriors reflect Larry's extensive home construction experience, painstaking research and talent as a fine artist.

Larry W. Garnett & Associates, Inc.

Starting as a designer of homes for Houston-area residents, Garnett & Associates has been marketing designs nationally for the past ten years. A well-respected design firm, the company's plans are regularly featured in *House Beautiful, Country Living, Home* and *Professional Builder*. Numerous accolades, including several from the Texas Institute of Building Design and the American Institute of Building Design, have been awarded to the company for excellence in architecture.

Home Planners, Inc.

Headquartered in Tucson, Arizona, with additional offices in Detroit, Home Planners is one of the longest-running and most successful home design firms in the United States. With over 2,500 designs in its portfolio, the company provides a wide range of styles, sizes and types of homes for the residential builder. All of Home Planners' designs are created with the care and professional expertise that fifty years of experience in the home-planning business affords. Their homes are designed to be built, lived in and enjoyed for years to come.

Donald A. Gardner, Architects, Inc.

The South Carolina firm of Donald A. Gardner was established in response to a growing demand for residential designs that reflect constantly changing lifestyles. The company's specialty is providing homes with refined, custom-style details and unique features such as passive-solar designs and open floor plans. Computer-aided design and drafting technology resulting in trouble-free construction documents places the firm at the leading edge of the home plan industry.

The Sater Group, Inc.

The Sater Group, Inc. has a long established tradition of providing South Florida's most diverse and extraordinary custom designed homes. Their goal is to fulfill each client's particular need for an exciting approach to design by merging creative vision with elements that satisfy a desire for a distinctive lifestyle. This philosophy is proven, as exemplified by over 50 national design awards, numerous magazine features and, most important, satisfied clients. The result is an elegant statement of lasting beauty and value.

Southern Farmhouses

With its porches and unpretentious warmth, the farmhouse lends itself well to Southern lifestyles. Where rains could prevent opening windows to coax breezes indoors, the Southern Farmhouse features wrapping porches to provide protection and the perfect spot for that favorite rocking chair or porch swing. This "high and dry" characteristic is extended to the actual foundation of the house, which is often raised off wet and soggy ground. And such additions as a rear deck with a spa add not only an air of modernism, but fit well with the outdoor sensibilities present in such a temperate climate. Abundant woodlands lend themselves to the building of these houses; wood siding, shingles, posts and columns are found on many designs. With 1½ or two stories of livability, central gathering areas and split sleeping arrangements characterize the comfort inherent in these designs.

In Design EE9623, the covered porch extends almost all the way around the house. Further earmarking this house as a fine example of Southern Farmhouse design is its wood siding, dormer windows and tall chimney stacks.

As a true testament to the variety of influences in Southern architecture, Design EE9087 stands out as exemplary. Proportioned to 1½ stories and adorned with a wraparound porch and two secondary porches, this house utilizes brick for its exterior and adds to its appeal with well-defined columns supporting the roof overhang that creates the porches.

With a variety of designs from which to choose, this section on Southern Farmhouses offers a wealth of fine home-building opportunities.

Design EE9621

First Floor: 1,325 square feet
Second Floor: 453 square feet
Total: 1,778 square feet

● For the economy-minded family, this compact design has all the amenities available in larger plans with little wasted space. In addition, a front Palladian window, dormers and rear arched windows provide exciting visual elements to the exterior. The spacious great room has a fireplace, a cathedral ceiling and clerestory windows. A second-level balcony overlooks this gathering area. The kitchen is centrally located for maximum flexibility in layout and features a pass-through to the great room. Besides the generous master suite with its well appointed full bath, there are two family bedrooms located on the second level sharing a full bath with a double vanity. Please specify basement or crawlspace foundation when ordering.

FRONT

REAR

Design by
Donald A.
Gardner,
Architects, Inc.

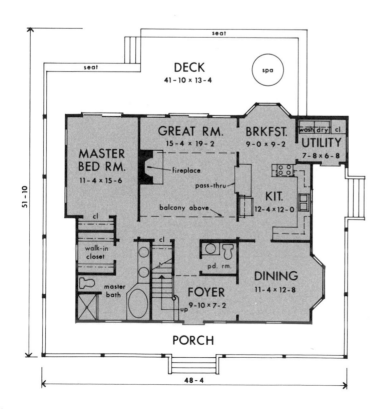

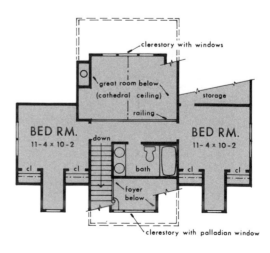

6

Design EE9632

First Floor: 1,756 square feet
Second Floor: 565 square feet
Total: 2,321 square feet

Design by
Donald A.
Gardner,
Architects, Inc.

● A wraparound covered porch at the front and sides of this house and an open deck at the back provide plenty of outside living area. The spacious great room features a fireplace, cathedral ceiling, and clerestory with an arched window. The first-floor master bedroom contains a generous closet and a master bath with garden tub, double-bowl vanity, and shower. The second floor sports two bedrooms and a full bath with double-bowl vanity. This plan includes a crawl-space foundation.

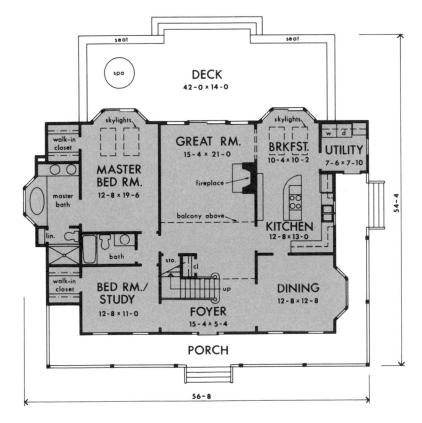

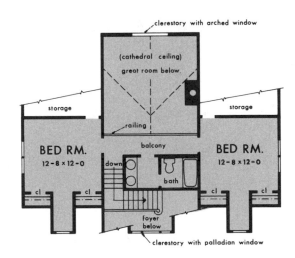

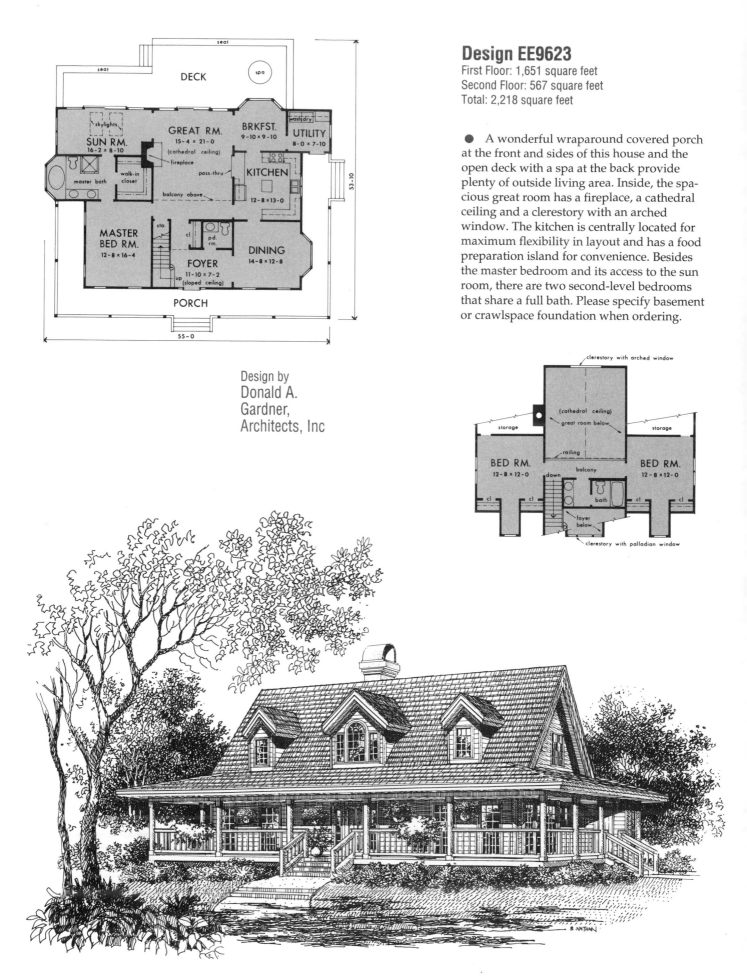

seat

seat

DECK

spa

skylights

SUN RM.
16-2 × 8-10

master bath

GREAT RM.
15-4 × 21-0
(cathedral ceiling)
fireplace

walk-in closet

pass-thru

balcony above

BRKFST.
9-10 × 9-10

wash dry

UTILITY
8-0 × 7-10

KITCHEN

12-8 × 13-0

MASTER BED RM.
12-8 × 16-4

sto.

cl

FOYER
11-10 × 7-2
(sloped ceiling)

up

p.d. rm.

DINING
14-8 × 12-8

PORCH

53-10

55-0

Design EE9623

First Floor: 1,651 square feet
Second Floor: 567 square feet
Total: 2,218 square feet

● A wonderful wraparound covered porch at the front and sides of this house and the open deck with a spa at the back provide plenty of outside living area. Inside, the spacious great room has a fireplace, a cathedral ceiling and a clerestory with an arched window. The kitchen is centrally located for maximum flexibility in layout and has a food preparation island for convenience. Besides the master bedroom and its access to the sun room, there are two second-level bedrooms that share a full bath. Please specify basement or crawlspace foundation when ordering.

Design by
Donald A. Gardner, Architects, Inc

clerestory with arched window

(cathedral ceiling)
great room below

storage

storage

railing

BED RM.
12-8 × 12-0

BED RM.
12-8 × 12-0

balcony

down

cl

cl

cl

cl

bath

foyer below

clerestory with palladian window

B. NATHAN

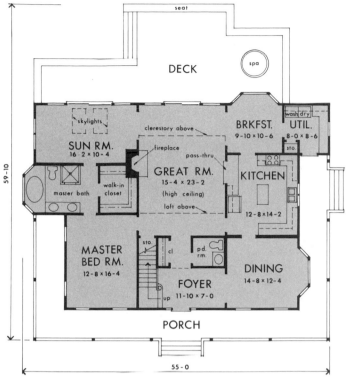

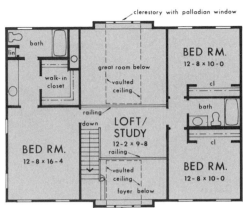

Design EE9616

First Floor: 1,734 square feet
Second Floor: 958 square feet
Total: 2,692 square feet

● A wraparound covered porch at the front and sides of this home and the open deck with spa and seating provide plenty of outside living area. A central great room features a vaulted ceiling, fireplace and clerestory windows above. The loft/study on the second floor over-looks this gathering area. Besides a formal dining room, kitchen, breakfast room and sun room on the first floor, there is also a generous master suite with garden tub. Three second-floor bedrooms complete sleeping accommodations. The plan includes a crawl-space foundation.

Design by
Donald A.
Gardner,
Architects, Inc.

FRONT

REAR

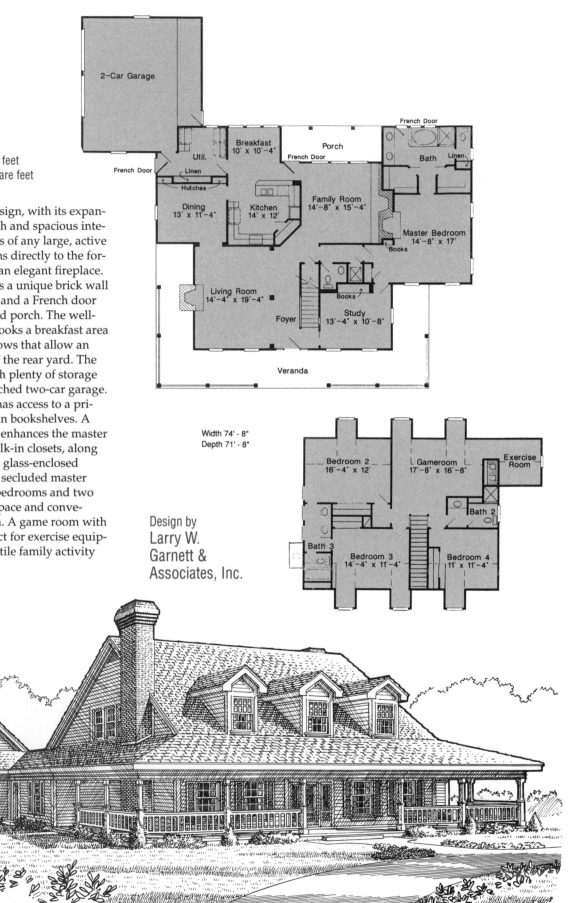

Design EE9004

First Floor: 2,166 square feet
Second Floor: 1,169 square feet
Total: 3,335 square feet

● This farmhouse design, with its expansive wraparound porch and spacious interior, will suit the needs of any large, active family. The foyer opens directly to the formal living room with an elegant fireplace. The family room offers a unique brick wall with built-in fireplace and a French door opening onto a covered porch. The well-planned kitchen overlooks a breakfast area with full-length windows that allow an uninterrupted view of the rear yard. The large utility room, with plenty of storage space, leads to an attached two-car garage. The master bedroom has access to a private study with built-in bookshelves. A third fireplace further enhances the master area. His and Hers walk-in closets, along with a garden tub and glass-enclosed shower, complete this secluded master suite. Upstairs, three bedrooms and two baths offer plenty of space and convenience for the children. A game room with an alcove that is perfect for exercise equipment provides a versatile family activity area.

Design by
Larry W.
Garnett &
Associates, Inc.

2-Car Garage

Breakfast
10' x 10'-4"
Util.
French Door
Porch
French Door
French Door
Linen
Bath
Linen
Hutches
Dining
13' x 11'-4"
Kitchen
14' x 12'
Family Room
14'-8" x 15'-4"
Master Bedroom
14'-8" x 17'
Books
Living Room
14'-4" x 19'-4"
Foyer
Books
Study
13'-4" x 10'-8"
Veranda

Width 74'-8"
Depth 71'-8"

Bedroom 2
16'-4" x 12'
Gameroom
17'-8" x 16'-8"
Exercise Room
Bath 2
Bath 3
Bedroom 3
14'-4" x 11'-4"
Bedroom 4
11' x 11'-4"

Design EE9001

First Floor: 1,308 square feet
Second Floor: 751 square feet
Total: 2,059 square feet

● A wraparound veranda and simple, uncluttered lines give this home an unassuming elegance that is characteristic of its farmhouse heritage. The kitchen overlooks an octagon-shaped breakfast room with full-length windows. The master bedroom features plenty of closet space and an elegant bath. Located within an oversized bay window is a garden tub with adjacent planter and glass-enclosed shower. Upstairs, two bedrooms share a bath with separate dressing and bathing areas. The balcony sitting area is perfect as a playroom or study. Plans for a detached two-car garage are included.

Design by
Larry W.
Garnett &
Associates, Inc.

Width 53'
Depth 45' - 4"

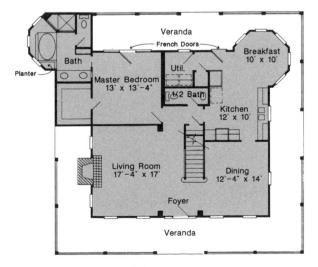

Veranda
French Doors
Bath
Planter
Master Bedroom
13' x 13'-4"
Util.
½ Bath
Breakfast
10' x 10'
Kitchen
12' x 10'
Living Room
17'-4" x 17'
Dining
12'-4" x 14'
Foyer
Veranda

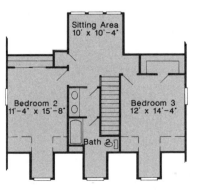

Sitting Area
10' x 10'-4"
Bedroom 2
11'-4" x 15'-8"
Bedroom 3
12' x 14'-4"
Bath

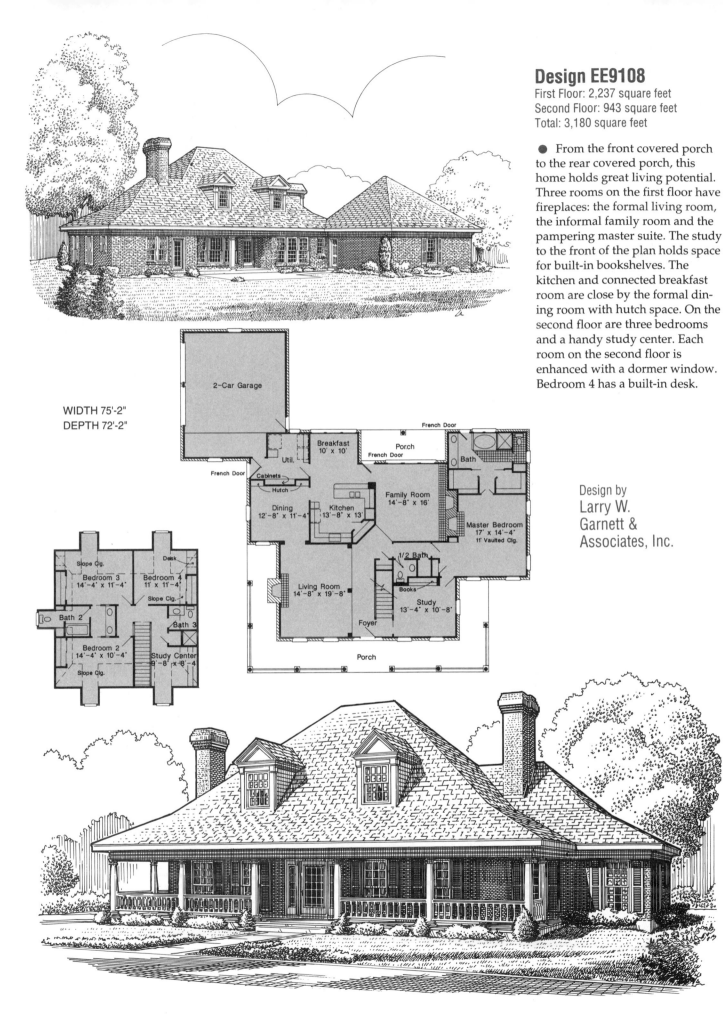

Design EE9108
First Floor: 2,237 square feet
Second Floor: 943 square feet
Total: 3,180 square feet

● From the front covered porch to the rear covered porch, this home holds great living potential. Three rooms on the first floor have fireplaces: the formal living room, the informal family room and the pampering master suite. The study to the front of the plan holds space for built-in bookshelves. The kitchen and connected breakfast room are close by the formal dining room with hutch space. On the second floor are three bedrooms and a handy study center. Each room on the second floor is enhanced with a dormer window. Bedroom 4 has a built-in desk.

Design by
Larry W.
Garnett &
Associates, Inc.

WIDTH 75'-2"
DEPTH 72'-2"

2-Car Garage

Breakfast 10' x 10'
Porch
Util.
Bath
French Door
Cabinets
Hutch
Dining 12'-8" x 11'-4"
Kitchen 13'-8" x 13'
Family Room 14'-8" x 16'
Master Bedroom 17' x 14'-4" 11' Vaulted Clg.
1/2 Bath
Living Room 14'-8" x 19'-8"
Books
Study 13'-4" x 10'-8"
Foyer
Porch

Slope Clg.
Desk
Bedroom 3 14'-4" x 11'-4"
Bedroom 4 11' x 11'-4"
Slope Clg.
Bath 2
Bath 3
Bedroom 2 14'-4" x 10'-4"
Study Center 9'-8" x 8'-4"
Slope Clg.

Design EE9087

First Floor: 2,263 square feet
Second Floor: 787 square feet
Total: 3,050 square feet

Design by
**Larry W.
Garnett &
Associates, Inc.**

● Excellent outdoor living is yours with this 1½-story home. The wrapping covered front porch gives way to a center hall entry with flanking living and dining rooms. The living room features a media center, two-way fireplace and columned entry. The attached garden room has French doors to the front porch and French doors to a smaller covered porch that is also accessed through the master bedroom suite. The family room is complemented by a fireplace, built-in bookshelves and another covered porch. An angled island counter separates it from the kitchen. Upstairs are three bedrooms and two full baths. Bedroom 4 has a beautiful bumped out window while Bedrooms 2 and 3 have dormer windows.

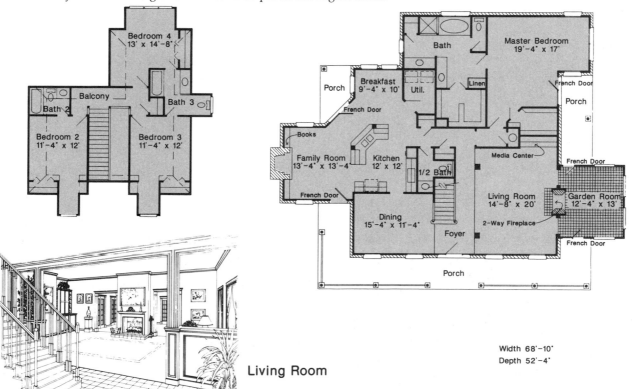

Living Room

Width 68'-10"
Depth 52'-4"

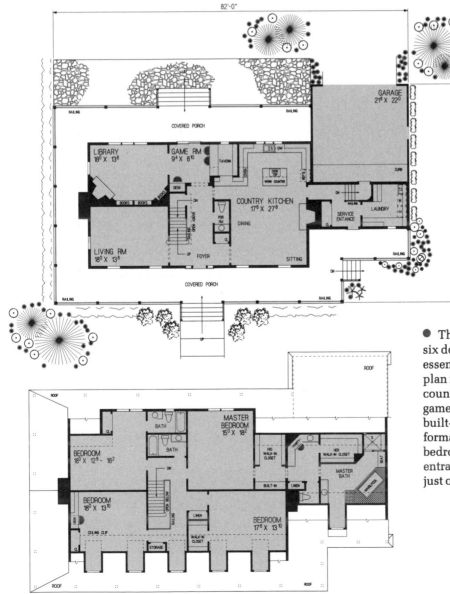

Quote One™

Cost to build? See page 232
to order complete cost estimate
to build this house in your area!

Design EE3399

First Floor: 1,716 square feet
Second Floor: 2,102 square feet
Total: 3,818 square feet

Design by
Home Planners,
Inc.

● This is the ultimate in farmhouse living — six dormer windows and a porch that stretches essentially around the entire house. Inside, the plan is open and inviting. Besides the large country kitchen with fireplace, there is a small game room with attached tavern, a library with built-in bookshelves and a fireplace, and a formal living room. The second floor has four bedrooms and three full baths. The service entrance features a laundry area conveniently just off the garage.

Design EE3397

First Floor: 1,855 square feet
Second Floor: 1,241 square feet
Total: 3,096 square feet

Design by
Home Planners,
Inc.

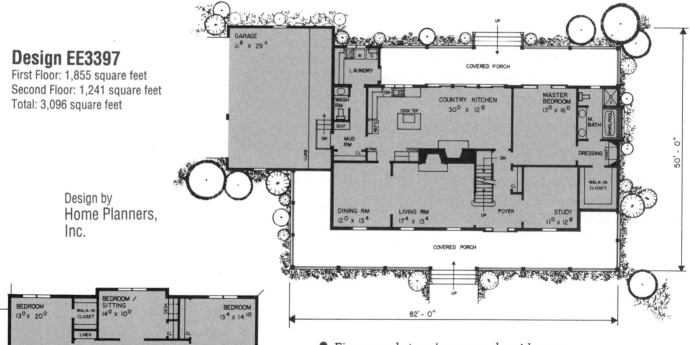

● Five second-story dormers and a wide covered front porch add to the charm of this farmhouse design. Inside, the entry foyer opens to the left to a formal living room with fireplace and attached dining room. To the right is a private study. The back of the plan is dominated by a huge country kitchen featuring an island cook top. On this floor is the master suite with a large walk-in closet. The second floor holds three bedrooms (or two and a sitting room) with two full baths.

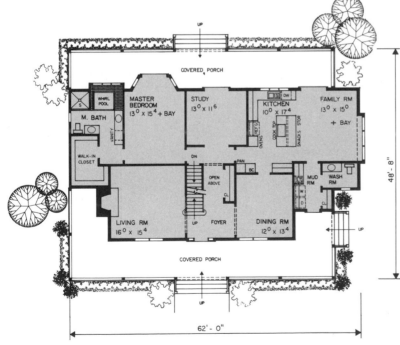

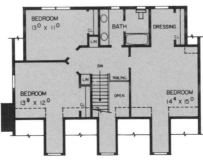

Design EE3396

First Floor: 1,829 square feet
Second Floor: 947 square feet
Total: 2,776 square feet

● Rustic charm abounds in this pleasant farm-house rendition. Covered porches to the front and rear enclose living potential for the whole family. Flanking the entrance foyer are the living and dining rooms. To the rear is the L-shaped kitchen with island cook top and snack bar. A small family room/breakfast nook is attached. A private study is tucked away on this floor next to the master suite. On the second floor are three bedrooms and a full bath. Two of the bedrooms have charming dormer windows.

Design by
Home Planners,
Inc.

Cost to build? See page 232
to order complete cost estimate
to build this house in your area!

61'-4"

TERRACE

DINING RM.
11⁴x10⁰

KITCHEN
11⁰x10⁰

FAMILY RM.
16⁴x15⁶

OVEN RANGE REF'G

38'-0"

LIVING RM.
15⁶x17⁰

GARAGE
21⁰x21⁴

SERVICE
ENTRANCE

UP DN

BRM.
CL.

PDR.
RM.

ENTRANCE

LAUNDRY

PORCH

Design by
Home Planners,
Inc.

WALK-IN
CLOSET

BATH BATH

LINEN

BED RM.
11⁶x10⁰

ROOF

MASTER.
BED RM.
15⁶x13⁴

DN

BED RM.
14⁶x10⁰

ROOF

ROOF

QUOTE ONE™

Cost to build? See page 232
to order complete cost estimate
to build this house in your area!

Design EE2776

First Floor: 1,134 square feet
Second Floor: 874 square feet
Total: 2,008 square feet

● This board-and-batten farmhouse design has all of the country charm of New England. The large front covered porch surely will be appreciated during the beautiful warm weather months. Immediately off the front entrance is the delightful corner living room. The dining room will be easily served by the U-shaped kitchen. Informal family living enjoyment will be obtained in the family room which features a raised-hearth fireplace, sliding glass doors to the rear terrace and easy access to the work center consisting of a powder room, a laundry room and a service entrance.

The second floor houses all of the sleeping facilities. There is a master bedroom with a private bath and a walk-in closet. Two other bedrooms share a bath. This is an excellent one-and-a-half-story design. For information on customizing this design, call 1-800-521-6797, ext. 800.

Design EE9290

First Floor: 1,322 square feet
Second Floor: 1,272 square feet
Total: 2,594 square feet

● Here's the luxury you've been
looking for—from the wraparound
covered front porch to the bright
sun room at the rear off the breakfast room. A sunken family room
with fireplace serves everyday casual gatherings, while the more formal
living and dining rooms are
reserved for special entertaining sit-
uations. The kitchen has a central
island with snack bar and is located
most conveniently for serving and
cleaning up. Upstairs are four bedrooms, one a lovely master suite
with French doors into the master
bath and a whirlpool tub in a dramatic bay window. A double vanity
in the shared bath easily serves the
three family bedrooms.

Design by
**Design
Basics,
Inc.**

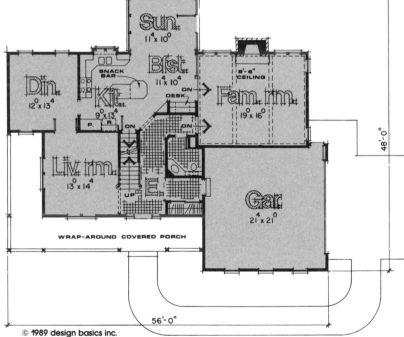

© 1989 design basics inc.

Design EE9214

First Floor: 1,188 square feet
Second Floor: 1,172 square feet
Total: 2,360 square feet

● Beginning with the interest of a wraparound porch, there's a feeling of country charm in this two-story plan. Formal dining and living rooms, visible from the entry, offer ample space for gracious entertaining. The large family room is truly a place of warmth and welcome with its gorgeous bay window, fireplace and French doors to the living room. The kitchen, with island counter, pantry and desk, makes cooking a delight. Upstairs, the secondary bedrooms share an efficient compartmented bath. The expansive master suite has its own luxury bath with double vanity, whirlpool, walk-in closet and dressing area.

Design by
Design
Basics,
Inc.

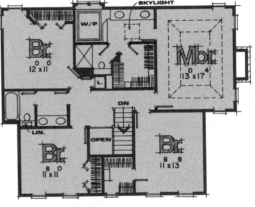

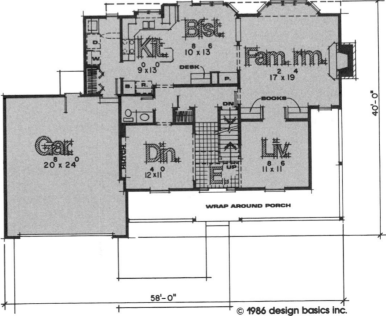

© 1986 design basics inc.

19

Design EE9298

First Floor: 1,881 square feet
Second Floor: 814 square feet
Total: 2,695 square feet

● Oval windows and an appealing covered porch lend character
to this 1½-story home. Inside, a
volume entry views the formal
living and dining rooms. Three
large windows and a raised-
hearth fireplace flanked by bookcases highlight a volume great
room. An island kitchen with
huge pantry and two Lazy
Susans serves a captivating gazebo dinette. In the master suite, a
cathedral ceiling, corner
whirlpool and roomy dressing
area deserve careful study. A
gallery wall for displaying family
mementos and prized heirlooms
graces the upstairs corridor. Each
secondary bedroom has convenient access to the bathrooms.
This home's charm and blend of
popular amenities will fit your
lifestyle.

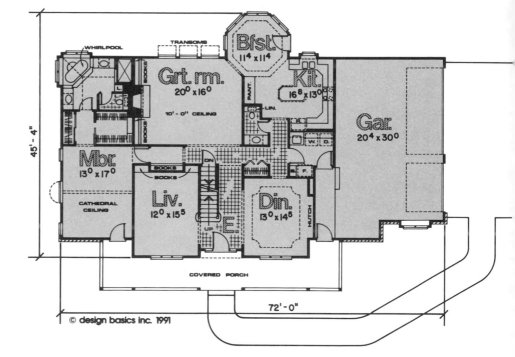

© design basics inc. 1991

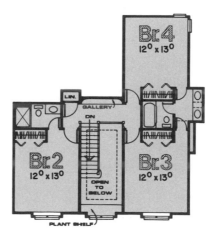

Design by
**Design
Basics,
Inc.**

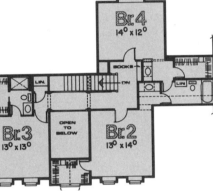

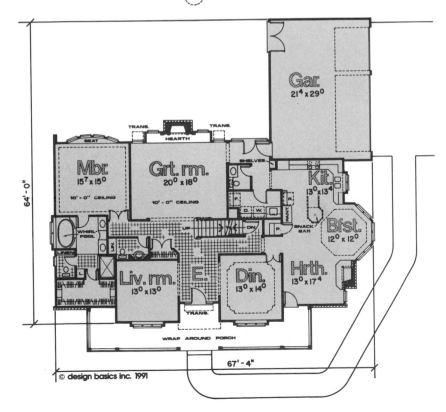

Br. 4
14⁰ x 12⁰

BOOKS

LIN. DN.

LIN.

Br. 3
13⁰ x 13⁰

OPEN TO BELOW

Br. 2
13⁰ x 14⁰

Gar.
21⁴ x 29⁰

TRANS.   HEARTH   TRANS.

SEAT

Mbr.
15⁷ x 15⁰
10'- 0" CEILING

Grt. rm.
20⁰ x 18⁰
10'- 0" CEILING

SHELVES

Kit.
13⁰ x 13⁴

WHIRL-POOL

LINEN

UP   DN

PANT.

SNACK BAR

Bfst.
12⁰ x 12⁰

Liv. rm.
13⁰ x 13⁰

E.

Din.
13⁰ x 14⁰

Hrth.
13⁰ x 17⁴

TRANS.

WRAP AROUND PORCH

64'- 0"

67'- 4"

© design basics inc. 1991

Design EE9297

First Floor: 2,280 square feet
Second Floor: 1,014 square feet
Total: 3,294 square feet

● Bright windows and a wraparound porch enhance the elevation of this four-bedroom, 1½-story home. Formal living and dining rooms are surveyed from the entry. A flush-hearth fireplace and transom windows highlight a volume great room planned for daily living. In the hearth room, catch a glimpse of the decorative fireplace and the convenient access to the front porch. Nearby, a sunny bayed dinette is served by an island kitchen with snack bar and two pantries. The main-floor master bedroom features a 10-foot ceiling and window seat. In the master bath, an oval whirlpool, dual vanities and walk-in closet pamper the home-owners. Upstairs, each secondary bedroom has a walk-in closet. Bedroom 3 has a private bath while Bedrooms 2 and 4 share a Hollywood bath. At 3,294 square feet, this prairie farmhouse adds distinction to any location.

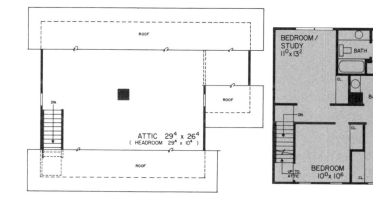

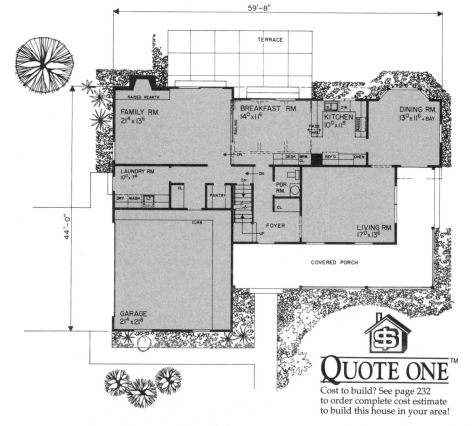

Design EE2774

First Floor: 1,366 square feet
Second Floor: 969 square feet
Total: 2,335 square feet

● Here's a popular farmhouse adaptation with all the most up-to-date features. Beginning with the formal areas, this design offers pleasures for the entire family. There is the quiet corner living room which has an opening to the sizable dining room. This room will enjoy plenty of natural light from the delightful bay window overlooking the rear yard. It is also conveniently located with the efficient U-shaped kitchen just a step away. The kitchen features many built-ins with a pass-through to the beamed ceiling breakfast room. Sliding glass doors to the terrace are fine attractions in both the sunken family room and breakfast room. The service entrance to the garage is flanked by a clothes closet and a large, walk-in pantry. There is a secondary entrance through the laundry room. Recreational activities and hobbies can be pursued in the basement area. Four bedrooms and two baths are upstairs. For information on customizing this design, call 1-800-521-6797, ext. 800.

Design by
Home Planners,
Inc.

QUOTE ONE™

Cost to build? See page 232
to order complete cost estimate
to build this house in your area!

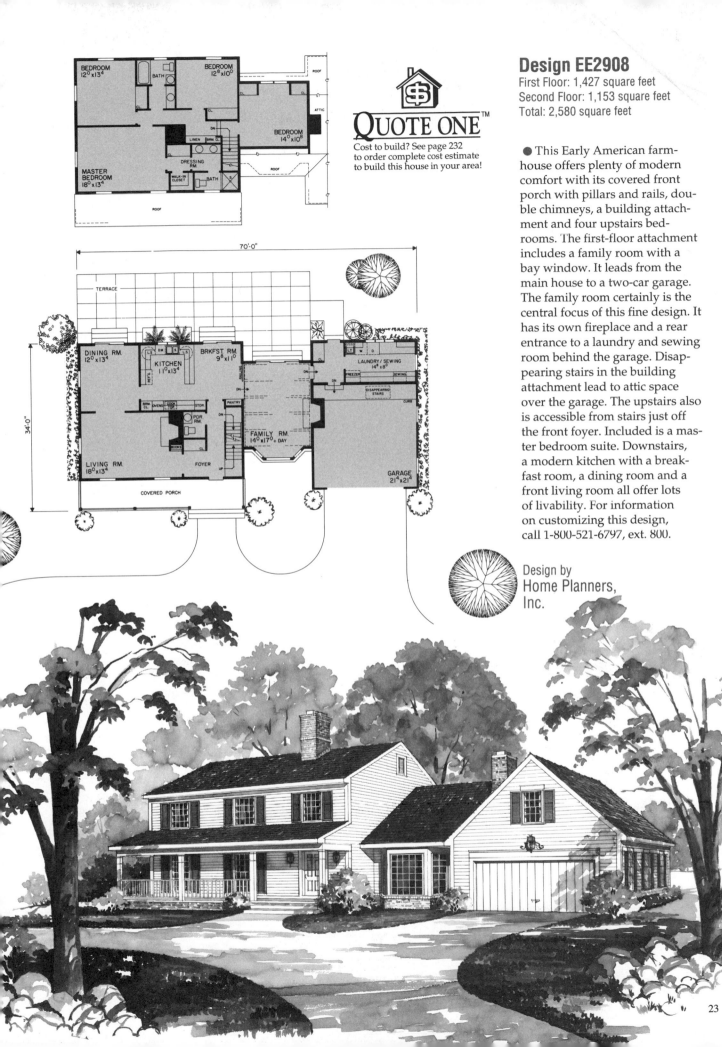

Floor plan labels (second floor):
BEDROOM 12⁰x13⁴ — BATH — BEDROOM 12⁸x10⁰ — ROOF — ATTIC — CL — CL — DN — LINEN — BRM. CL — DRESSING RM. — BEDROOM 14⁰x10⁸ — MASTER BEDROOM 18⁰x13⁴ — WALK-IN CLOSET — BATH — ROOF — ROOF

Quote One:

QUOTE ONE™

Cost to build? See page 232 to order complete cost estimate to build this house in your area!

Floor plan labels (first floor):
70'-0" — 34'-0" — TERRACE — DINING RM. 12⁰x13⁴ — KITCHEN 11⁰x13⁴ — BRKFST RM. 9⁸x11⁰ — LAUNDRY / SEWING 14⁸x8⁰ — FREEZER — SEWING — DW — REF'S. — OVENS — COOK TOP — STOR. — PANTRY — DISAPPEARING STAIRS — CURB — BRM. CL — POR. RM. — BOOKS — CL — DN — DN — MAIN HALL — FAMILY RM. 14⁰x17⁰+ BAY — LIVING RM. 18⁰x13⁴ — FOYER — UP — GARAGE 21⁴x21⁴ — COVERED PORCH

Design EE2908

First Floor: 1,427 square feet
Second Floor: 1,153 square feet
Total: 2,580 square feet

● This Early American farm-house offers plenty of modern comfort with its covered front porch with pillars and rails, double chimneys, a building attachment and four upstairs bedrooms. The first-floor attachment includes a family room with a bay window. It leads from the main house to a two-car garage. The family room certainly is the central focus of this fine design. It has its own fireplace and a rear entrance to a laundry and sewing room behind the garage. Disappearing stairs in the building attachment lead to attic space over the garage. The upstairs also is accessible from stairs just off the front foyer. Included is a master bedroom suite. Downstairs, a modern kitchen with a breakfast room, a dining room and a front living room all offer lots of livability. For information on customizing this design, call 1-800-521-6797, ext. 800.

Design by
Home Planners, Inc.

Design by
Home Planners,
Inc.

Design EE2694

First Floor: 2,026 square feet
Second Floor: 1,386 square feet
Total: 3,412 square feet

● This two-story design faithfully recalls the 18th-Century homestead of Sec. of Foreign Affairs John Jay. Downstairs features include a large country kitchen, clutter room, music alcove, and library wing. Upstairs are three sizable bedrooms, including a master suite with whirlpool.

QUOTE ONE

Cost to build? See page 232
to order complete cost estimate
to build this house in your area

QUOTE ONE™

Cost to build? See page 232 to order complete cost estimate to build this house in your area!

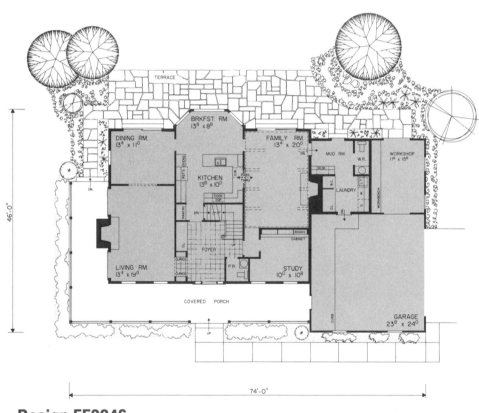

Design by
Home Planners,
Inc.

Design EE2946

First Floor: 1,581 square feet; Second Floor: 1,344 square feet; Total: 2,925 square feet

● Here's a traditional design that's made for down-home hospitality, the pleasures of casual conversation and the good grace of pleasant company. The star attractions are the large covered porch and terrace—perfect for family gatherings. Inside, the design is truly a hard worker. Separate living and family rooms—each with a fireplace—a formal dining room, a large kitchen and breakfast area with bay windows, a separate study, a workshop with plenty of room to maneuver, a mud room and four bedrooms all define the livability of this home. Not to be overlooked are the curio niches, the powder room, the built-in bookshelves, the kitchen pass-through, the pantry, the planning desk, the workbench and the stairs to the basement. For information on customizing this design, call 1-800-521-6797, ext. 800.

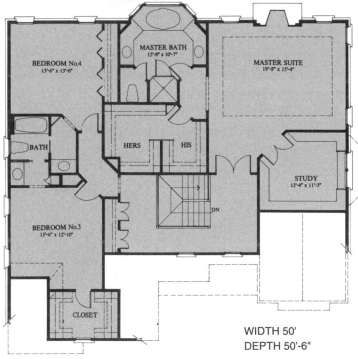

WIDTH 50'
DEPTH 50'-6"

BEDROOM No.4
13'-6" x 13'-0"

MASTER BATH
12'-8" x 10'-7"

MASTER SUITE
19'-8" x 15'-4"

BATH

HERS   HIS

STUDY
12'-4" x 11'-3"

DN

BEDROOM No.3
13'-6" x 12'-10"

CLOSET

Design EE9819

First Floor: 1,678 square feet
Second Floor: 1,677 square feet
Total: 3,355 square feet

Design by
Design Traditions

DECK

BREAKFAST
9'-4" x 10'-0"

GUEST ROOM
13'-6" x 12'-0"

FAMILY ROOM
19'-8" x 15'-4"

KITCHEN
15'-0" x 11'-8"

LAUNDRY
9'-8" x 5'-10"

PANTRY

DINING ROOM
14'-9" x 10'-9"

UP

FOYER
6'-6" x 18'-8"

DN

LIVING ROOM
12'-4" x 12'-7"

TWO-CAR GARAGE
21'-4" x 23'-4"

POWDER

VLT.CLG.

STOOP

● This home features a dramatic brick and stucco exterior accented by a gabled roof line and artful half-timbering. Inside, the foyer opens to the formal living room accented with a vaulted ceiling and a boxed-bay window. The dining room flows directly off the living room and features its own angled bay window. Through the double doors lies the center of family activity. An entire wall of glass, accented by a central fireplace, spans from the family room through to the breakfast area and kitchen. For your guests, a bedroom and bath are located on the main level. The second floor provides two additional bedrooms and a bath for children. The master suite—with its tray ceiling, fireplace and private study—is a true retreat. This home is designed with a basement foundation.

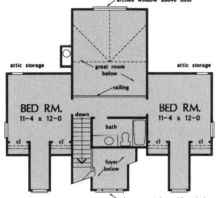

arched window above door

attic storage   attic storage

great room below

railing

BED RM.
11-4 x 12-0

BED RM.
11-4 x 12-0

down

bath

cl cl   cl cl

foyer below

clerestory window with arched top

skylights

BONUS RM.
13-4 x 24-0

down

Width 65'-4"
Depth 67'-10"

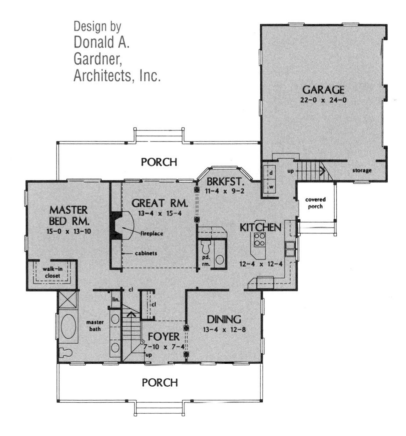

Design by
**Donald A.
Gardner,
Architects, Inc.**

GARAGE
22-0 x 24-0

storage

PORCH

d
w

up

covered porch

BRKFST.
11-4 x 9-2

**MASTER
BED RM.**
15-0 x 13-10

GREAT RM.
13-4 x 15-4

fireplace

cabinets

pd. rm.

KITCHEN
12-4 x 12-4

walk-in closet

lin.

cl

cl

master bath

DINING
13-4 x 12-8

FOYER
7-10 x 7-4
up

PORCH

Design EE9732

First Floor: 1,506 square feet; Second Floor: 513 square feet
Total: 2,019 square feet; Bonus Room: 397 square feet

● This three-bedroom, country home with front and rear porches offers an open plan layout with minimal wasted space. A front Palladian window dormer and a rear arched window along with the overall massing of the home adds to its exterior visual intrigue. The entrance foyer rises with a sloped ceiling and enjoys an abundance of light from a Palladian window clerestory. In the spacious great room, a fireplace, a cathedral ceiling and a clerestory with an arched window all add to appeal. A second-level balcony overlooks the great room. The master suite features all of the amenities while two secondary bedrooms reside on the second level. A bonus room offers room to grow.

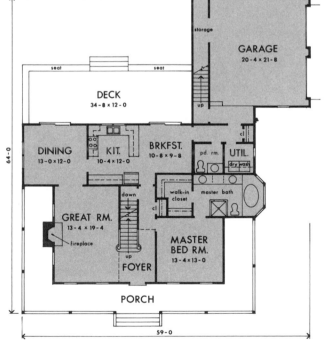

DECK
34-8 x 12-0

DINING
13-0 x 12-0

KIT.
10-4 x 12-0

BRKFST.
10-8 x 9-8

UTIL.

GARAGE
20-4 x 21-8

storage

pd. rm.

master bath

walk-in closet

GREAT RM.
13-4 x 19-4

fireplace

MASTER
BED RM.
13-4 x 13-0

FOYER

PORCH

64-0

59-0

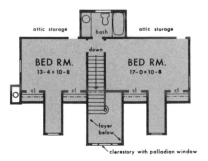

attic storage

bath

attic storage

BED RM.
13-4 x 10-8

BED RM.
17-0 x 10-8

down

foyer below

clerestory with palladian window

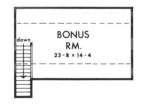

BONUS RM.
23-8 x 14-4

down

Design EE9645

First Floor: 1,356 square feet
Second Floor: 542 square feet
Total: 1,898 square feet

● The welcoming charm of this country farmhouse is expressed by its many windows and its covered, wraparound porch. A two-story entrance foyer is enhanced by a Palladian window in a clerestory dormer above to allow natural lighting. A first-floor master suite allows privacy and accessibility. The master bath includes a whirlpool tub, a shower and a double-bowl vanity along with a walk-in closet. The first floor features a nine-foot ceiling throughout with the exception of the kitchen area which features an eight-foot ceiling. The second floor provides two additional bedrooms, a full bath and plenty of storage space. An unfinished basement and bonus room provide room to grow. Please specify basement or crawlspace foundation when ordering.

Design by
Donald A.
Gardner,
Architects, Inc.

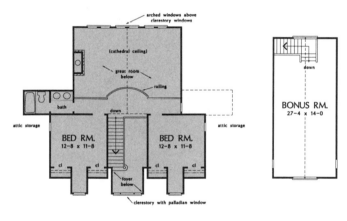

arched windows above clerestory windows

(cathedral ceiling)

great room below

railing

bath

attic storage

attic storage

BED RM. 12-8 x 11-8

BED RM. 12-8 x 11-8

cl

cl

cl

cl

down

foyer below

clerestory with palladian window

down

BONUS RM. 27-4 x 14-0

Design EE9723

First Floor: 2,064 square feet
Second Floor: 594 square feet
Total: 2,658 square feet
Bonus Room: 464 square feet

● You'll find country living at its best when meandering through this spacious four-bedroom farmhouse with wraparound porch. A front Palladian window dormer and rear clerestory windows at the great room add exciting visual elements to the exterior while providing natural light to the interior. The large great room boasts a fireplace, bookshelves and a raised cathedral ceiling, allowing a curved balcony overlook above. The great room, master bedroom and breakfast room are accessible to the rear porch for greater circulation and flexibility. Special features such as the large cooktop island in the kitchen, the wet bar, the bedroom/study and the generous bonus room over the garage and ample storage set this plan apart.

Design by
Donald A.
Gardner,
Architects, Inc.

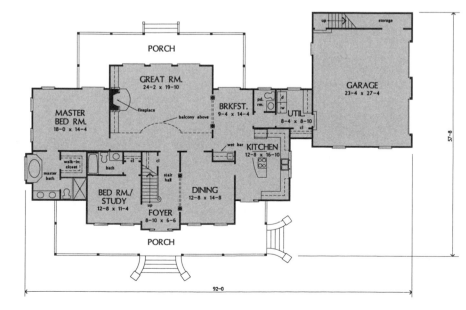

PORCH

GREAT RM. 24-2 x 19-10

fireplace

balcony above

MASTER BED RM. 18-0 x 14-4

BRKFST. 9-4 x 14-4

pd. rm.

UTIL. 8-4 x 8-10

cl

up

storage

GARAGE 23-4 x 27-4

57-8

walk-in closet

bath

master bath

cl

wet bar

KITCHEN 12-8 x 16-10

BED RM./ STUDY 12-8 x 11-4

stair hall

DINING 12-8 x 14-8

FOYER 8-10 x 6-6

up

PORCH

92-0

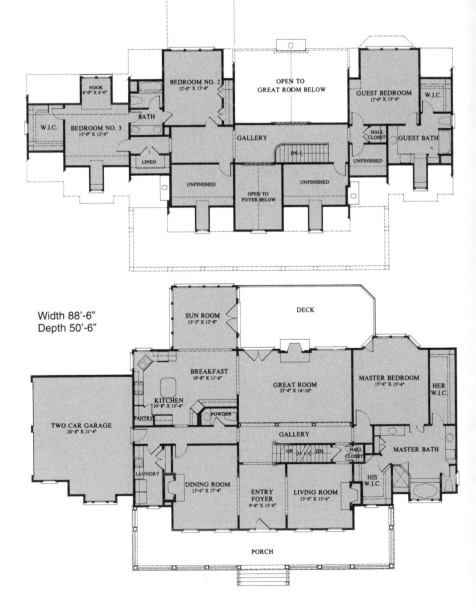

Design by
Design Traditions

Design EE9910

First Floor: 2,565 square feet
Second Floor: 1,375 square feet
Total: 3,940 square feet

● A symmetrical facade with twin chimneys makes a grand statement. A covered porch welcomes visitors and provides a pleasant place to spend cool evenings. The entry foyer is flanked by formal living areas: a dining room and a living room, each with a fireplace. A third fireplace is the highlight of the expansive great room to the rear. The deck is accessible through the great room, the sun room or the master bedroom. The second floor offers three bedrooms, two full baths and plenty of storage space. This home is designed with a basement foundation.

Width 88'-6"
Depth 50'-6"

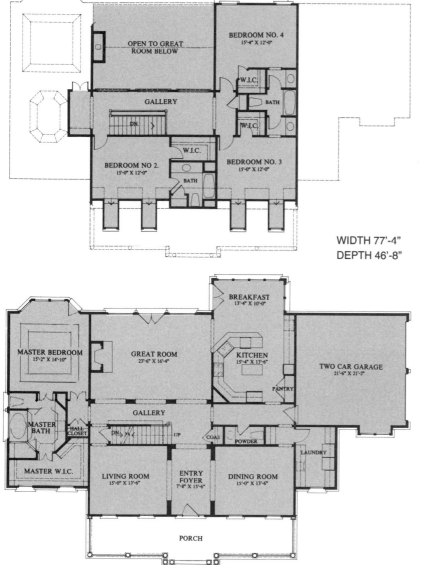

Design EE9912

First Floor: 2,315 square feet
Second Floor: 1,200 square feet
Total: 3,515 square feet

● This grand home displays the finest in farmhouse design. Dormer windows and a traditional brick and siding exterior lend a welcoming facade. Inside, the entry foyer opens to a formal zone consisting of a living room to the left and a dining room to the right. Both share the same dimensions, thus creating a balance that will function well for entertaining. The kitchen enjoys a pass-through to the breakfast area—the great room is just a step away. Here, a fireplace graces the far end of the room while a wall of glass allows light to penetrate the interior of the room. Double doors grant passage to the back yard. Beyond the first-floor gallery, the master bedroom boasts a tray ceiling, a window bay and a lavish bath. Upstairs, three secondary bedrooms all have walk-in closets and direct access to a bath. This home is designed with a basement foundation.

Design by
Design Traditions

WIDTH 77'-4"
DEPTH 46'-8"

OPEN TO GREAT ROOM BELOW

BEDROOM NO. 4
15'-4" X 12'-0"

W.I.C.

BATH

GALLERY

DN.

W.I.C.

BEDROOM NO 2.
15'-0" X 12'-0"

W.I.C.

BEDROOM NO. 3
15'-0" X 12'-0"

BATH

MASTER BEDROOM
15'-2" X 14'-10"

GREAT ROOM
23'-6" X 16'-4"

BREAKFAST
13'-4" X 10'-0"

KITCHEN
15'-4" X 13'-6"

TWO CAR GARAGE
21'-6" X 21'-2"

PANTRY

MASTER BATH

HALL CLOSET

GALLERY

DN.

COAT

POWDER

LAUNDRY

MASTER W.I.C.

LIVING ROOM
15'-0" X 13'-6"

ENTRY FOYER
7'-8" X 13'-6"

DINING ROOM
15'-0" X 13'-6"

PORCH

Design EE9851 First Floor: 2,210 square feet
Second Floor: 1,070 square feet; Total: 3,280 square feet

● A generous front porch enhances the living area of this home with its sheltering welcome and Americana detailing. The classic style is also echoed in the use of wood siding, shuttered windows and stone finish work on two chimneys. The main level begins with a two-story foyer with a tray ceiling. Double doors open into the study with an exposed beam ceiling and fireplace. Left of the foyer lies the dining room drenched in natural sunlight. Across the hall, the great room with a fireplace, a wet bar and two sets of French doors provides a great gathering place. The master suite located at the end of the main hallway. It features a tray ceiling and a complete master bath with a separate shower, a water closet and dual vanities. The large walk-in closet completes the suite. The two-car garage is at the rear of the home, with convenient access from the expansive kitchen and breakfast area. Staircases from the great room and foyer lead to the upper level. Two additional bedrooms, each with a walk-in closet and a vanity, share the tub area. A third bedroom has a generous walk-in closet and a private bath. This home is designed with a basement foundation.

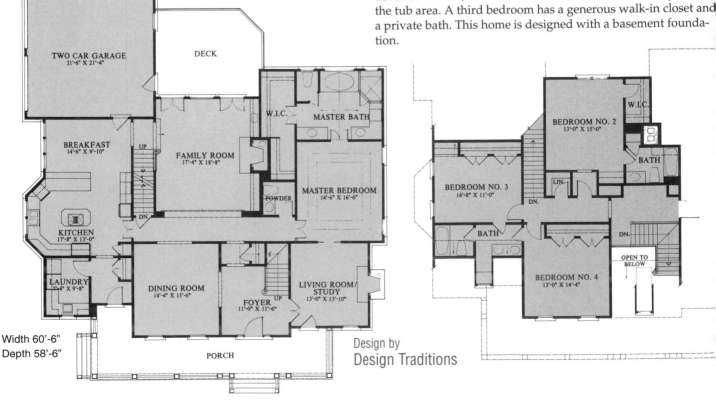

Width 60'-6"
Depth 58'-6"

Design by
Design Traditions

Southern Country Designs

Sporting many of the same attributes of the Southern Farmhouse, the Southern Country house lends itself to slightly different interpretations. In some instances, it takes on a much more ground-hugging, unassuming appearance, due in large part to not having to be raised above wet farmlands. With clapboard siding, as well as a prominent chimney, these homes are much more likely to conform to a rolling landscape, not unlike a ranch house does. The first designs in this section — such as EE9622 — display these endearing qualities along with expansive decks or terraces for enjoying prime weather. Front porches still offer home owners the opportunity to sit, relax and chat with neighbors.

Because the need for utility, once so prevalent on working farms, is gone, Southern Country designs veer from farmhouse designs with a tendency to more closely mirror the fancies of city dwellers. Thus, elements of other styles often show up with more prominence. Gothic columns, Palladian windows, French doors and Greek Revival detailing all provide desirable effects. Exterior materials also give way to variations, with more houses sporting combinations of brick and stucco. This is exemplified in Design EE8039 where a columned porch with arches, a brick and stucco exterior, quoins, a sloping roof and multi-pane windows work in chorus to present a charming country home.

Tackling livability issues without any problems, Design EE9822 greets visitors with true Southern hospitality. A sheltering front porch — note the use of columns here — provides the first indication of a welcoming interior. Pedimented gables and wood siding combine to form interesting planes; wood shingles highlight sweeping roof lines while dormer windows offer additional dimension to this pleasing facade.

Whatever your fancy, the many designs in this section all provide the very best in country livability.

FRONT

REAR

Design EE9602
Square Footage: 1,899

● Multi-paned windows, dormers, a covered porch and two projected windows with shed roofs at the dining room and study offer a welcoming front exterior to this home. The great room has a cathedral ceiling, paddle fan, built-in cabinets and book shelves, and has direct access to the sunroom through two sliding glass doors. The convenient kitchen features a center island cook top and provides service to both the formal dining room and breakfast area. It is connected to the great room by a pass-through. Overlooking the private rear deck is the sumptuous master suite with double-bowl vanity, shower and garden tub. Two other bedrooms are located at the other end of the house for privacy (the front bedroom could double as a study). The two-car garage has ample storage space.

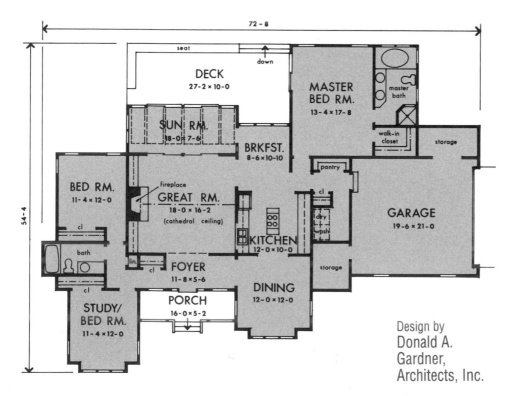

Design by
Donald A.
Gardner,
Architects, Inc.

34

REAR

Design by
Donald A.
Gardner,
Architects, Inc.

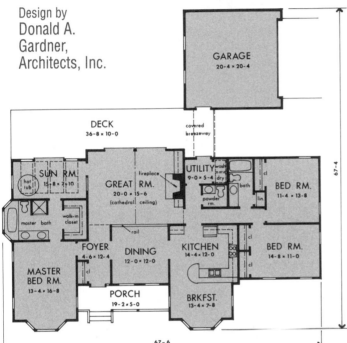

GARAGE
20-4 × 20-4

DECK
36-8 × 10-0

covered
breezeway

SUN RM.
15-8 × 7-10

hot
tub

GREAT RM.
20-0 × 15-6
(cathedral ceiling)

fireplace

UTILITY
9-0 × 5-4

wash
dry

bath

powder
rm.

cl

lin.

BED RM.
11-4 × 13-8

master bath

walk-in
closet

rail

FOYER
4-6 × 12-4

DINING
12-0 × 12-0

KITCHEN
14-4 × 12-0

BED RM.
14-8 × 11-0

MASTER
BED RM.
13-4 × 16-8

cl

PORCH
19-2 × 5-0

BRKFST.
13-4 × 7-8

67-4

67-6

Design EE9619
Square Footage: 2,021

● Multi-pane windows, shutters, dormers, bay
windows and a delightful covered porch grace
the facade of this country cottage. Inside, the
floor plan is no less appealing. Note that the
great room has a fireplace, a cathedral ceiling
and sliding glass doors with an arched window
above to allow for natural illumination of the
room. A sun room with a hot tub leads to an
adjacent deck. This space can also be reached
from the master bath. The generous master
bedroom has a walk-in closet and a spacious
bath with a double-bowl vanity, a shower and
a garden tub. Two additional bedrooms are
located at the other end of the house for privacy. The garage is connected to the house by a
breezeway. Please specify basement or crawlspace foundation when ordering.

FRONT

FRONT

Design EE9622
Square Footage: 1,782

● What visual excitement is created in this country ranch with the combined use of exterior building materials and shapes! The angular nature of the plan allows for flexibility in design—lengthen the great room or family room, or both, to suit individual space needs. Notice the cathedral ceilings in both rooms and the fireplace in the great room. An amenity-filled master bedroom features a cathedral ceiling, a private deck and a master bath with a whirlpool tub. Two other bedrooms share a full bath. An expansive deck area with a hot tub wraps around interior family gathering areas for enhanced outdoor living. Please specify basement or crawlspace foundation when ordering.

hot tub

DECK

down

GREAT RM.
15-4 x 17-8
(cathedral ceiling)

fireplace

FAMILY RM.
12-0 x 10-0
(cathedral ceiling)

DINING
12-4 x 11-4

down

GARAGE
21-0 x 21-0

KITCHEN
12-0 x 9-8

UTILITY

storage

BED RM.
11-0 x 12-0

ref.

drywash

FOYER

PORCH
27-8 x 4-0

storage

down

DECK

BED RM.
11-0 x 12-0

bath

MASTER
BED RM.
16-4 x 18-8
(cathedral ceiling)

master bath

tub

walk-in closet

walk-in closet

61-8

92-4

Design by
Donald A.
Gardner,
Architects, Inc.

REAR

36

Design EE9679
Square Footage: 1,512

● A multi-pane bay window, dormers, a cupola, a covered porch and a variety of building materials all combine to dress up this intriguing country cottage. The generous entry foyer leads to a formal dining room and an impressive great room with a cathedral ceiling and a fireplace. The kitchen includes a breakfast area with a bay window overlooking the deck. The great room and master bedroom also access the deck. The master bath has a double-bowl vanity, a shower and a garden tub. Two additional bedrooms are located at the front of the house for privacy and share a full bath.

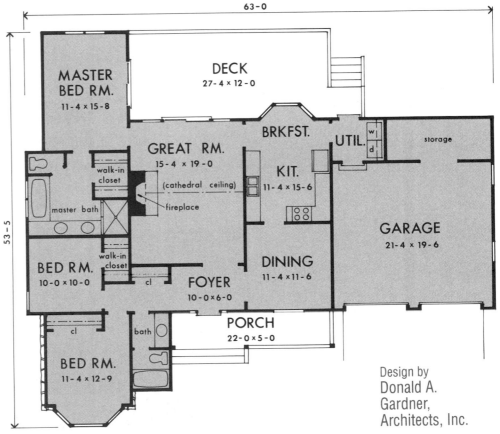

63-0

MASTER BED RM.
11-4 x 15-8

DECK
27-4 x 12-0

BRKFST.

UTIL.

storage

w d

GREAT RM.
15-4 x 19-0

KIT.
11-4 x 15-6

(cathedral ceiling)

walk-in closet

master bath

fireplace

GARAGE
21-4 x 19-6

53-5

BED RM.
10-0 x 10-0

walk-in closet

cl

DINING
11-4 x 11-6

FOYER
10-0 x 6-0

cl

bath

BED RM.
11-4 x 12-9

PORCH
22-0 x 5-0

Design by
Donald A.
Gardner,
Architects, Inc.

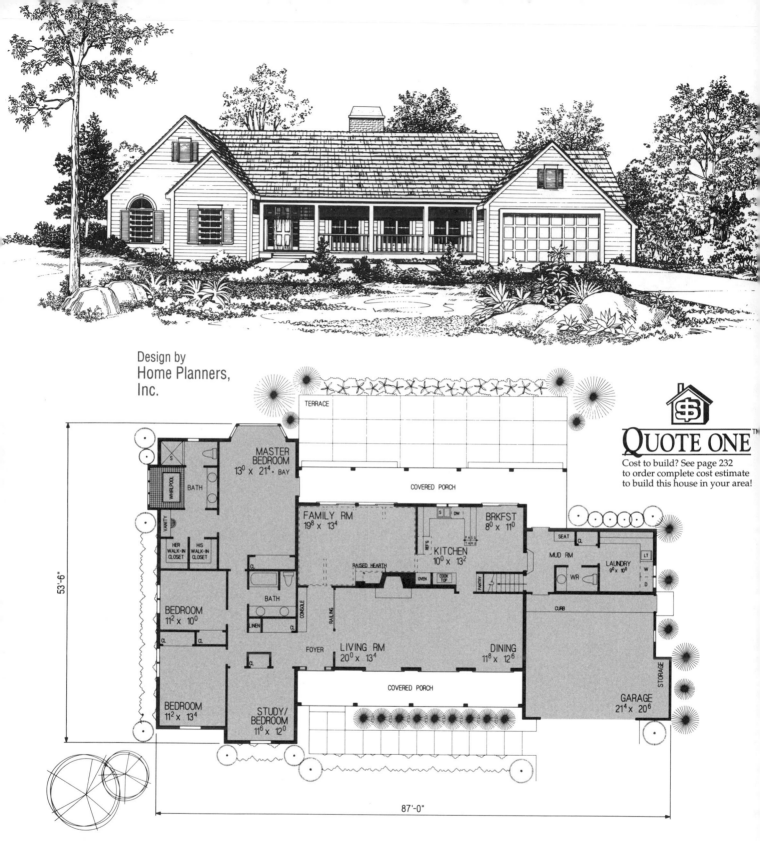

Design by
Home Planners,
Inc.

TERRACE

COVERED PORCH

MASTER
BEDROOM
13⁰ x 21⁴ • BAY

BATH

WHIRLPOOL

VANITY

HER
WALK-IN
CLOSET

HIS
WALK-IN
CLOSET

FAMILY RM
19⁸ x 13⁴

KITCHEN
10⁰ x 13²

BRKFST
8⁰ x 11⁰

SEAT

MUD RM

LAUNDRY
9⁰ x 10⁰

WR

W
D

LT

53'-6"

BEDROOM
11² x 10⁰

BATH

LINEN

CONSOLE

RAISED HEARTH

OVEN

COOK
TOP

PANTRY

CURB

RAILING

BEDROOM
11² x 13⁰

STUDY/
BEDROOM
11⁶ x 12⁰

FOYER

LIVING RM
20⁰ x 13⁴

DINING
11⁸ x 12⁶

STORAGE

GARAGE
21⁴ x 20⁶

COVERED PORCH

87'-0"

Design EE3348
Square Footage: 2,549

● Covered porches front and rear will be the envy of the neighborhood when this house is built. The interior plan meets family needs perfectly in well-zoned areas: a sleeping wing with four bedrooms and two baths, a living zone with formal and informal gathering space, and a work zone with U-shaped kitchen and laundry with washroom. The master bedroom with deluxe bath, including His and Hers walk-in closets, is noteworthy. Open planning and fireplaces enhance the living areas. Extra storage space is provided in the two-car garage.

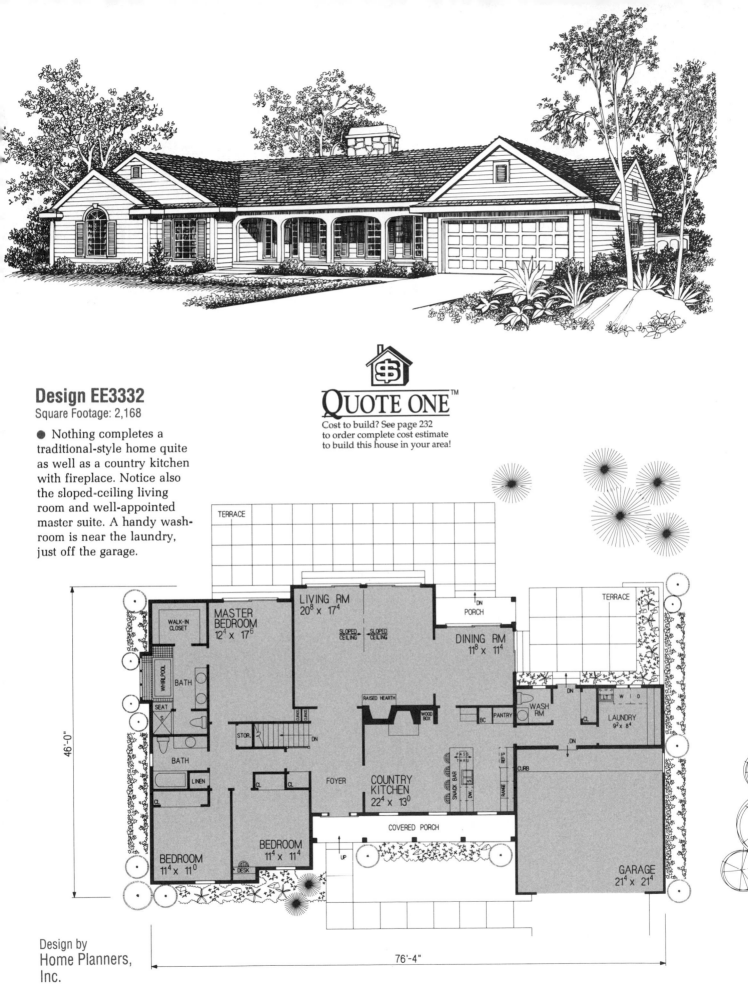

Design EE3332

Square Footage: 2,168

● Nothing completes a traditional-style home quite as well as a country kitchen with fireplace. Notice also the sloped-ceiling living room and well-appointed master suite. A handy washroom is near the laundry, just off the garage.

Quote One™

Cost to build? See page 232 to order complete cost estimate to build this house in your area!

Design by
Home Planners,
Inc.

Floor plan labels

TERRACE

MASTER BEDROOM 12⁴ x 17⁶

WALK-IN CLOSET

WHIRLPOOL

SEAT

BATH

BATH

LINEN

LIVING RM 20⁸ x 17⁴

SLOPED CEILING SLOPED CEILING

RAISED HEARTH

WOOD BOX

STOR.

DN

FOYER

COUNTRY KITCHEN 22⁴ x 13⁰

DESK

BEDROOM 11⁴ x 11⁰

BEDROOM 11⁴ x 11⁴

COVERED PORCH

UP

DINING RM 11⁸ x 11⁴

PORCH

DN

PANTRY

BC

WASH RM

SNACK BAR

PASS THRU

RANGE

REF'G

CURB

WASH RM

LAUNDRY 9² x 8⁴

W/D

CL

TERRACE

GARAGE 21⁴ x 21⁴

46'-0"

76'-4"

39

© The Sater Group, Inc.

Jenkins

Design EE6600

Square Footage: 1,795

● This engaging three-bedroom split plan promotes casual living both inside and out, offering contemporary amenities for convenient living. The foyer opens to the formal dining room on the right, and straight ahead, the great room complete with a fireplace and a built-in entertainment center. Double French doors unfold onto a large veranda. The kitchen includes a large walk-in pantry, an eating bar and a bayed breakfast nook. The relaxing master suite enjoys access to a screened porch, His and Hers walk-in closets and a private bath with a glass-enclosed shower. Two secondary bedrooms offer privacy and plenty of storage.

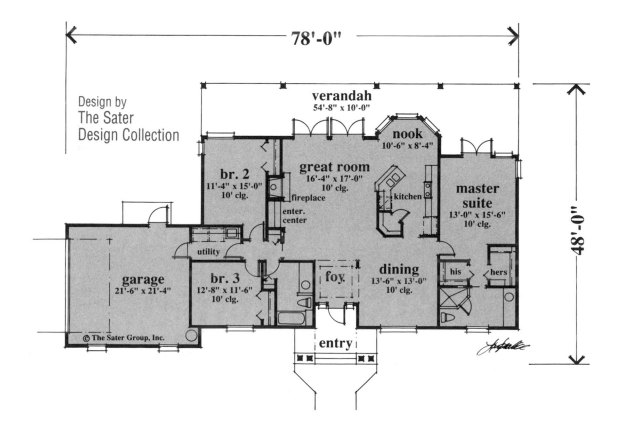

Design by
The Sater
Design Collection

78'-0"

48'-0"

verandah
54'-8" x 10'-0"

nook
10'-6" x 8'-4"

br. 2
11'-4" x 15'-0"
10' clg.

great room
16'-4" x 17'-0"
10' clg.

fireplace

enter. center

kitchen

master suite
13'-0" x 15'-6"
10' clg.

utility

garage
21'-6" x 21'-4"

br. 3
12'-8" x 11'-6"
10' clg.

foy.

dining
13'-6" x 13'-0"
10' clg.

his

hers

© The Sater Group, Inc.

entry

Design EE3461

First Floor: 1,391 square feet
Second Floor: 611 square feet
Total: 2,002 square feet

● A Palladian window set in a dormer provides a nice introduction to this 1½-story country home. The two-story foyer draws on natural light and a pair of columns to set a comfortable, yet elegant mood. The living room, to the left, presents a grand space for entertaining. From full-course dinners to family suppers, the dining room will serve its purpose well. The kitchen delights with an island work station and openness to the keeping room. Here, a raised-hearth fireplace provides added comfort. Sleeping accommodations are comprised of four bedrooms, one a first-floor master suite. With a luxurious private bath, including dual lavatories, this room will surely be a favorite retreat. Upstairs, three secondary bedrooms meet the needs of the growing family.

Design by
Home Planners,
Inc.

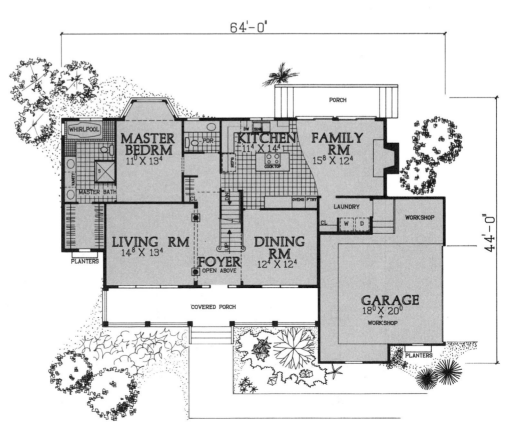

Cost to build? See page 232
to order complete cost estimate
to build this house in your area!

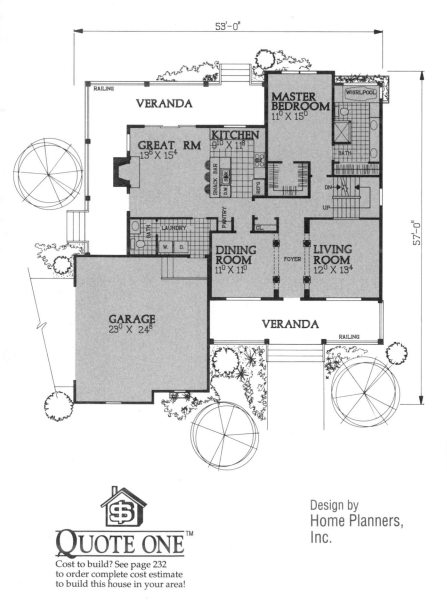

Design EE3462

First Floor: 1,395 square feet
Second Floor: 813 square feet
Total: 2,208 square feet

● Get off to a great start with this handsome family farmhouse. Covered porches front and rear assure comfortable outdoor living while varied roof planes add visual interest. Inside, distinct formal and informal living zones provide the best accommodations for any occasion. The columned foyer opens to both the dining and living rooms. The central kitchen services the large family room with an island work counter and snack bar. For everyday chores, a laundry room is conveniently located and also provides access to the garage. On the first floor you'll find the master bedroom suite. It enjoys complete privacy and luxury with its double closets and master bath with double-bowl vanity, whirlpool tub and separate shower. Upstairs, three family bedrooms extend fabulous livability.

Design by
Home Planners, Inc.

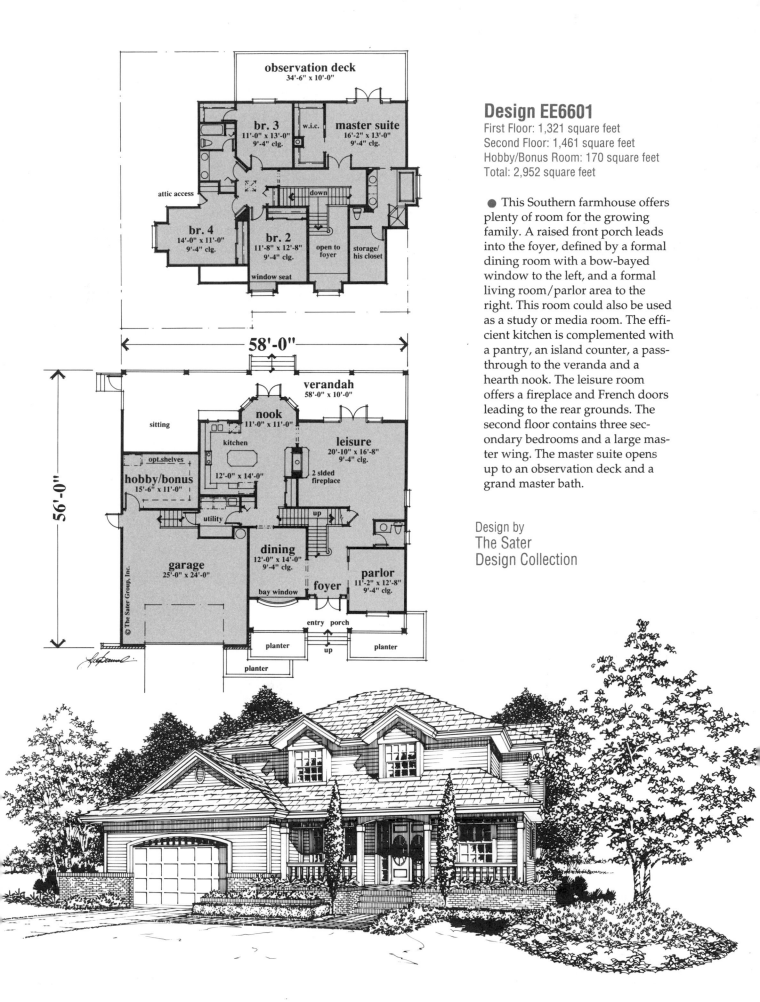

observation deck
34'-6" x 10'-0"

br. 3
11'-0" x 13'-0"
9'-4" clg.

w.i.c.

master suite
16'-2" x 13'-0"
9'-4" clg.

attic access

br. 4
14'-0" x 11'-0"
9'-4" clg.

down

br. 2
11'-8" x 12'-8"
9'-4" clg.

open to foyer

storage/his closet

window seat

58'-0"

56'-0"

verandah
58'-0" x 10'-0"

sitting

nook
11'-0" x 11'-0"

kitchen

12'-0" x 14'-0"

opt.shelves

hobby/bonus
15'-6" x 11'-0"

utility

leisure
20'-10" x 16'-8"
9'-4" clg.

2 sided fireplace

up

garage
25'-0" x 24'-0"

dining
12'-0" x 14'-0"
9'-4" clg.

foyer

parlor
11'-2" x 12'-8"
9'-4" clg.

bay window

entry porch

planter

up

planter

planter

© The Sater Group, Inc.

Design EE6601

First Floor: 1,321 square feet
Second Floor: 1,461 square feet
Hobby/Bonus Room: 170 square feet
Total: 2,952 square feet

● This Southern farmhouse offers plenty of room for the growing family. A raised front porch leads into the foyer, defined by a formal dining room with a bow-bayed window to the left, and a formal living room/parlor area to the right. This room could also be used as a study or media room. The efficient kitchen is complemented with a pantry, an island counter, a pass-through to the veranda and a hearth nook. The leisure room offers a fireplace and French doors leading to the rear grounds. The second floor contains three secondary bedrooms and a large master wing. The master suite opens up to an observation deck and a grand master bath.

Design by
**The Sater
Design Collection**

Design EE9312

First Floor: 1,150 square feet
Second Floor: 1,120 square feet
Total: 2,270 square feet

● Lap siding, special windows and a covered porch enhance
the elevation of this popular style. The spacious two-story
entry surveys the formal dining room with hutch space. An
entertainment center, through-fireplace and bayed windows
add appeal to the great room. Families will love the spacious
kitchen, breakfast and hearth room. Enhancements to this
casual living area include a through-fireplace, gazebo dinette,
wrapping counters, an island kitchen and planning desk. An
efficient U-shaped staircase routes traffic throughout.
Comfortable secondary bedrooms and a sumptuous master
suite feature privacy by design. Bedroom 3 is highlighted by a
half round window, volume ceiling and double closets while
Bedroom 4 features a built-in desk. The master suite has a
vaulted ceiling, large walk-in closet, His and Hers vanities,
compartmented stool/shower area and an oval whirlpool tub.

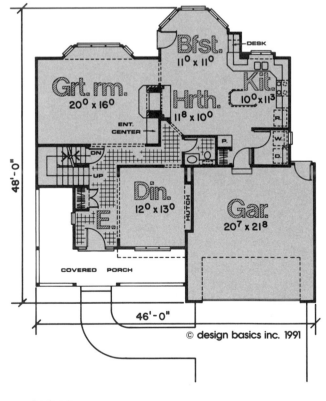

© design basics inc. 1991

Design by
Design
Basics,
Inc.

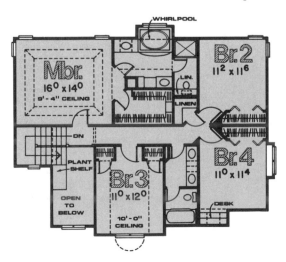

Design EE9235

First Floor: 919 square feet
Second Floor: 927 square feet
Total: 1,846 square feet

● Wonderful country design
begins with the wraparound
porch of this plan. Explore
further and find a two-story
entry with a coat closet and
plant shelf above and a strate-
gically placed staircase along-
side. The island kitchen with a
boxed window over the sink
is adjacent to a large bay-windowed dinette. The great
room includes many windows
and a fireplace. A powder
bath and laundry room are
both conveniently placed on
the first floor. Upstairs, the
large master suite contains
His and Hers walk-in closets,
corner windows and a bath
area featuring a double vanity
and whirlpool tub. Two pleasant secondary bedrooms have
interesting angles and a third
bedroom in the front features
a volume ceiling and arched
window.

© 1989 design basics inc.

Design by
Design
Basics,
Inc.

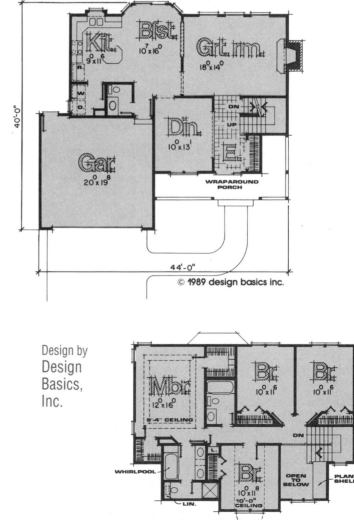

Design EE9284 First Floor: 1,348 square feet
Second Floor: 603 square feet; Total: 1,951 square feet

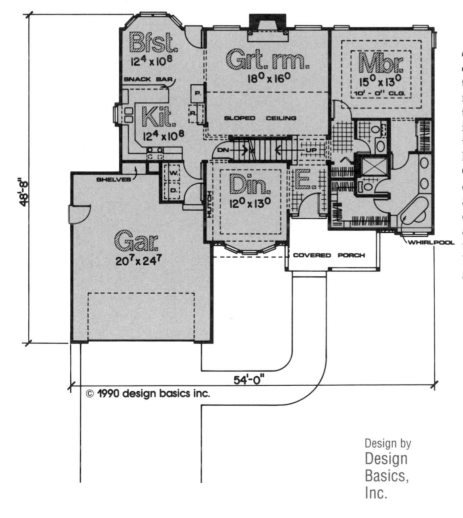

© 1990 design basics inc.

54'-0"

Design by
Design
Basics,
Inc.

● Highlighting the elevation of this window-brightened 1½-story home is a covered porch. Upon entering the home, enjoy the view to the spacious great room, ideal for daily living. Adding to the comfort of this informal area are bright windows flanking the fireplace. An elegant bayed window in the formal dining room with hutch space is also seen from the entry. Cooks will enjoy the thoughtfully designed kitchen with snack bar, pantry and window above the sink and the sunny dinette. A pampering master suite features a tiered ceiling, double vanity, corner whirlpool and large walk-in closet. Upstairs, three secondary bedrooms share a hall bath.

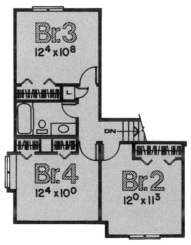

Design EE9314

First Floor: 1,679 square feet
Second Floor: 1,990 square feet
Total: 3,669 square feet

● Designed to be a country estate residence, this two-story home combines a sophisticated floor plan with a charming elevation. Throughout the home, beautiful windows bring the outdoors in. From the covered front porch, move inside to view a spectacular two-story entry with curving staircase. French doors lead into the library with a bayed window, built-in desk and bookcases. To the right, note the formal dining room. A great room benefits from the 10-foot spider-beamed ceiling, plus a wet bar and built-in entertainment center. Home owners will relish the combination breakfast/hearth room and kitchen concept. Upstairs, a balcony between the bedrooms overlooks the entry below. Segregation of the secondary bedrooms with walk-in closets provides privacy. Special finishing touches include the formal ceiling and bayed sitting area in the master suite. The master dressing/bath area is enhanced by His and Hers vanities, an oval whirlpool beneath the arched window and a deluxe walk-in closet with windows.

Design by
Design Basics, Inc.

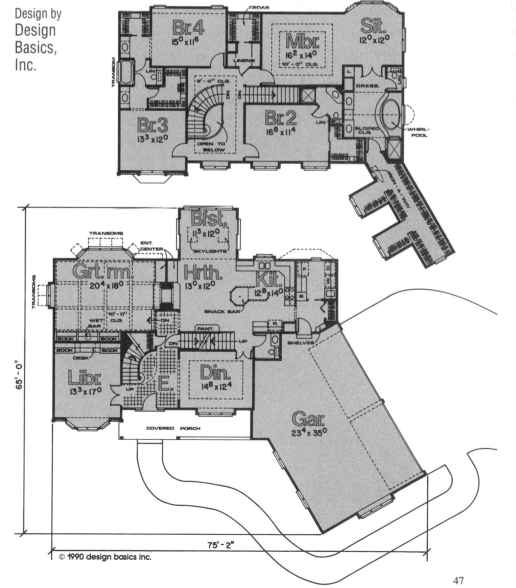

© 1990 design basics inc.

47

Design by
Donald A.
Gardner,
Architects, Inc.

Design EE9662

First Floor: 1,025 square feet
Second Floor: 911 square feet
Total: 1,936 square feet

● The exterior of this three-bedroom home is enhanced by its many gables, arched windows and wraparound porch. A large great room with impressive fireplace leads to both the dining room and screened porch with access to the deck. An open kitchen offers a country-kitchen atmosphere. The second-level master suite has two walk-in closets and an impressive bath. There is also bonus space over the garage. The plan is available with a crawl-space foundation.

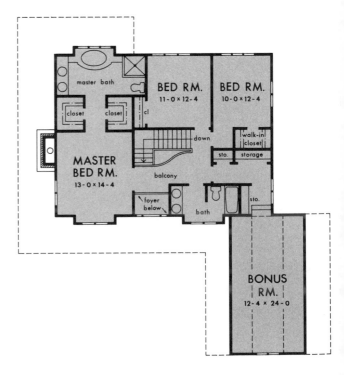

B. NATHAN.

Floor Plans

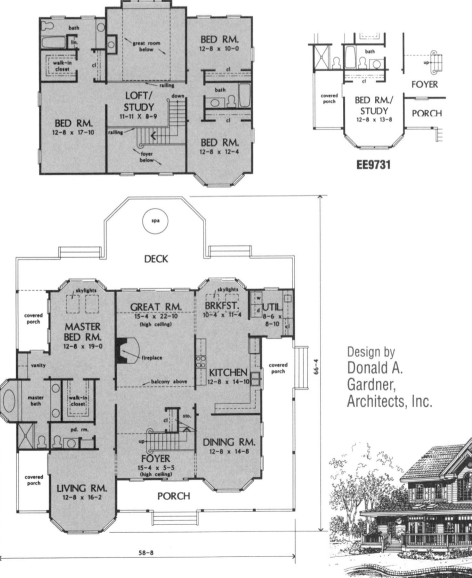

Second Floor

bath
lin.
walk-in closet
cl
clerestory with palladian window
great room below
railing
BED RM.
12-8 x 10-0
cl
bath
cl
LOFT/ STUDY
11-11 X 8-9
down
BED RM.
12-8 x 17-10
railing
foyer below
BED RM.
12-8 x 12-4

EE9731

bath
cl
up
FOYER
covered porch
BED RM./ STUDY
12-8 x 13-8
PORCH

EE9731

First Floor

spa
DECK
skylights
GREAT RM.
15-4 x 22-10
(high ceiling)
skylights
BRKFST.
10-4' x 11-4
UTIL
8-6 x 8-10
w d
cl
covered porch
MASTER BED RM.
12-8 x 19-0
fireplace
vanity
balcony above
covered porch
KITCHEN
12-8 x 14-10
66-4
master bath
walk-in closet
pd. rm.
cl
sto.
up
DINING RM.
12-8 x 14-8
covered porch
FOYER
15-4 x 5-5
(high ceiling)
LIVING RM.
12-8 x 16-2
PORCH
58-8

Design EE9730/EE9731

First Floor: 1,976 square feet
Second Floor: 970 square feet
Total: 2,946 square feet

● This stylish country farmhouse offers flexibility in the total number of bedrooms while maximizing use of space. Choose between a living room with a half bath (Design EE9730) or a bedroom/study with a full bath (Design EE9731) depending on your family needs. A loft/study on the second floor overlooks the elegant foyer and the great room below. The master bedroom and the breakfast area admit natural light through bay windows and skylights. Private covered porches are accessible from the master bedroom and the living room/study. Three bedrooms and two full baths occupy the second floor.

Design by
Donald A. Gardner, Architects, Inc.

Design EE9722

First Floor: 1,923 square feet
Second Floor: 598 square feet
Total: 2,521 square feet

● This stately four-bedroom home is reinforced by the symmetry of the front elevation along with the arched windows, intricately detailed columns and copper roofing over bay windows. The interior offers a wealth of architectural excitement as shown in the great room with its cathedral ceiling spanning from the clerestory windows on one side to the curved second-level balcony on the other. This open plan is packed with the latest design features including kitchen with large island, wet bar, bedroom/study combo on the first level and gorgeous master suite with large walk-in closet and spacious master bath containing whirlpool tub, shower and two vanities. Two bedrooms sharing a bath are on the second level along with ample attic space for storage. A large front porch and rear deck that is partially covered offer maximum outdoor living flexibility. There is also a large bonus room over the garage.

Design by
Donald A.
Gardner,
Architects, Inc.

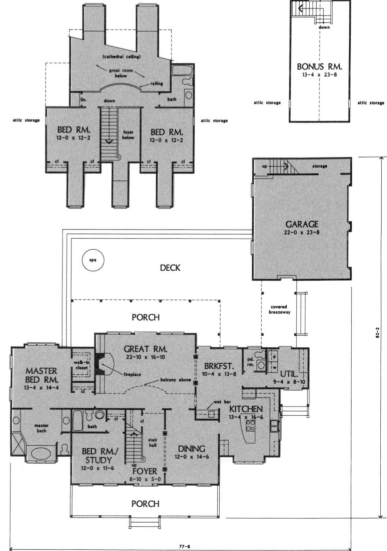

Design EE9743

First Floor: 2,176 square feet; Second Floor: 861 square feet; Total: 3,037 square feet; Bonus Room: 483 square feet

● Country living is at its best in this spacious four-bedroom farmhouse with a wraparound porch. A front Palladian window dormer and rear clerestory windows in the great room add exciting visual elements to the exterior as well as provide natural light to the interior. In the great room, a fireplace, bookshelves, a cathedral ceiling and a balcony overlook create a comfortable atmosphere. The formal zones of the living and dining rooms offer additional living space. Special features such as a large cooktop island in the kitchen, a wet bar, a bedroom/study combo, a generous bonus room over the garage and ample storage space set this plan apart from others. You'll also love the fact that the master bedroom suite, the great room and the breakfast room all directly access the rear porch.

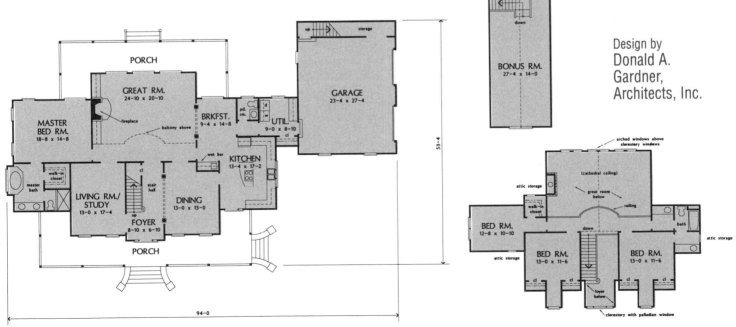

Design by
Donald A.
Gardner,
Architects, Inc.

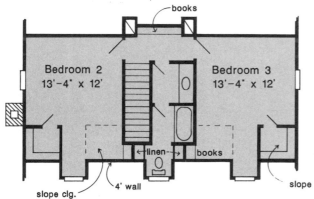

books

Bedroom 2
13'-4" x 12'

Bedroom 3
13'-4" x 12'

linen

books

slope clg.

4' wall

slope clg.

Design EE9121

First Floor: 1,266 square feet
Second Floor: 639 square feet
Total: 1,905 square feet

● Complete with dormers and a covered front porch, the facade details of this home are repeated at the side-loaded garage, making it a perfectly charming plan from any angle. From the raised foyer, step down into the living room with fireplace. This area opens to a dining room which has a French door to the rear yard. Close by is a kitchen with pantry and access to a utility room and the garage. The master suite is on the first floor for convenience. Note the two large walk-in closets here. Upstairs there are two secondary bedrooms and a full compartmented bath. An entry near the garage contains a staircase to an optional storage room. This space could be developed later as a mother-in-law suite or home office.

Design by
Larry W.
Garnett &
Associates, Inc.

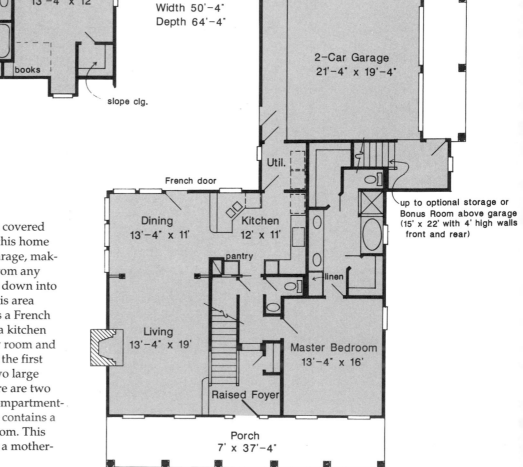

Width 50'-4"
Depth 64'-4"

2-Car Garage
21'-4" x 19'-4"

Util.

French door

up to optional storage or
Bonus Room above garage
(15' x 22' with 4' high walls
front and rear)

Dining
13'-4" x 11'

Kitchen
12' x 11'

pantry

linen

Living
13'-4" x 19'

Master Bedroom
13'-4" x 16'

Raised Foyer

Porch
7' x 37'-4"

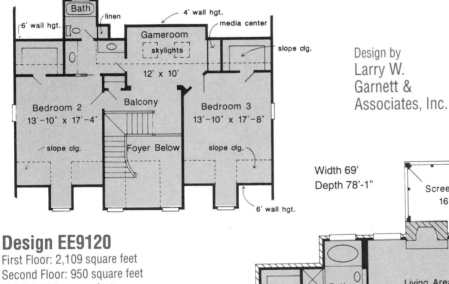

Bath

6' wall hgt.

linen

4' wall hgt.

media center

Gameroom

skylights

12' x 10'

slope clg.

Bedroom 2
13'-10" x 17'-4"

Balcony

Bedroom 3
13'-10" x 17'-8"

slope clg.

Foyer Below

slope clg.

6' wall hgt.

Design by
Larry W.
Garnett &
Associates, Inc.

Width 69'
Depth 78'-1"

2-Car Garage
26' x 19'-4"

12' x 26' unfinished area
above garage

Screened Porch
16' x 10'

French doors

Util.

up

Storage

Bath

Breakfast
12' x 11'

cabinet

Bath

linen

Closet
6' x 15'

seat

drawers

Living Area
19' x 16'

Kitchen
13' x 11'

pantry

Bedroom 4
11' x 12'-8"

Master Bedroom
13'-4" x 18'-8"

Foyer

Dining
13'-4" x 15'

Porch
40' x 10'

Design EE9120

First Floor: 2,109 square feet
Second Floor: 950 square feet
Total: 3,059 square feet

● This distinctive Greek Revival Style home works well in a 1½-story plan. The 10'-deep covered porch of this home opens to an entry foyer that connects the dining room and living room and contains the stairway to the second floor. Stairs at the breakfast room provide access to a 12' x 26' future room. The master bedroom is complemented by a bath with many amenities. Tucked away to the right of the plan is a bedroom that works well as guest quarters or could hold a home office or study. For additional sleeping space, there are two bedrooms with dormer windows and walk-in closets, plus a full bath on the second floor.

Design EE8060

First Floor: 3,545 square feet
Second Floor: 1,751 square feet
Total: 5,296 square feet

● Reminiscent of the South, this stately home is designed for the growing family. The living room displays a large masonry fireplace flanked by built-in cabinets and shelves. The kitchen features a cooktop island, a walk-in pantry and a screened porch, providing a wonderful setting for outdoor meals. Nearby, the family and breakfast rooms share a two-way gas fireplace. An amenity-filled master suite includes a corner fireplace and a master bath with an exercise room, a corner whirlpool and His and Hers walk-in closets. Her closet features a secondary cedar closet for extra-special storage. Three bedrooms, two baths, a multi-purpose loft and a future playroom encompass the second floor.

Design by
Larry E. Belk
Designs

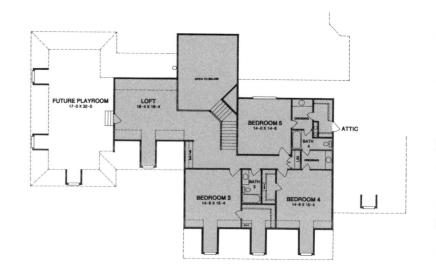

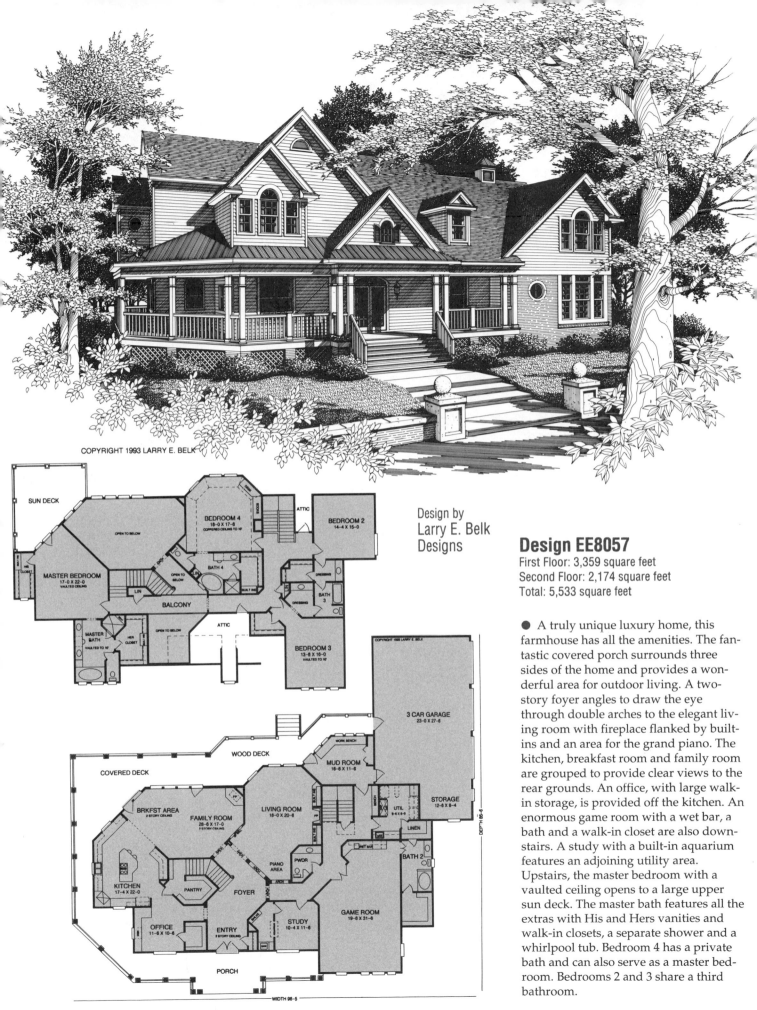

COPYRIGHT 1993 LARRY E. BELK

SUN DECK

BEDROOM 4
18-0 X 17-6
COPPERED CEILING TO 10'

ATTIC

BEDROOM 2
14-4 X 15-0

MASTER BEDROOM
17-0 X 22-0
VAULTED CEILING

OPEN TO BELOW

BATH 4

OPEN TO BELOW

LIN

BATH 3

DRESSING

BALCONY

MASTER BATH
VAULTED TO 10'

HER CLOSET

OPEN TO BELOW

ATTIC

BEDROOM 3
13-8 X 16-0
VAULTED TO 10'

COPYRIGHT 1993 LARRY E. BELK

3 CAR GARAGE
23-0 X 27-6

WORK BENCH

WOOD DECK

MUD ROOM
18-6 X 11-6

COVERED DECK

STORAGE
12-6 X 8-4

BRKFST AREA
2 STORY CEILING

FAMILY ROOM
28-6 X 17-0
2 STORY CEILING

LIVING ROOM
18-0 X 20-6

UTIL

LINEN

KITCHEN
17-4 X 22-0

PANTRY

PIANO AREA

PWDR

WET BAR

BATH 2

FOYER

OFFICE
11-6 X 10-6

ENTRY
2 STORY CEILING

STUDY
10-4 X 11-6

GAME ROOM
19-8 X 31-8

PORCH

WIDTH 96-5

DEPTH 85-6

Design by
Larry E. Belk
Designs

Design EE8057
First Floor: 3,359 square feet
Second Floor: 2,174 square feet
Total: 5,533 square feet

● A truly unique luxury home, this farmhouse has all the amenities. The fantastic covered porch surrounds three sides of the home and provides a wonderful area for outdoor living. A two-story foyer angles to draw the eye through double arches to the elegant living room with fireplace flanked by built-ins and an area for the grand piano. The kitchen, breakfast room and family room are grouped to provide clear views to the rear grounds. An office, with large walk-in storage, is provided off the kitchen. An enormous game room with a wet bar, a bath and a walk-in closet are also downstairs. A study with a built-in aquarium features an adjoining utility area. Upstairs, the master bedroom with a vaulted ceiling opens to a large upper sun deck. The master bath features all the extras with His and Hers vanities and walk-in closets, a separate shower and a whirlpool tub. Bedroom 4 has a private bath and can also serve as a master bedroom. Bedrooms 2 and 3 share a third bathroom.

55

COPYRIGHT 1991 LARRY E. BELK

Design by
Larry E. Belk
Designs

Design EE8039 First Floor: 2,600 square feet
Second Floor: 383 square feet; Total: 2,983 square feet

● An inviting country elevation welcomes you to this comfortable home. Inside, twelve-foot ceilings in the entry, living room and dining room create a feeling of spaciousness. Columns with connecting arches define the dining room and make a stunning visual statement at the entry. The kitchen, breakfast room and family room are conveniently grouped for family gatherings and entertaining. The master suite is located on the opposite side of the home for privacy. An angled bay window in this bedroom highlights a sitting area overlooking the rear grounds. Two additional bedrooms and a bath are located off the family room. Upstairs, a loft, a bedroom and a bath combine to form the perfect arrangement for the teenager in the family.

Width 77'-5"
Depth 78'-6"

56

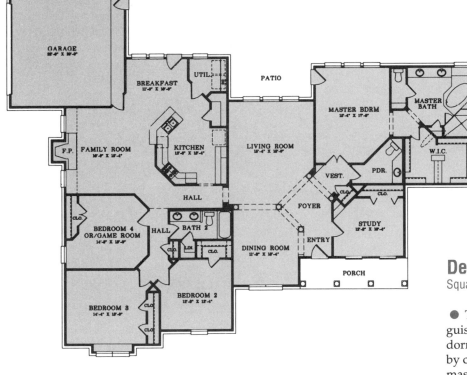

Design EE8018
Square Footage: 2,846

● This Southern Colonial home is distinguished by its columned porch and double dormer. Inside, the angled foyer is defined by columns and connecting arches. The master suite is located away from the other bedrooms for privacy and includes a large master bath and a walk-in closet. Three additional bedrooms are located adjacent to the family room. The kitchen, breakfast area and family room are open and perfect for informal entertaining and family gatherings. The foyer, living room and dining room have twelve-foot ceilings. Ten-foot ceilings are used in the family room, kitchen, breakfast area and master suite to give this home an open, spacious feeling. This plan is available with either a crawlspace or slab foundation. Please specify when ordering.

Width 84'-6"
Depth 64'-2"

Design by
Larry E. Belk
Designs

Copyright 1992 Stephen S. Fuller, Inc.

Design EE9870 First Floor: 2,155 square feet
Second Floor: 1,020 square feet; Total: 3,175 square feet

● To highlight the exterior of this home, wood siding and paneled shutters have been artfully combined with arched transoms, gables and a sweeping roof line to define the beautiful glass entry. The open foyer at once reveals the large living and dining rooms and a classic great room with a coffered ceiling and a hearth. Double doors open to the master bedroom with its unique tray ceiling and fireplace. The master bath includes knee space with double vanities and a shower, a corner garden tub and His and Hers closets. The exercise room can be accessed from either

the master bedroom or the great room and opens onto the p at the rear of the home. The generous corner breakfast area opens to the porch. The large kitchen with a cook-top island pantry and a laundry room complete the main level. The ga features built-in bookshelves and a computer/study nook w easy access from all three bedrooms on the upper level. An ished bonus room with attic access offers room for expansic This home is designed with a basement foundation.

Design by
Design Traditions

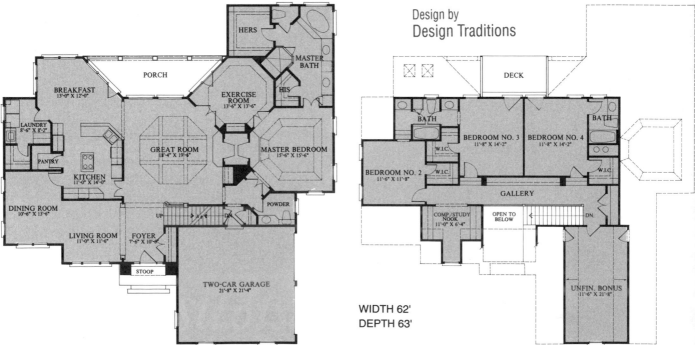

WIDTH 62'
DEPTH 63'

Copyright 1992 Stephen S. Fuller, Inc.

Design by
Design Traditions

PORCH

BEDROOM/
OFFICE
10'-4" X 11'-0"

BREAKFAST
13'-4" X 9'-0"

GREAT ROOM
17'-0" X 17'-8"

KITCHEN
13'-4" X 10'-6"

MASTER
BATH

MASTER BEDRDOOM
16'-4" X 13'-6"

BEDROOM NO. 2
10'-4" X 12'-0"

BATH

LAUNDRY

DN.

BATH

TWO CAR GARAGE
20'-6" X 19'-6"

DINING ROOM
11'-4" X 12'-10"

FOYER
5'-4" X
12'-10"

BEDROOM/
STUDY
11'-2" X 12'-0"

PORCH

Width 61'
Depth 70'-6"

Design EE9853
Square Footage: 2,090

● This traditional home features board-and-batten and cedar shingles in an attractively proportioned exterior. Finishing touches include a covered entrance and porch with column detailing and an arched transom, flower boxes and shuttered windows. The foyer opens to both the dining room and great room beyond with French doors opening onto the porch. Through the double doors to the right of the foyer is the combination bedroom/study. A short hallway leads to a full bath and a secondary bedroom with ample closet space. The master bedroom is spacious, with walk-in closets on both sides of the entrance to the master bath. With separate vanities, a shower and a toilet, the master bath forms a private retreat at the rear of the home. Convenient to both the great room and dining room, the kitchen opens to an attractive breakfast area featuring a bay window. An additional room is remotely located off the kitchen, providing a retreat for today's at-home office or guest. This home is designed with a basement foundation.

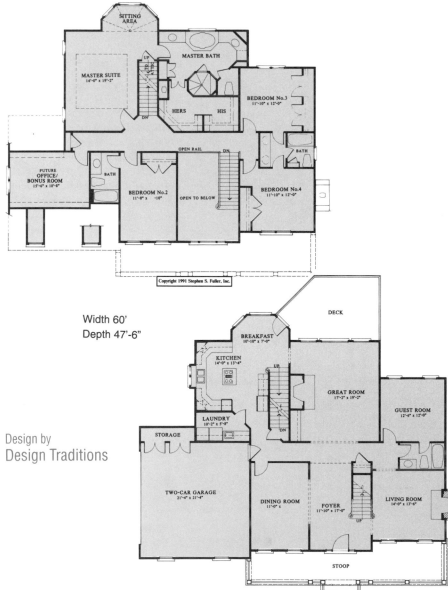

SITTING AREA

MASTER BATH

MASTER SUITE
14'-0" x 19'-2"

UP ATTIC

DN

HERS   HIS

BEDROOM No.3
11'-10" x 12'-0"

OPEN RAIL   DN

BATH

FUTURE
OFFICE/
BONUS ROOM
15'-6" x 10'-8"

BATH

BEDROOM No.2
11'-8" x '10"

OPEN TO BELOW

BEDROOM No.4
11'-10" x 12'-0"

Copyright 1991 Stephen S. Fuller, Inc.

Width 60'
Depth 47'-6"

Design by
Design Traditions

DECK

BREAKFAST
10'-10" x 7'-0"

KITCHEN
14'-0" x 13'-4"

UP

GREAT ROOM
17'-2" x 19'-2"

GUEST ROOM
12'-6" x 12'-0"

LAUNDRY
10'-2" x 5'-8"

STORAGE

DN

TWO-CAR GARAGE
21'-4" x 31'-4"

DINING ROOM
11'-0" x

FOYER
11'-10" x 17'-0"

LIVING ROOM
14'-0" x 13'-6"

UP

STOOP

Design EE9909

First Floor: 1,700 square feet
Second Floor: 1,585 square feet
Total: 3,285 square feet

● The covered front stoop of this
two-story, traditionally styled
home gives way to the foyer and
formal areas inside. A cozy living
room with a fireplace sits on the
right and an elongated dining
room—perfect for an elegant table
—is on the left. For fine family living, a great room—also with a fireplace—and a kitchen/breakfast
area account for the rear of the
first-floor plan. Notice the deck off
the breakfast room. A guest room
with a nearby full bath finishes off
the accommodations. Upstairs, four
bedrooms include a master suite fit
for a king. In it are a bayed sitting
area and a private bath with His
and Hers closets, dual lavatories, a
spa tub, an octagonal shower stall
and a compartmented toilet. A
bonus room rests near Bedroom 3
and would make a great office or
additional bedroom. This home is
designed with a basement
foundation.

Design EE9852 First Floor: 1,840 square feet
Second Floor: 950 square feet; Total: 2,790 square feet

Design by
Design Traditions

● The appearance of this Early American home brings the past to mind with its wraparound porch, wood siding and flower-box detailing. The uniquely shaped foyer leads to the dining room accented by columns, a vaulted ceiling and a bay window. Columns frame the great room as well, while a ribbon of windows creates a wall of glass at the back of the house from the great room to the breakfast area. The asymmetrical theme continues through the kitchen as it leads back to the hallway, accessing the laundry and two-car garage. Left of the

foyer lies the living room with a warming fireplace. The master suite begins with double doors that open to a large living space with an octagonal tray ceiling and a bay window. The spacious master bath and walk-in closet complete the suite. Stairs to the second level lead from the breakfast area to an open landing overlooking the great room. Three additional bedrooms with large walk-in closets and a variety of bath arrangements complete this level. This home is designed with a basement foundation.

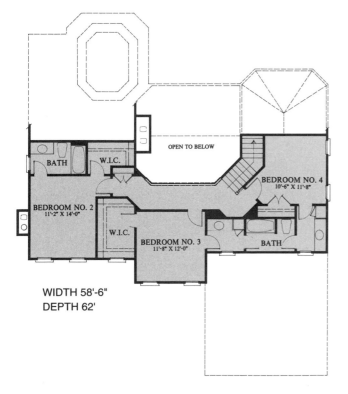

WIDTH 58'-6"
DEPTH 62'

Design EE9822

First Floor: 1,944 square feet
Second Floor: 954 square feet
Total: 2,898 square feet

● This story-and-a-half home combines warm informal materials with a modern livable floor plan to create a true Southern classic. The dining room, study and great room work together to create one large, exciting space. Just beyond the open rail, the breakfast room is lined with windows. Plenty of counter space and storage make the kitchen truly usable. The master suite, with its tray ceiling and decorative wall niche, is a gracious and private owners' retreat. Upstairs, two additional bedrooms each have their own vanity within a shared bath while the third bedroom or guest room has its own bath and a walk-in closet. This home is designed with a basement foundation.

Design by
Design Traditions

WIDTH 51'-6"
DEPTH 73'

Victorian & Folk Designs

For the South, with its appreciation of the finer things in life, the Victorian Age did not go unnoticed. As a matter of fact, the common denominators of Victorian design — verandas, dormer windows and an extensive use of woodwork — fit into the Southern architectural landscape with little trouble.

In the Victorian age, advances in construction technology and an improved economic climate allowed for homes with intricate detail, complex shapes and a grand nature. Some would say the Victorian Age produced the only true American housing style. In the South, where influences were centuries old and from several countries, this recognition of Victorian design does not pass without significance.

Basic Victorian elements often include asymmetrical forms, steeply pitched roofs and a multitude of decorative detail, and the South readily embraced these elements as it explored such Victorian styles as Second Empire, Italianate and Queen Anne. In the two former, proportions tend toward the vertical; decoration includes carved balusters, repeating columns and intricate window and door surrounds. Design EE9015 reflects some of these features with a facade offset by a gable and curved spindlework that ties together a very charming front porch.

Providing the largest landscape for stylistic innovations, the Queen Anne style features steeply pitch roof lines, oftentimes a front-facing gable and a turret, fan and side lights around doors and a variety of exterior materials. Clapboard is the most common of these and usually combines with shingles, masonry and even terra-cotta. Then, of course, come the spandrels, spindlework, finials and corner brackets to act as icing on the cake.

With considerable proportions and comfortable living patterns, Design EE2953 captures much of the magic of the Queen Anne style. Decorated with covered porches on three sides, this home welcomes all into a fantastic interior.

Folk Victorian traditions also come through in this section with a fine precedent set by Design EE9067. Among its quiet features: a wrapping veranda, a front gable with a Palladian window and chimneys on either side of the house for an additional sense of balance.

No matter what Victorian fancy comes to mind, the designs presented here will undoubtedly make dream homes come true!

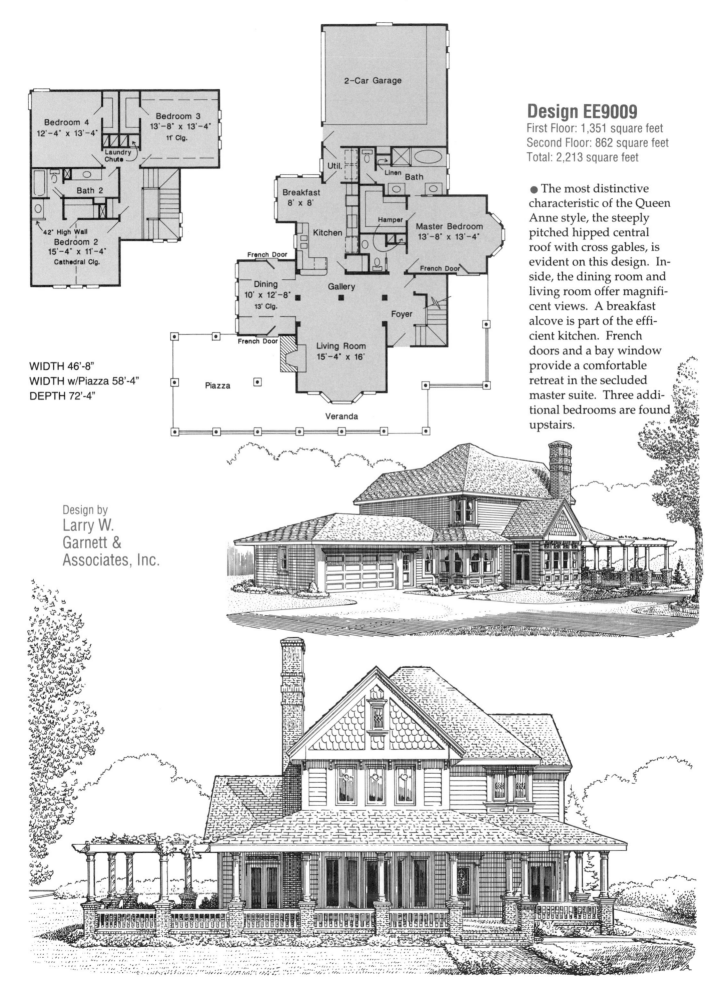

Bedroom 4
12'-4" x 13'-4"

Bedroom 3
13'-8" x 13'-4"
11' Clg.

Laundry Chute

Bath 2

42" High Wall
Bedroom 2
15'-4" x 11'-4"
Cathedral Clg.

2-Car Garage

Util.

Linen   Bath

Breakfast
8' x 8'

Kitchen

Hamper

Master Bedroom
13'-8" x 13'-4"

French Door

Dining
10' x 12'-8"
13' Clg.

Gallery

French Door

Foyer

French Door

Living Room
15'-4" x 16'

WIDTH 46'-8"
WIDTH w/Piazza 58'-4"
DEPTH 72'-4"

Piazza

Veranda

Design EE9009

First Floor: 1,351 square feet
Second Floor: 862 square feet
Total: 2,213 square feet

● The most distinctive characteristic of the Queen Anne style, the steeply pitched hipped central roof with cross gables, is evident on this design. Inside, the dining room and living room offer magnificent views. A breakfast alcove is part of the efficient kitchen. French doors and a bay window provide a comfortable retreat in the secluded master suite. Three additional bedrooms are found upstairs.

Design by
Larry W.
Garnett &
Associates, Inc.

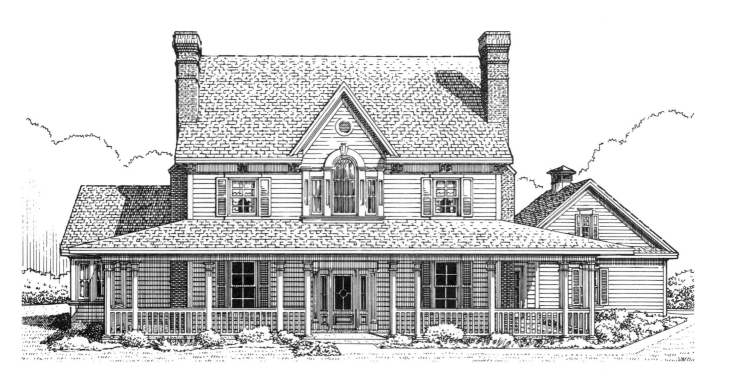

Design EE9067

First Floor: 1,999 square feet
Second Floor: 933 square feet
Total: 2,932 square feet

● The wraparound veranda and simple lines give this home an unassuming elegance that is characteristic of its Folk Victorian heritage. Opening directly to the formal dining room, the two-story foyer offers extra space for large dinner parties. Double French doors lead to the study with raised paneling and a cozy fireplace. Built-in bookcases conceal a hidden security vault. The private master suite features a corner garden tub, glass-enclosed shower and a walk-in closet. Overlooking the family room and built-in breakfast nook is the central kitchen. A rear staircase provides convenient access to the second floor from the family room. The balcony provides a view of the foyer below and the Palladian window. Three additional bedrooms complete this exquisite home.

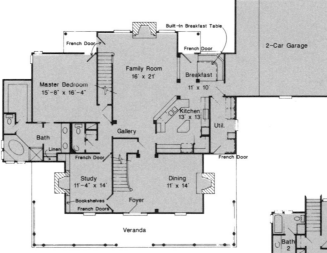

9' Clg. Throughout

Design by
**Larry W.
Garnett &
Associates, Inc.**

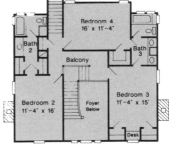

REAR VIEW

WIDTH 79' 8"
DEPTH 59'

65

Design EE9063 First Floor: 1,236 square feet
Second Floor: 835 square feet; Total: 2,071 square feet

● The living area of this spectacular Queen Anne Style home features a fireplace and a bay-windowed alcove. The centrally located kitchen overlooks a dining area with full-length windows and a French door. The master bedroom has a large walk-in closet and French doors opening to the rear veranda. The master bath provides additional closet space, along with a glass-enclosed shower and an oval tub in an octagon-shaped alcove. Upstairs, French doors open into a game room. Bedroom 2 has a walk-in closet and a ten-foot sloped ceiling. Bedroom 3 also has a walk-in closet and a raised octagon-shaped ceiling. Plans are included for a detached, two-car garage and an optional screened porch.

Design by
Larry W.
Garnett &
Associates, Inc.

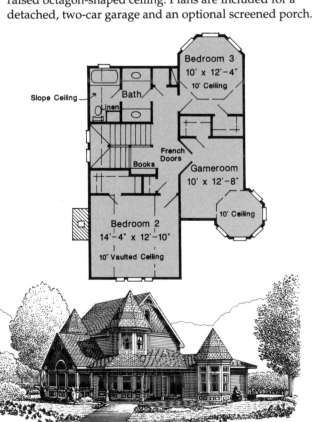

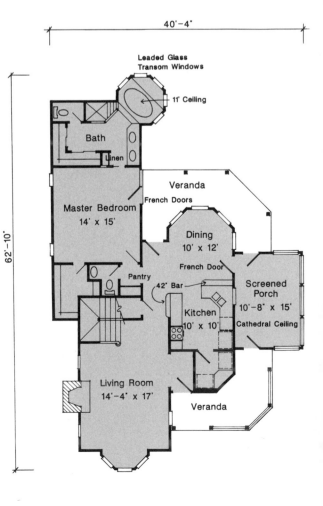

Design EE9014

First Floor: 1,565 square feet
Second Floor: 1,598 square feet
Total: 3,163 square feet

● The angled entry of this home opens to a grand foyer and a formal parlor with expansive windows and a French door leading to the side yard. The formal dining area features a built-in hutch. Double French doors open from the foyer to the large study with bookcases and full-length windows. The spacious family room with a fireplace and wet bar is a superb entertainment area. The kitchen with its work island and abundant cabinet space overlooks the octagon-shaped breakfast room. Upstairs, the master bedroom has French doors which open onto a rear deck. The distinctive bath features a bay-windowed tub area and glass enclosed shower. Three additional bedrooms each have walk-in closets. Plans for two-car detached garage are included.

Design by
Larry W.
Garnett &
Associates, Inc.

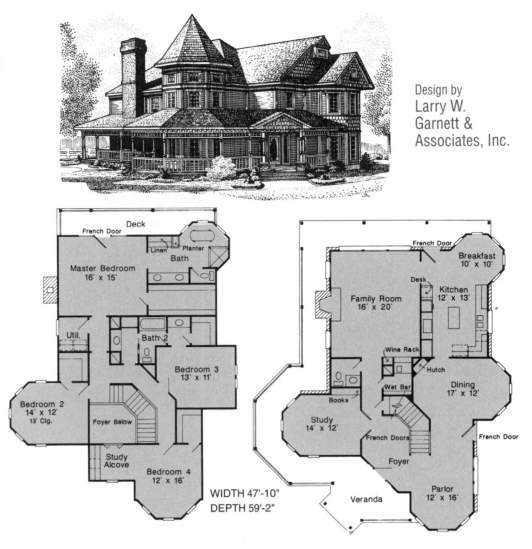

WIDTH 47'-10"
DEPTH 59'-2"

Design EE9055

First Floor: 997 square feet
Second Floor: 1,069 square feet
Total: 2,066 square feet

● With its exceptional detail and proportions, this home is reminiscent of the Queen Anne Style. Turned posts resting on brick pedestals support a raised-gable entry to the veranda. The foyer opens to a living area with a bay-windowed alcove and a fireplace with flanking bookshelves. A large walk-in pantry and box window at the sink are special features in the kitchen. Natural light fills the breakfast area with a full-length bay window and a French door. Upstairs, the master bedroom offers unsurpassed elegance and convenience.

The sitting area has an eleven-foot ceiling with arch-top windows. The bath area features a large walk-in closet, His and Hers lavatories, and plenty of linen storage. Plans for a two-car detached garage are included.

Design by
Larry W.
Garnett &
Associates, Inc.

Width 39' 8"
Depth 39' 2"

Design EE9013
First Floor: 2,385 square feet
Second Floor: 1,467 square feet
Total: 3,852 square feet

● This Victorian-inspired home can take advantage of a building site that offers views in every direction. Built-in bookcases and double French doors opening from the living room and the gallery make the study a perfect retreat. The conveniently located wet bar serves both the living area and the gallery. Overlooking the breakfast area, the kitchen features a work island, a walk-in pantry and plenty of cabinet space. The spacious master bedroom has French doors opening onto the veranda. Upstairs, the game room overlooks the foyer and the main staircase. A staircase leads to an optional third floor. Bedrooms 2 and 4 each have private dressing areas with window seats. Bedroom 3 has a large walk-in closet and shares a hall bath. A rear staircase, which leads to the breakfast area, has a plant ledge and a skylight. A two-car detached garage design is included with the plan.

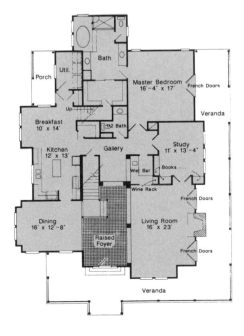

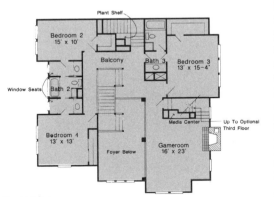

Design by
Larry W.
Garnett &
Associates, Inc.

Width 54' - 4"
Depth 75'

Design EE9012

First Floor: 1,357 square feet
Second Floor: 1,079 square feet
Total: 2,436 square feet

● An inviting wraparound veranda with delicate spindlework and a raised turret with leaded-glass windows recall the grand Queen Anne Victorians of the late 1880s. Double doors open from the dramatic two-story foyer to a private study with built-in bookcases and a bay window. The gallery, with decorative wood columns and an arched ceiling, overlooks both the large formal dining and living rooms. French doors open from the living room to the front veranda and to the screened porch. A fireplace adds warmth to the breakfast area and the island kitchen. Above the two-car garage is an optional area that is perfect for a home office or guest quarters. Upstairs, the master suite, with His and Hers walk-in closets, leads to a luxurious bath with a garden tub and glass-enclosed shower. An optional exercise loft and plant shelves complete this elegant master bath. Two additional bedrooms, one with a private deck and the other with a cathedral ceiling, share a dressing area and bath.

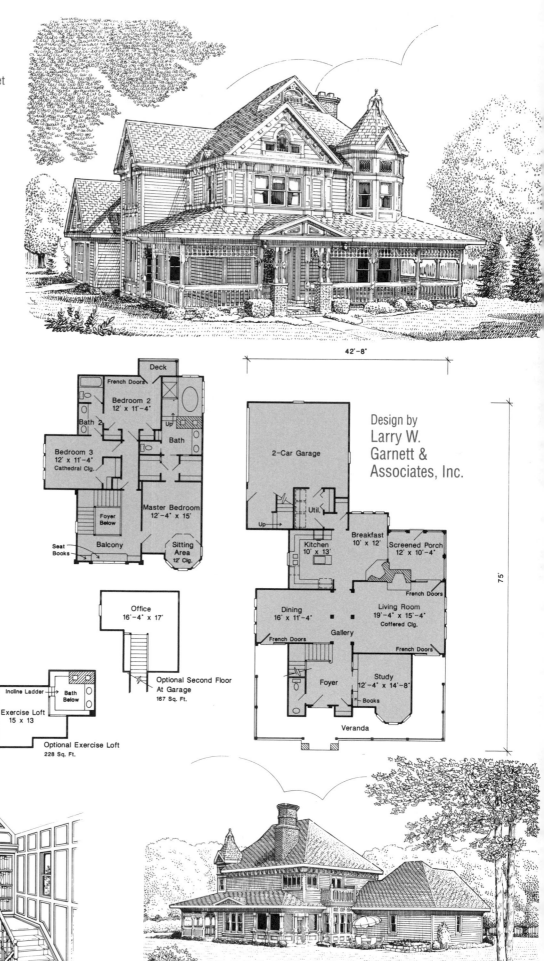

Design by
Larry W. Garnett & Associates, Inc.

42'-8"

75'

Deck
French Doors
Bedroom 2
12' x 11'-4"
Bath 2
Up
Bath
Bedroom 3
12' x 11'-4"
Cathedral Clg.
Foyer Below
Master Bedroom
12'-4" x 15'
Seat Books
Balcony
Sitting Area
12' Clg.

2-Car Garage
Util.
Up
Kitchen
10' x 13'
Breakfast
10' x 12'
Screened Porch
12' x 10'-4"
French Doors
Dining
16' x 11'-4"
French Doors
Living Room
19'-4" x 15'-4"
Coffered Clg.
Gallery
French Doors
Foyer
Study
12'-4" x 14'-8"
Books
French Doors
Veranda

Office
16'-4" x 17'

Optional Second Floor At Garage
167 Sq. Ft.

Incline Ladder
Bath Below
Exercise Loft
15 x 13

Optional Exercise Loft
228 Sq. Ft.

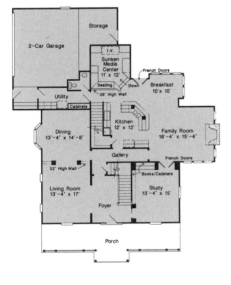

Width 59' - 4"
Depth 72' - 8"

Design EE9015

First Floor: 1,948 square feet
Second Floor: 1,891 square feet
Total: 3,839 square feet

● As authentic as the exterior of this design is, the interior offers all the luxury and elegance that today's homeowners could desire. The formal living and dining rooms are separated by detailed wood columns. Built-in bookcases and cabinets highlight the block-paneled study. The centrally located kitchen becomes the focal point of a truly outstanding family living center which includes a sunken media area, breakfast alcove, and a family room with a fireplace. Adjacent to the kitchen is a large hobby room with a built-in desk, a space for a freezer, and generous cabinet storage. A rear staircase provides convenient access to the second floor. The secluded master suite is beyond compare, with such extras as a fireplace with flanking window seats and cabinets, an enormous walk-in closet, and a private deck. The luxurious bath features a dressing table, a whirlpool tub with a gazebo-shaped ceiling above, and an oversized shower. Finally, there is a private exercise room with a bay-window seat. Three additional bedrooms and a laundry room complete the second floor. A staircase leads to an optional third floor area.

Design by
Larry W.
Garnett &
Associates, Inc.

Design EE9270

First Floor: 1,113 square feet
Second Floor: 965 square feet
Total: 2,078 square feet

● Elegant detail, a charming veranda and the tall brick chimney create a pleasing facade on this four-bedroom Victorian home. Yesterday's simpler lifestyle is reflected throughout this plan. A large bayed parlor with sloped ceiling is visible from the entry. Step down to enter the gathering room with a fireplace and plenty of windows. Note the pantry cabinet and built-in desk in the kitchen and breakfast area. The formal dining room opens to the parlor for entertaining ease. The second-floor master suite is segregated for privacy and provides a dressing and bath area with double lavatories, skylight and whirlpool tub.

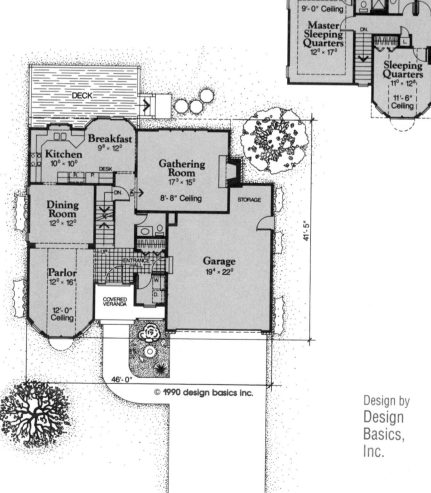

© 1990 design basics inc.

Design by

Design
Basics,
Inc.

Design EE9251

First Floor: 1,653 square feet
Second Floor: 700 square feet
Total: 2,353 square feet

● Beautiful arches and elaborate detail give the elevation of this four-bedroom, 1½-story home an unmistakable elegance. Inside the floor plan is equally appealing. Note the formal dining room with bay window, visible from the entrance hall. The large great room has a fireplace and a wall of windows out the back. A hearth room, with bookcase, adjoins the kitchen area with walk-in pantry. The master suite on the first floor features His and Hers wardrobes, a large whirlpool and double lavatories. Upstairs quarters share a full bath with compartmented sinks.

Design by
Design Basics, Inc.

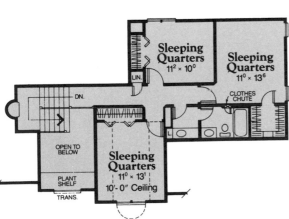

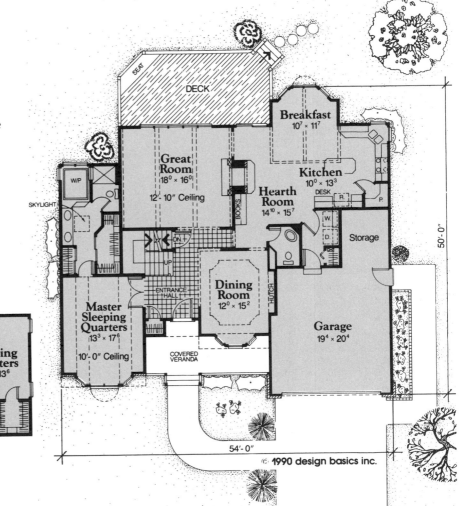

Design EE9277

First Floor: 1,553 square feet
Second Floor: 725 square feet
Total: 2,278 square feet

● The intricate detailing,
tall brick chimney and stately
veranda on the elevation of
this four-bedroom, 1½-story
home blend effortlessly into
Victorian elegance. Other
preferred features include:
two-story entrance hall, bay
window in formal dining
room, open island kitchen
with pantry and desk, private master suite with vaulted ceiling, two-person
whirlpool in master bath.
This versatile plan is designed for practical living
with guest rooms or chil-
dren's bedrooms located on
the upper level. One of these
second-story bedrooms has a
walk-in closet.

Design by
**Design
Basics,
Inc.**

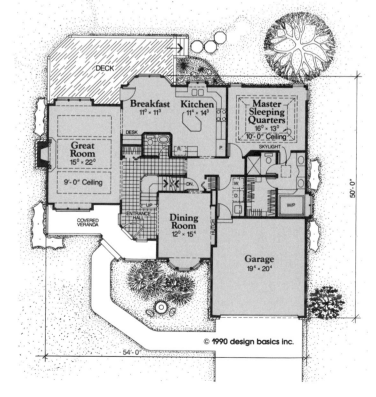

Design EE9268
First Floor: 1,308 square feet
Second Floor: 1,107 square feet; Total: 2,415 square feet

Design by
Design Basics, Inc.

● Embellished with interesting detail, this four-bedroom, two-story home offers an alternative to the ordinary. The covered veranda welcomes all to a marvelous floor plan. Thoughtful amenities include a dining room with added hutch space, a bay window in the parlor, a large gathering room with fireplace and plenty of windows and a featured-filled kitchen. The luxurious master bedroom has a vaulted ceiling and pampering bath with whirlpool, double lavatories and two closets. Three secondary bedrooms share a full bath with double lavatories.

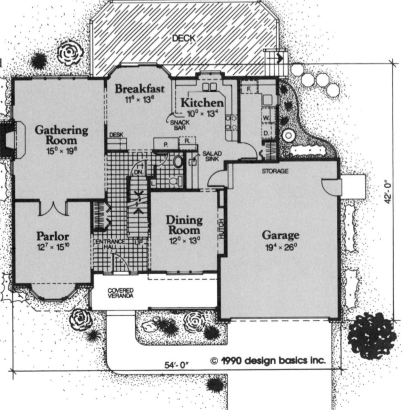

© 1990 design basics inc.

Design EE2970 First Floor: 1,538 square feet
Second Floor: 1,526 square feet; Third Floor: 658 square feet
Total: 3,722 square feet

● A porch, is a porch, is a porch. But, when it wraps around to a side, or even two sides, of the house, we have called it a veranda. This charming Victorian features a covered outdoor living area on all four sides! It even ends at a screened porch which features a sun deck above. This interesting plan offers three floors of livability. And what livability it is! Plenty of formal and informal living facilities to go along with the potential of five bedrooms. The master suite is just that. It is adjacent to an interesting sitting room. It has a sun deck and excellent bath/personal care facilities. The third floor will make a wonderful haven for the family's student members.

Design by
Home Planners, Inc.

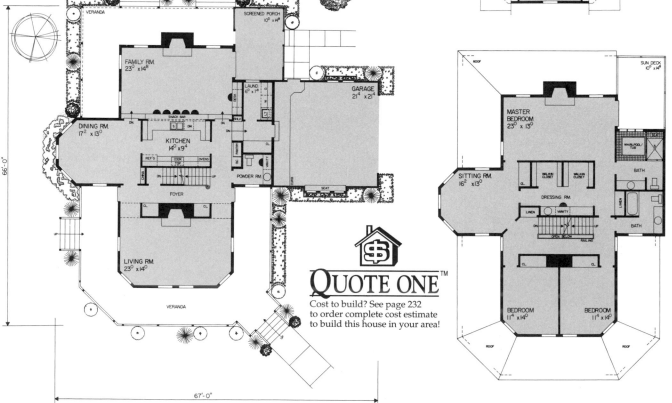

Quote One™

Cost to build? See page 232
to order complete cost estimate
to build this house in your area!

Design EE2974

First Floor: 911 square feet
Second Floor: 861 square feet
Total: 1,772 square feet

● Victorian houses are well known for their orientation on narrow building sites. And when this occurs nothing is lost to captivating exterior styling. This house is but 38 feet wide. Its narrow width belies the tremendous amount of livability found inside. And, of course, the ubiquitous porch/veranda contributes mightily to style as well as livability. The efficient, U-shape kitchen is flanked by the informal breakfast room and formal dining room. The rear living area is spacious and functions in an exciting manner with the outdoor areas. Bonus recreational, hobby and storage space is offered by the basement and the' attic.

QUOTE ONE™

Cost to build? See page 232
to order complete cost estimate
to build this house in your area!

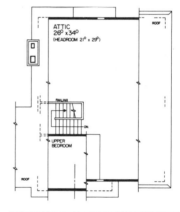

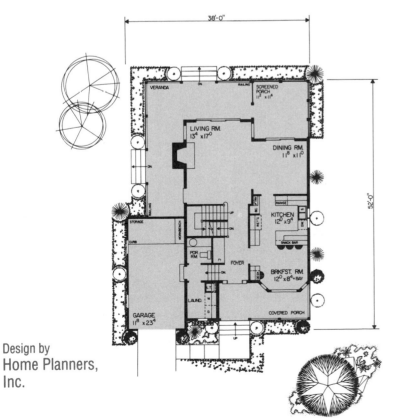

Design by
**Home Planners,
Inc.**

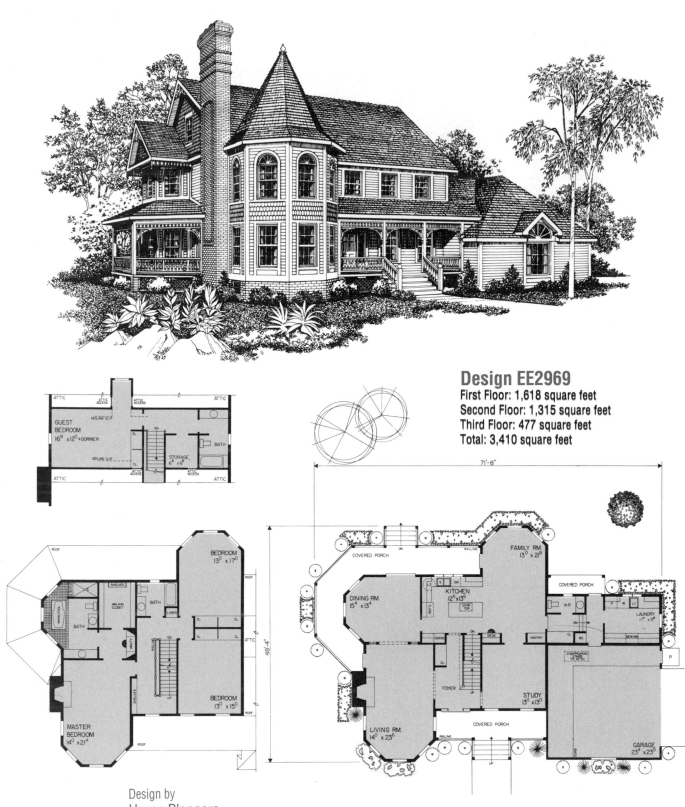

Design EE2969

First Floor: 1,618 square feet
Second Floor: 1,315 square feet
Third Floor: 477 square feet
Total: 3,410 square feet

Design by
Home Planners,
Inc.

● What could beat the charm of a turreted Victorian with covered porches to the front, side and rear? This delicately detailed exterior houses an outstanding family oriented floor plan. Projecting bays make their contribution to the exterior styling. In addition, they provide an extra measure of livability to the living, dining and family rooms, plus two of the bedrooms. The efficient kitchen, with its island cooking station, functions well with the dining and family rooms. A study provides a quiet first floor haven for the family's less active pursuits. Upstairs there are three big bedrooms and a fine master bath.

The third floor provides a guest suite and huge bulk storage area (make it a cedar closet if you wish). This house has a basement for the development of further recreational and storage facilities. Don't miss the two fireplaces, large laundry and attached two-car garage. A great investment.

Design EE3309

First Floor: 1,375 square feet
Second Floor: 1,016 square feet
Total: 2,391 square feet

● Covered porches, front and back, are a fine preview to the livable nature of this Victorian. Living areas are defined in a family room with fireplace, formal living and dining rooms, and a kitchen with breakfast room. An ample laundry room, garage with storage area, and powder room round out the first floor. Three second floor bedrooms are joined by a study and two full baths.

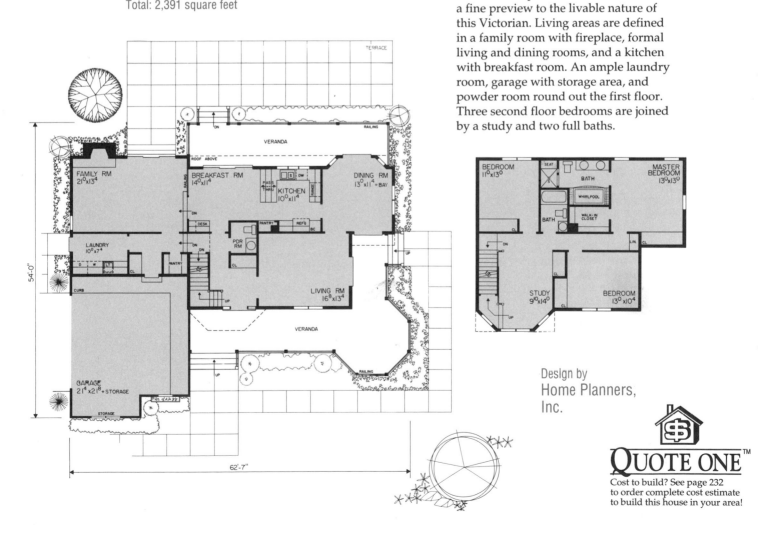

Design by
Home Planners,
Inc.

Quote One™
Cost to build? See page 232
to order complete cost estimate
to build this house in your area!

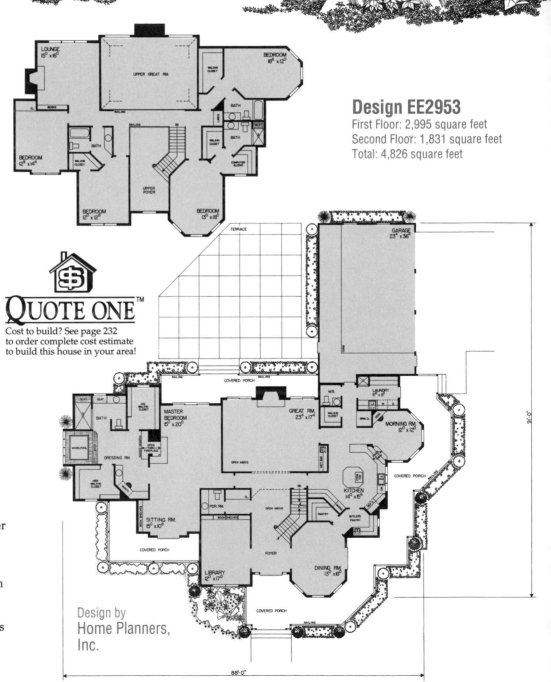

A magnificent, finely wrought covered porch wraps around this impressive Victorian estate home. The gracious two-story foyer provides a direct view past the stylish bannister and into the great room with large central fireplace. To the left of the foyer is a bookshelf-lined library and to the right is a dramatic, octagonal-shaped dining room. The island cooktop completes a convenient work triangle in the kitchen, and a pass-through connects this room with the Victorian-style morning room. A butler's pantry, walk-in closet, and broom closet offer plenty of storage space. A luxurious master suite is located on the first floor and opens to the rear covered porch. A through-fireplace warms the bedroom, sitting room, and dressing room, which includes His and Hers walk-in closets. The step-up whirlpool tub is an elegant focal point to the master bath. Four uniquely designed bedrooms, three full baths, and a restful lounge with fireplace are located on the second floor. Who says you can't combine the absolute best of today's amenities with the quaint styling and comfortable warmth of the Victorian past!

Design EE2953

First Floor: 2,995 square feet
Second Floor: 1,831 square feet
Total: 4,826 square feet

QUOTE ONE™

Cost to build? See page 232 to order complete cost estimate to build this house in your area!

Design by
Home Planners,
Inc.

Southern Colonial, Georgian & Plantation Styles

All the grandeur of the South comes through in our selection of styles ranging from Southern Colonial and Georgian to the distinguished Plantation style. Similarities of these houses include the use of brick — oftentimes to ward off the evils of rain on wood—columns and pedimented structures.

The Southern Colonial, for example, displays symmetry with a covered stoop flanked by equal sets of windows. Quoins enhance the exterior as in Design EE9364. This house features a family room wing on the left to balance a modern garage wing on the right. The floor plan remains true to order.

To expand on such stateliness, EE3303 utilizes a roof overhang supported by six columns to create a portico. Balance reigns, again, through matching wings on both sides of the main house. In this design, the wings function in truly modern terms with one for the family vehicles and one to accommodate the master bedroom suite.

Symmetry continues to be the watchword in Georgian variations, with a central structure often flanked by wings. However, these wings tend to carry more living space with one wing carrying all sleeping quarters and another, utility areas (usually coupled with the garage). Brick continues as the primary exterior material, especially appropriate for the South. As displayed in Design EE2693, Georgians are less vertical and have a lower pitched roof. Four chimneys dominate the exterior elevation and are placed in an orderly fashion. Entryways remain a focus with columns and pediments introducing a very livable interior.

Of all the styles prominent in the South, perhaps the most distinguished is the Southern Plantation home. Steeped in Southern history, this style exhibits classic architectural proportions. Because plantations were often set in the moist, fertile areas of the South — especially Louisiana — concern over water tables came into play. As a result, houses incorporated a raised basement and a story or a story-and-a-half for living. This is exemplified in Design EE3505. It also shows how today's adaptations still sport verandas that stretch around the house for enjoying cool breezes — or any breezes at all. And because plantation living meant wealth, this design and others in this section still offer large proportions and embellishments such as the grand and picturesque columns that help define the style.

This section offers all this and more — including historical homes, with modern interpretations, such as Jefferson's Poplar Forest home, Design EE3509. All in all, the spirit of the South couldn't be more alive than in these homes!

Design EE2693

Square Footage: 3,462

● This elegant Georgian manor is reminiscent of historic Rose Hill, built 1818 in Lexington, Kentucky. It is typical of the classic manors with Greek Revival features built in Kentucky as the 19th Century dawned. Note the classical portico of four Ionic columns plus the fine proportions. Also noteworthy is the updated interior, highlighted by a large country kitchen with fireplace and an efficient work center that includes an island cooktop. The country kitchen leads directly into a front formal dining room, just off the foyer. On the other side of the foyer is a front living room. A large library is located in the back of the house. It features built-in bookcases plus a fireplace, one of four fireplaces.

Design by
Home Planners, Inc.

Design EE2977 First Floor: 4,104 square feet; Second Floor: 979 square feet; Total: 5,083 square feet

Design by
Home Planners, Inc.

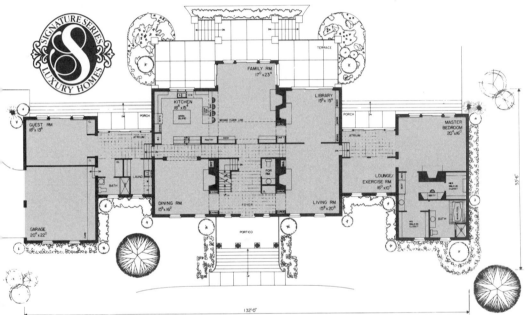

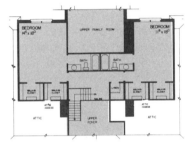

● Both front and rear facades of this elegant brick manor depict classic Georgian symmetry. A columned, Greek entry opens to an impressive two-story foyer. Fireplaces, built-in shelves, and cabinets highlight each of the four main gathering areas: living room, dining room, family room, and library.

Design EE2981

First Floor: 2,104 square feet
Second Floor: 2,015 square feet
Total: 4,119 square feet

Design by
Home Planners,
Inc.

● This formal two-story recalls a Louisiana plantation house, Land's End, built in 1857. The Ionic columns of the front porch and the pediment gable echo the Greek Revival style. Highlighting the interior is the bright and cheerful spaciousness of the informal family room area. It features a wall of glass stretching to the second story sloping ceiling. Enhancing the drama of this area is the adjacent glass area of the breakfast room. Note the "His/Her" areas of the master bedroom.

Quote One™

Cost to build? See page 232
to order complete cost estimate
to build this house in your area!

Design EE3505

First Floor: 2,899 square feet
Second Floor: 1,519 square feet
Total: 4,418 square feet
Bonus Room: 540 square feet

● A sweeping veranda with tapered columns supports the low-pitched roof and its delicately detailed cornice work. The wood railing effectively complements the lattice-work below. Horizontal siding and double-hung windows with muntins and shutters enhance the historic appeal of the 1½-story home. Inside, the spacious central foyer has a high ceiling and a dramatic, curving staircase to the second floor. Two formal areas flank the foyer and include the living room to the left and the dining room to the right. the U-shaped kitchen easily services the later through a butler's pantry. A library and gathering room flank the kitchen and will delight the family. Sleeping accommodations excel with spacious master suite. Here, a private bath and two closets—one a walk-in—guarantee satisfaction. At the top of the dramatic staircase to the second floor is a generous sitting area which looks down on the foyer. Three bedrooms are directly accessible form this area. A bonus room further enhances this fabulous family home.

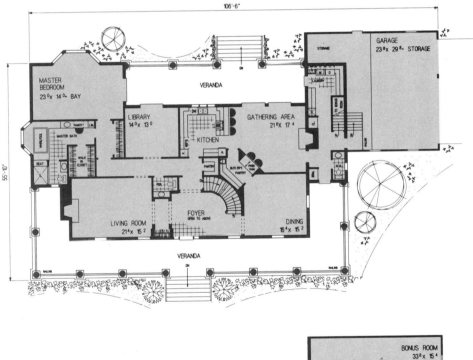

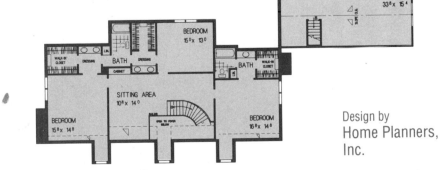

Design by
Home Planners, Inc.

Design EE2668 First Floor: 1,206 square feet
Second Floor: 1,254 square feet; Total: 2,460 square feet

● This elegant exterior houses a very livable plan. Every bit of space has been put to good use. The front country kitchen is a good place to begin. It is efficiently planned with its island cook top, built-ins and pass-thru to the dining room. The large great room will be the center of all family activities. Quiet times can be enjoyed in the front library. Study the second floor sleeping areas.

Design by
Home Planners,
Inc.

Design EE2683

First Floor: 2,126 square feet
Second Floor: 1,882 square feet
Total: 4,008 square feet

● This historical Georgian home has its roots in the 18th-Century. Dignified symmetry is a hallmark of both front and rear elevations. The elegant gathering room, three steps down from the rest of the house, has ample space for entertaining on a grand scale. It fills an entire wing and is dead-ended so that traffic does not pass through it. Guests and family alike will enjoy the two rooms flanking the foyer, the study and formal dining room. Each of these rooms will have a fireplace as its highlight. The breakfast room, kitchen, powder room and laundry are arranged for maximum efficiency. This area will always have that desired light and airy atmosphere with the sliding glass door and the triple window over the kitchen sink. The second floor houses the family bedrooms. Take special note of the spacious master bedroom suite. It has a deluxe bath, fireplace and sunken lounge with dressing room and walk-in closet.

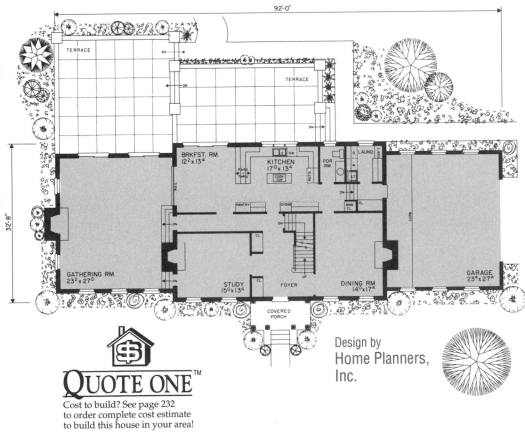

Design by
Home Planners,
Inc.

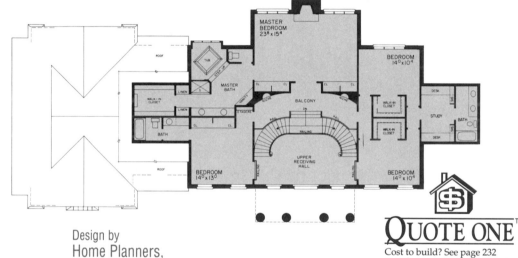

Design by
**Home Planners,
Inc.**

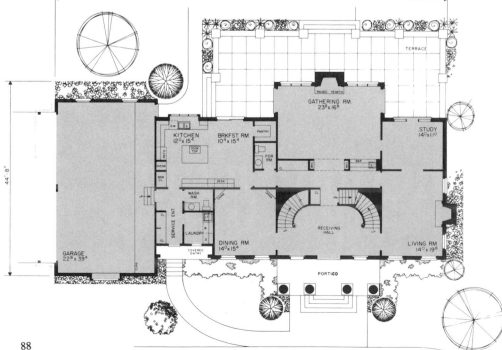

Design EE2889

First Floor: 2,349 square feet
Second Floor: 1,918 square feet
Total: 4,267 square feet

● This is truly a classic design. Some of the exterior highlights of this two-story include the pediment gable with cornice work and dentils, the beautifully proportioned columns, the front door detailing and the window treatment. Behind the facade of this design is an equally elegant interior. Imagine greeting your guests in the large receiving hall. It is graced by two curving staircases and opens to the formal living and dining rooms. Beyond the living room is the study. It has access to the rear terrace. Those large, informal occasions for family get-togethers or entertaining will be enjoyed in the spacious gathering room. It has a centered fireplace flanked by windows on each side, access to the terrace and a wet bar. The work center is efficient: a kitchen with island cooktop, breakfast room, washroom, laundry and service entrance. The second floor also is outstanding. Three family bedrooms and two full baths are joined by the feature-filled master bedroom suite.

QUOTE ONE™
Cost to build? See page 232
to order complete cost estimate
to build this house in your area!

Design EE2984

First Floor: 3,116 square feet
Second Floor: 1,997 square feet
Total: 5,113 square feet

● An echo of Whitehall, built in 1765 in Anne Arundel County, Maryland, resounds in this home. Its classic symmetry and columned facade herald a grand interior. There's no lack of space whether entertaining formally or just enjoying a family get-together, and all are kept cozy with fireplaces in the gathering room, study, and family room. An island kitchen with attached breakfast room handily serves the nearby dining room. Four second floor bedrooms include a large master suite with another fireplace, a whirlpool, and His and Hers closets in the bath. Three more full baths are found on this floor.

Design by
Home Planners,
Inc.

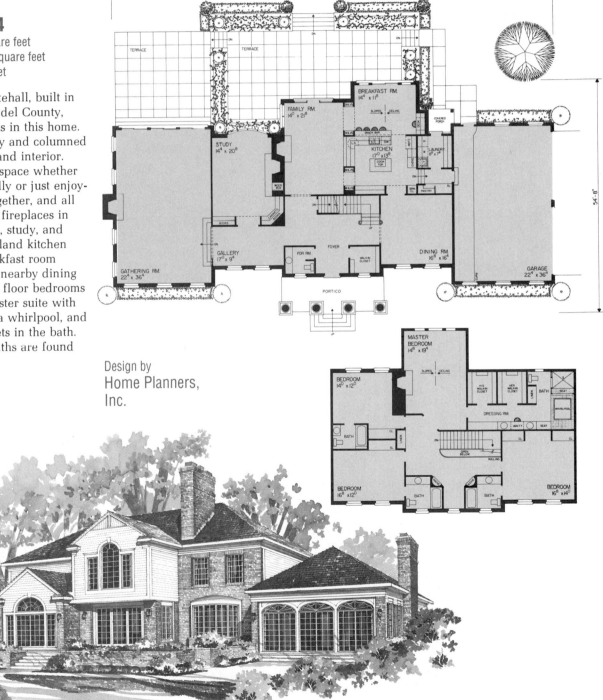

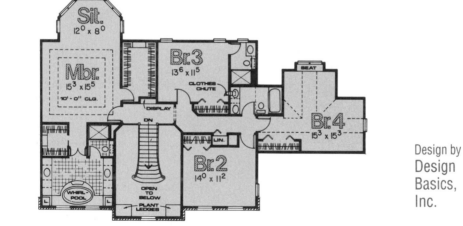

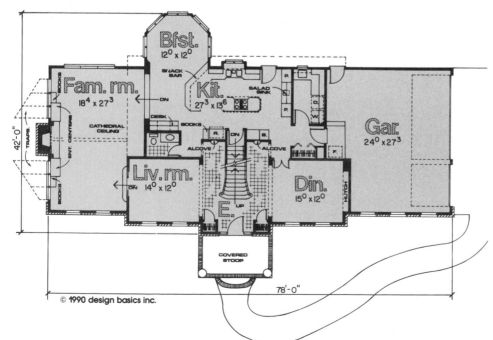

Design by
**Design
Basics,
Inc.**

Design EE9364

First Floor: 1,717 square feet
Second Floor: 1,518 square feet
Total: 3,235 square feet

● This beautiful Southern Colonial is highlighted by stately columns. The open entry allows views into formal areas and the tapering staircase. Alcoves flank the staircase in the entry while elegant formal rooms are enhanced by arched cased openings. The formal dining room with hutch space accesses the kitchen area through double doors. The living room accesses the family room through attractive pocket doors. Step down into the huge family room to find large windows, a fireplace, built-in entertainment center and bookcases. The kitchen adjoins the semi-gazebo breakfast area. Secondary bedrooms have two bath areas. The private master suite features a tiered ceiling, two walk-in closets and a roomy bayed sitting area.

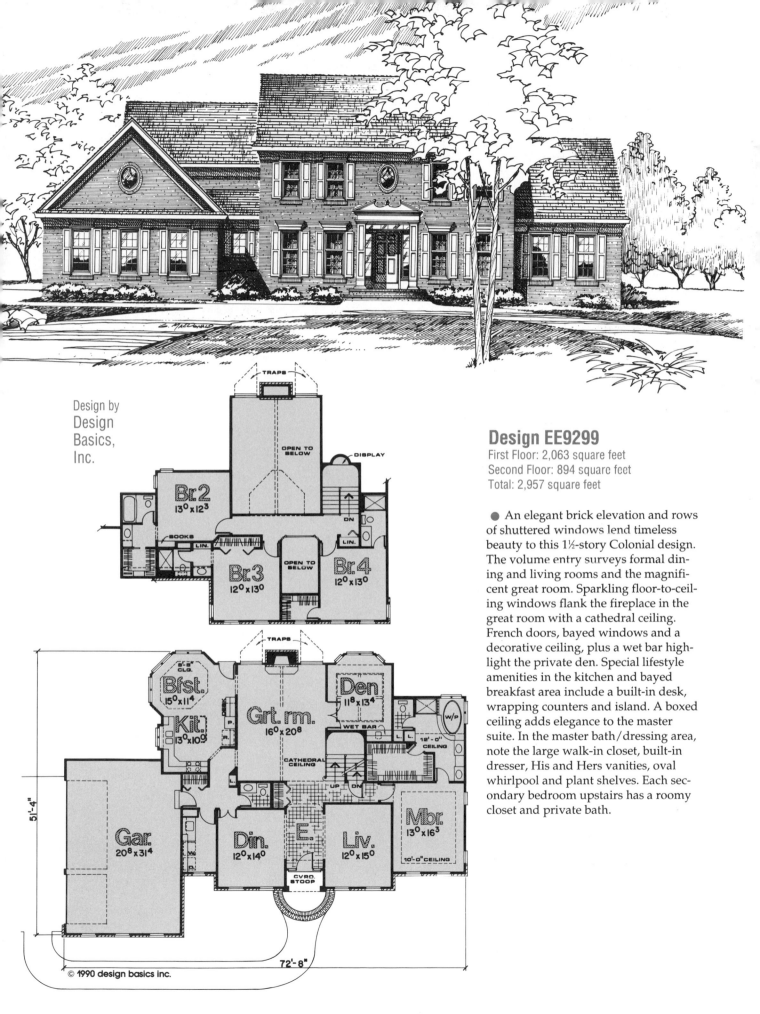

Design by
Design Basics, Inc.

© 1990 design basics inc.

Design EE9299

First Floor: 2,063 square feet
Second Floor: 894 square feet
Total: 2,957 square feet

● An elegant brick elevation and rows of shuttered windows lend timeless beauty to this 1½-story Colonial design. The volume entry surveys formal dining and living rooms and the magnificent great room. Sparkling floor-to-ceiling windows flank the fireplace in the great room with a cathedral ceiling. French doors, bayed windows and a decorative ceiling, plus a wet bar highlight the private den. Special lifestyle amenities in the kitchen and bayed breakfast area include a built-in desk, wrapping counters and island. A boxed ceiling adds elegance to the master suite. In the master bath/dressing area, note the large walk-in closet, built-in dresser, His and Hers vanities, oval whirlpool and plant shelves. Each secondary bedroom upstairs has a roomy closet and private bath.

Design EE7208

First Floor: 1,675 square feet
Second Floor: 1,605 square feet
Total: 3,280 square feet

● A grand and glorious split staircase makes a lasting first impression in this stately two-story home. The striking family room is lit by a beveled wall of windows while a wet bar, built-in book cases and an entertainment center provide the finishing touches. The spacious kitchen is sure to please, featuring an island cooktop with a snack bar, a planning desk and a sunny bayed breakfast area. Quiet and private, the second floor accommodates the sleeping areas. Each secondary bedroom enjoys a walk-in closet, two bedrooms share a Hollywood bath and a third enjoys a private bath. The master suite offers uncommon elegance with French doors opening into the master bedroom with its tray ceiling, a gazebo sitting area and a separate off-season closet. Enter the master bath through French doors and enjoy its relaxing whirlpool tub, an open shower and built-dressers in the large walk-in closet.

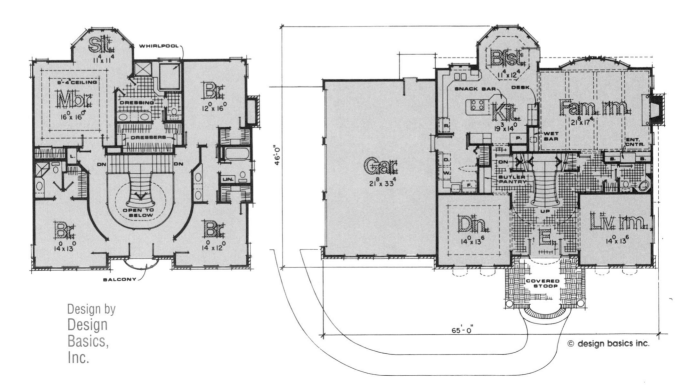

Design by
Design
Basics,
Inc.

Design EE9367 First Floor: 2,500 square feet; Second Floor: 973 square feet; Total: 3,473 square feet

● Step between the columns and into the entry of this grandiose design. The first floor offers maximum livability with 2,500 square feet. Large living and dining rooms flank a formal staircase. One of the most dramatic rooms in the house is the great room with a fourteen-foot-high beamed ceiling, a fireplace and wonderful views. Fancy the octagon-shaped break-fast nook or the kitchen with abundant counter space. This house incorporates four bedrooms with the master bedroom on the first floor. A tiered ceiling, two walk-in closets and a luxurious bath with His and Hers vanities, shower and a spa tub all characterize this room. On the second floor you'll find three bedrooms: two share a full bath, one has a private bath.

Design by
Design Basics, Inc.

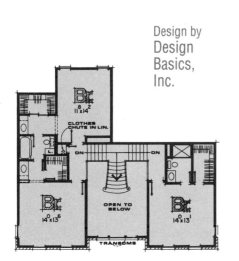

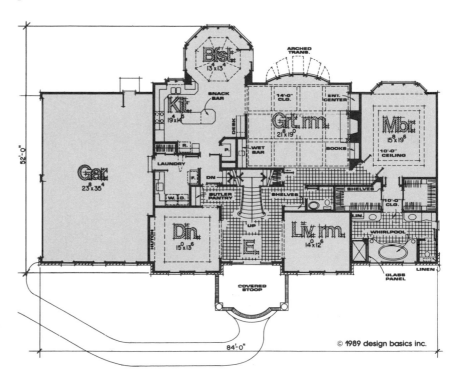

© 1989 design basics inc.

Design by
Design Traditions

Design EE9923

First Floor: 3,509 square feet
Second Floor: 1,564 square feet
Total: 5,073 square feet

● Classical details, symmetry of design and a stately brick exterior accentuate the grace and timeless beauty of this traditional style home. The entry begins with a wide and welcoming staircase which is framed by the large columns and intricately detailed door surrounds. Once inside, the ornate entryway yields to the large two-story foyer which opens to the large study/living room and beyond to an impressive great room. The master suite is secluded and complete with a dressing area, a large vaulted bath with a sauna, a lengthy closet and a private sitting room. The sitting room mirrors the breakfast area on the opposite end to complete the same symmetrical balance that is shown in the front elevation. The back stair provides an easy, yet private, access to the three large bedrooms above. Each bedroom is complete with its own bath and walk-in closet. This home is designed with a basement foundation.

Width 86'-6"
Depth 67'-3"

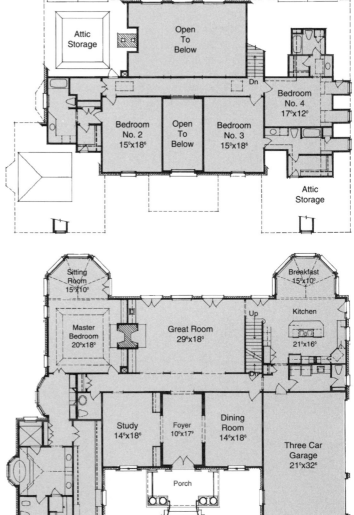

Design EE9924

First Floor: 3,365 square feet
Second Floor: 1,456 square feet
Total: 4,821 square feet
Bonus Room: 341 square feet

● The lines of this formal Georgian brick manor are graceful and flowing. The classical details complement the historical and stately elegance of this beautiful home. The inviting two-story foyer is highlighted by its view through the living room to the large patio. The tasteful entertaining area of the home is complemented by the spacious living area which includes the kitchen, the breakfast room and the den. Upstairs are three large bedrooms with either private or semi-private shared baths. Access to a bonus room is achieved from the back stairs located at the entrance of the kitchen. This home is designed with a basement foundation.

Width 81'
Depth 71'-9"

Design by
Design Traditions

95

Design EE9842 First Floor: 1,053 square feet; Second Floor: 1,053 square feet; Total: 2,106 square feet

● Brick takes a bold stand in grand traditional style in this treasured design. From the front entry to the rear deck, the floor plan serves family needs in just over 2,000 square feet. The front study has a nearby full bath, making it a handy guest bedroom. The family room with a fireplace opens to a cozy breakfast area. For more formal entertaining there's a dining room just off the entry. The kitchen features a prep island and a huge pantry. Upstairs, the master bedroom has its own sitting room and a giant-sized closet. Two family bedrooms share a full bath. This home is designed with a basement foundation.

Design by
Design Traditions

WIDTH 52'
DEPTH 34'

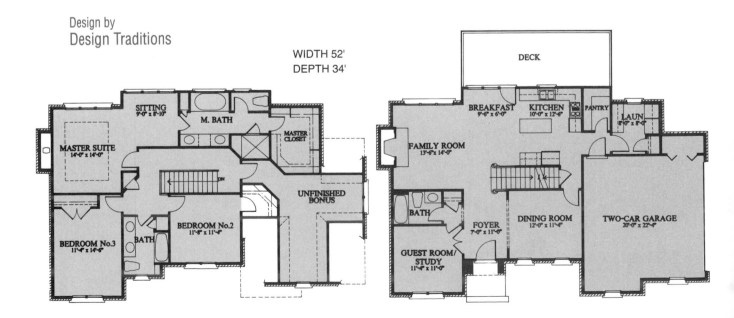

Design EE9823 First Floor: 1,960 square feet
Second Floor: 905 square feet; Total: 2,865 square feet

● The classical styling of this Colonial home will be appreciated by traditionalists. The foyer opens to both a banquet-sized dining room and a formal living room with a fireplace. Just beyond is the two-story great room. The entire right side of the main level is taken up by the master suite. The other side of the main level includes a large kitchen and a breakfast room just steps away from the detached garage. Upstairs, each bedroom features ample closet space and direct access to bathrooms. The detached garage features an unfinished office or studio on its second level. This home is designed with a basement foundation.

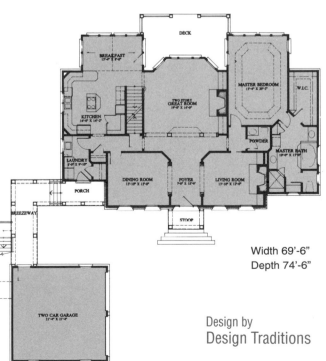

Width 69'-6"
Depth 74'-6"

Design by
Design Traditions

Design EE9828

First Floor: 1,455 square feet
Second Floor: 1,649 square feet
Total: 3,104 square feet

● The double wings, twin chimneys and center portico of this home
work in concert to create a classic
architectural statement. The
two-story foyer is flanked by the spacious dining room and formal
living room, each containing its own
fireplace. A large family room with a
full wall of glass beckons the outside
in while it opens conveniently onto
the sunlit kitchen and breakfast room.
The master suite features a tray ceiling
and French doors that open onto a
covered porch. A grand master bath
with all the amenities, including a garden tub and a huge closet, completes
the master suite. Two other bedrooms
share a bath while another has its own
private bath. The fourth bedroom also
features a sunny nook for sitting or
reading. This home is designed with a
basement foundation.

Design by
Design Traditions

WIDTH 53'
DEPTH 46'

WIDTH 77'-4"
DEPTH 58'-4"

Design EE9830

First Floor: 2,380 square feet
Second Floor: 1,295 square feet
Total: 3,675 square feet

● A blending of brick and finely crafted porches makes this home a classic in traditional living. Past the large French doors, the impressive foyer is flanked by both the formal living and dining rooms. Beyond the stairhall is a vaulted family room with a wall of glass, a fireplace and accompanying bookcases. From here the breakfast room and kitchen are easily accessible and open onto a private side porch. The master suite provides a large bath, two spacious closets, a fireplace and a private entry that opens to the covered rear porch. The second floor contains three bedrooms and a children's playroom. This home is designed with a basement foundation.

Design by
Design Traditions

COPYRIGHT 1994 LARRY E. BELK

Design by
Larry E. Belk
Designs

Design EE8028

First Floor: 2,270 square feet
Second Floor: 1,100 square feet
Total: 3,370 square feet

● A combination of stacked stone, brick and wood siding make this Southern traditional home a real beauty from the front curb. Designed for a golf course lot, the foyer steps up into a large great room with a view to the rear grounds. On the other side, steps lead down into the dining room with access to a side porch. The master suite includes a fabulous master bath—really two baths in one— with a His and Hers dressing area and a shared shower between. Up a short flight of stairs, a curved landing with windows to the rear is the perfect place for a piano. Continuing up the stairs, a large circular loft overlooks the great room and provides stunning views through high windows in the great room to the rear beyond. Three bedrooms and two baths are included in the upstairs layout. A permanent staircase located in the garage provides access to floored attic space.

Width 76'-6"
Depth 69'-4"

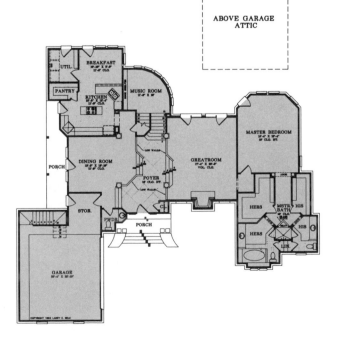

100

Design EE8036

First Floor: 2,682 square feet
Second Floor: 2,072 square feet
Total: 4,754 square feet

● This home reflects the traditional architecture of the South with the wide front porch supported by six massive columns. Inside, the two-story foyer is dominated by the staircase to the second floor. To the right is the dining room and to the left, through traditional square columns, is the large family room with a fireplace on the outer wall. Beyond the family room is the study—a perfect place for solitude and homework in the evenings. The plan incorporates a secondary front porch so that playing children may enter and go upstairs to the large game room located over the garage. Also upstairs are three large bedrooms and a finished storage area which may be used for an office or a hobby room. Two of the bedrooms feature dormer windows perfect for a built-in window seat or a toy chest. Please specify crawlspace or slab when ordering.

Design by
Larry E. Belk
Designs

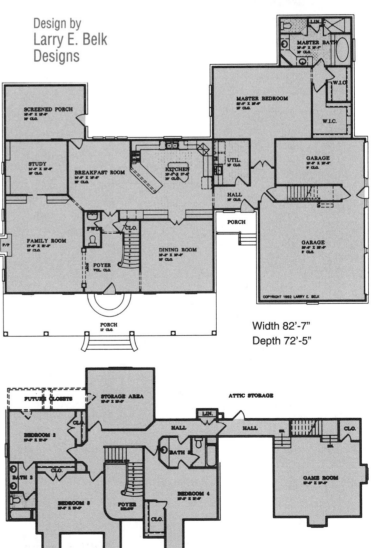

Width 82'-7"
Depth 72'-5"

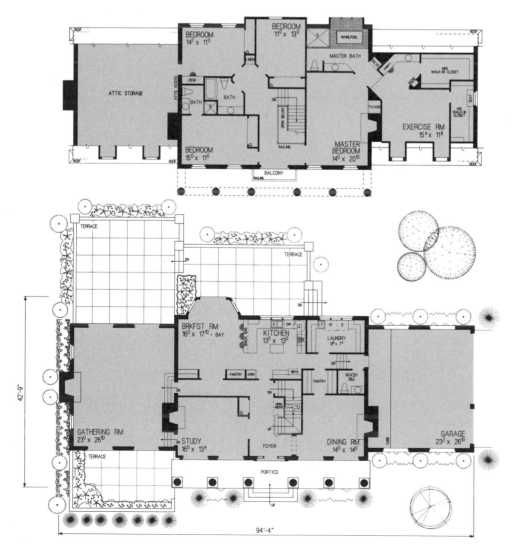

QUOTE ONE™

Cost to build? See page 232
to order complete cost estimate
to build this house in your area!

Design EE3337

First Floor: 2,167 square feet
Second Floor: 1,992 square feet
Total: 4,159 square feet

● The elegant facade of this design with its columned portico, fanlights, and dormers houses an amenity-filled interior. The gathering room, study and dining room, each with fireplace, provide plenty of room for relaxing and entertaining. A large work area contains a kitchen with breakfast room and snack bar, laundry room and pantry. The four-bedroom upstairs includes a master suite with a sumptuous bath and an exercise room.

Design by
Home Planners,
Inc.

Design EE3303

First Floor: 2,563 square feet
Second Floor: 1,496 square feet
Total: 4,059 square feet

● With its stately columns and one-story wings, this design is a fine representation of 18th Century adaptations. Formal living and dining areas flank the entry foyer at the front of the home. Look for a fireplace in the living room, china cabinet built-ins in the dining room. More casual living dominates the back section in a family room and kitchen/breakfast room combination that features access to the rear terrace and plenty of space for cooking and informal dining. The left wing garage is connected to the main structure by a service entrance adjacent to the laundry. The right wing contains the private master suite. Four second floor bedrooms share two full baths and each has its own walk-in closet.

QUOTE ONE™
Cost to build? See page 232 to order complete cost estimate to build this house in your area!

Design by
Home Planners,
Inc.

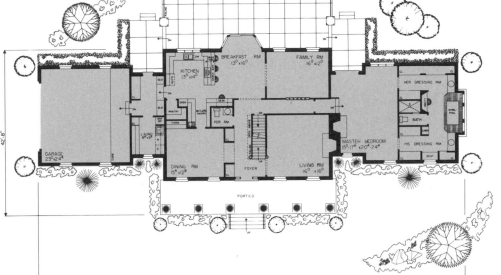

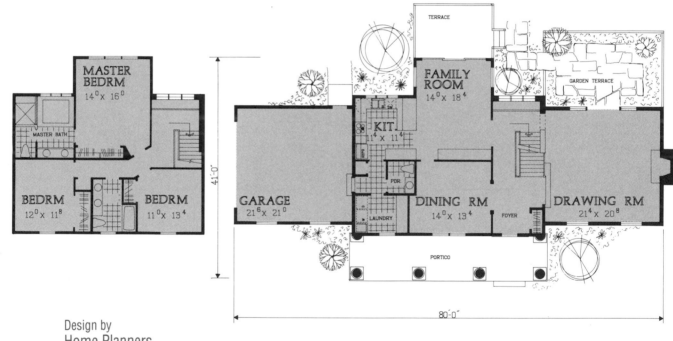

Design EE3317 First Floor: 1,507 square feet
Second Floor: 976 square feet; Total: 2,483 square feet

● Fine family living takes off in this traditional design. Step onto the portico and into the foyer where a graceful drawing room gains attention. It is set a few steps down from the foyer and features a central fireplace and access to a rear garden terrace, thus making elegant entertaining a cinch. In the family room, another terrace supports outdoor enjoyments. The efficient kitchen features a double sink and a Lazy Susan. Upstairs, three bedrooms include a master bedroom with its own bath. The two secondary bedrooms enjoy the use of a full bath with dual lavatories.

Design EE3508

First Floor: 2,098 square feet
Second Floor: 1,735 square feet
Total: 3,833 square feet

● Make history with this modern version of Louisiana's "Rosedown House." Like its predecessor—built in the 1800s—the modern adaptation exhibits splendid Southern styling, but with today's most sought-after amenities. The formal zone of the house is introduced by a foyer with a graceful, curving staircase. The dining and living rooms flank the foyer—each is highlighted by a fireplace. Off the living room, a library or music room offers comfort with a corner fireplace and a covered porch. This room also accesses the family room where more informal living takes off with a nearby breakfast room, expansive kitchen and rear covered porch. Upstairs, three bedrooms (one with its own bath) and a study (which may convert to an additional bedroom, if desired) include a gracious master suite. It opens with double doors and furthers this romantic feeling with a fireplace. A large dressing room with walk-in closets leads to the luxury bath. Two covered balconies complete the superb livability found in this plan.

Design by
Home Planners,
Inc.

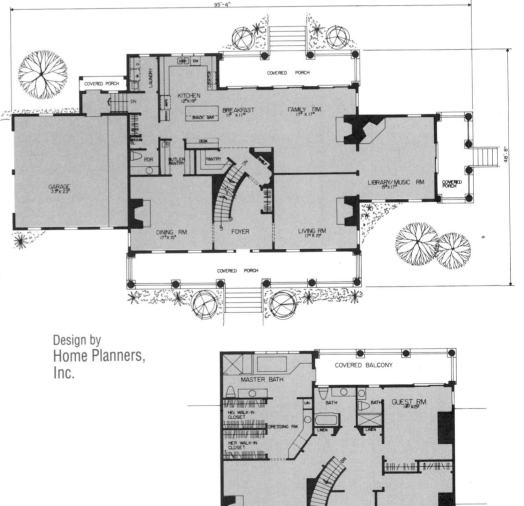

Design EE2993

First Floor: 2,440 square feet
Second Floor: 2,250 square feet
Total: 4,690 square feet

● This dramatically columned home delivers beautiful proportions and great livability on two levels. The main area of the house, the first floor, holds a gathering room, library, family room, dining room and gourmet kitchen. The master bedroom features a whirlpool tub and through fireplace. Two family bedrooms on the second floor share a full bath. A fourth bedroom is the perfect guest bedroom with its own private bath.

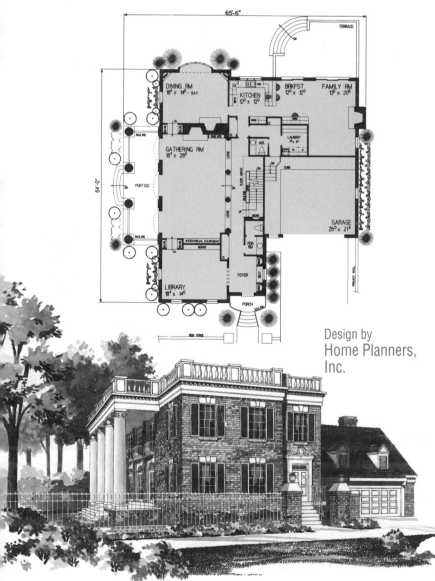

Design by
Home Planners,
Inc.

Quote One™
Cost to build? See page 232 to order complete cost estimate to build this house in your area!

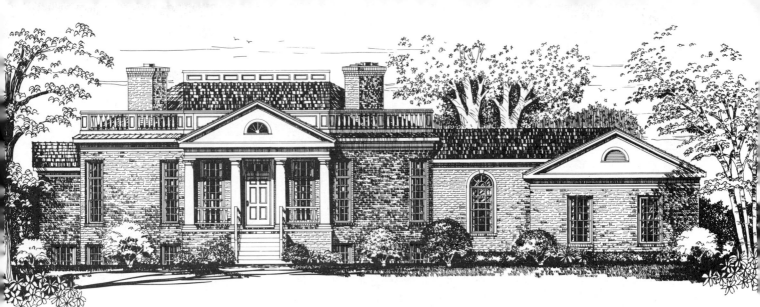

Design EE3509

First Floor: 2,434 square feet
Second Floor: 2,434 square feet
Total: 4,868 square feet

● If you're looking to do something a little different for your home-building experience, this adaptation of Jefferson's "Poplar Forest" home may be just the ticket. Originally built in the hills around Lynchburg, Virginia, Poplar Forest served Jefferson as a retreat from the hustle and bustle of a new country. Now, equipped with modern amenities, this home will be your perfect retreat. The entry gives way to a sitting or receiving area on the left and a library on the right. Fireplaces adorn all of the major living areas downstairs: drawing room, family room, living room and lounge. Upstairs bedrooms include a master suite with a fireplace and a private luxury bath.

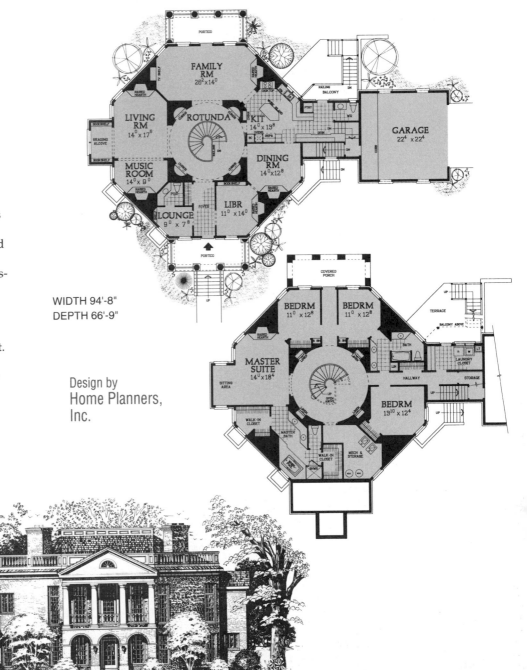

WIDTH 94'-8"
DEPTH 66'-9"

Design by
Home Planners,
Inc.

Design EE9804

First Floor: 2,199 square feet
Second Floor: 1,235 square feet
Total: 3,434 square feet

● The covered front porch of this home warmly welcomes family and visitors. To the right of the foyer is a versatile option room. On the other side is the formal dining room, located just across from the open great room with its skylights, French doors and fireplace—which also opens into the breakfast room. The kitchen, with its bay window, includes a cooking island/breakfast bar. Adjacent to the breakfast room is the sun room. At the rear of the main level is the master suite, which features a decorative tray ceiling and a lavish bath loaded with features. Just off the bedroom is a private deck. On the second level, three additional bedrooms and two baths are found. This home is designed with a basement foundation.

WIDTH 62'-6"
DEPTH 54'-3"

Design by
Design Traditions

Atlanta Classic & European Styles

When speaking of Atlanta, genteel living is a given. One of the South's belle cities, Atlanta exhibits a meshing and absorption of housing styles, especially those of European descent. Its houses sport great curb appeal and range from traditional clapboards to stuccoed French manors.

A true Atlanta Classic, the French-inspired Design EE9805 exudes elegance with a brick exterior, a highly pitched roof and a front covered porch with columns and arches. Dormer windows provide airiness to the interior as well as expansive views of the city and surrounding country.

Appealing, with more of a country flavor, Design EE9803 speaks to a quiet lifestyle. A covered porch, perfect for thoughtful reflection, introduces a floor plan that reaps satisfaction. A parlor provides the perfect spot for moving conversations from the porch to the indoors.

Like much of the South, Atlanta draws on many characteristics of European architecture. Warmer climes encourage the building of many stuccoed and sunny designs. Palladian windows and rear terraces offer further appeal and enhance indoor/outdoor livability. Heightened roof lines give way to better air circulation within the homes.

With Norman roots, Design EE8031 offers many of these features. Familiar columns and arches combine in an impressive entry. These arches harmonize with the famous Palladian design of the windows. Interior spaces rise to two stories to provide a feeling of loftiness as well as to play a part in expelling Southern summer heat.

With designs such as EE3558 and its abundance of windows and pizazz, this section furnishes a great deal of architectural excitement.

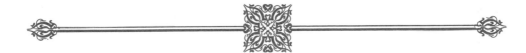

Design EE9918

First Floor: 1,710 square feet
Second Floor: 1,470 square feet
Total: 3,180 square feet

● Many generously sized, shuttered windows flood this stunning home with the clear, warming light of outdoors—captivating with its classic styling. The two-story foyer with its tray ceiling makes a dramatic entrance. To the right, a banquet-sized dining room offers space for a buffet, while the large kitchen allows easy access to the bay-windowed breakfast room. To the left is a versatile room which can serve as a living room, a study or a guest room. Beyond the foyer is the great room which sports a cheering fireplace flanked by bookcases. An open-railed stairway leads to three bedrooms on the second floor. The exquisite master suite is truly a room to live in, with its stylish tray ceiling and warming fireplace. Its elegance is intensified right down to the bay window and huge walk-in closet with a built-in dressing table. This home is designed with a basement foundation.

Design by
Design Traditions

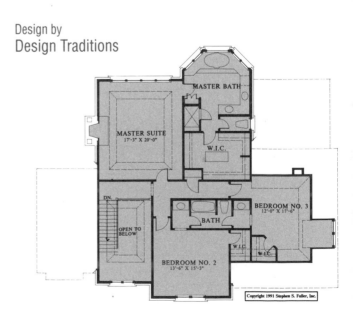

Design EE9837

First Floor: 1,847 square feet
Second Floor: 1,453 square feet
Total: 3,300 square feet

● To suit those who favor classic European styling, this English Manor home features a dramatic brick exterior which is further emphasized by the varied roofline and the finial atop the uppermost gable. The main level opens with a two-story foyer and formal rooms on the right. The living room contains a fireplace set in a bay window. The dining room is separated from the living room by a symmetrical column arrangement. The more casual family room is to the rear. For guests, a bedroom and bath are located on the main level. The second floor provides additional bedrooms and baths for family as well as a magnificent master suite. This home is designed with a basement foundation.

Design by
Design Traditions

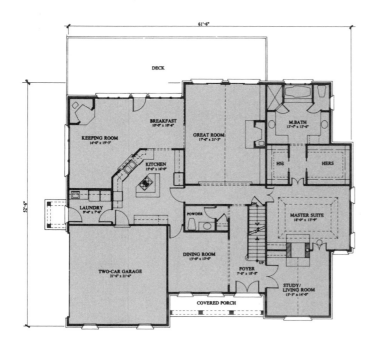

Design EE9805

First Floor: 2,355 square feet
Second Floor: 987 square feet
Total: 3,342 square feet

● The front of this traditional home is characterized by an arch pattern evident in the windows, doorway and above the columned front porch. Left of the foyer is the formal dining area and a great room with a fireplace and a vaulted ceiling. The large kitchen is conveniently situated with a cooking island, adjoining breakfast room and a keeping room with a corner fireplace. The master suite includes a study with a vaulted ceiling just off the foyer, with a dual-opening fireplace that also warms the bedroom. Beyond the large closets is the bath with dual vanities. Upstairs are three more bedrooms and two baths. This home is designed with a basement foundation.

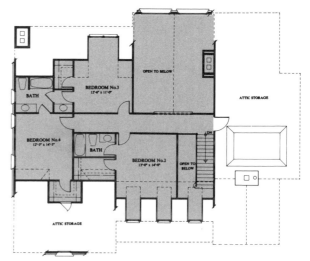

Design by
Design Traditions

Design EE9803

First Floor: 1,850 square feet
Second Floor: 1,760 square feet
Total: 3,610 square feet

● This American Country-styled home, with wood siding and shuttered windows, echoes images of the warmth and strength of traditional Southern living. The two-story foyer opens to a dining room and a formal parlor. Then pass the open rail stairs to the large family room with its fireplace and hearth, flanking bookcases, and squared column supports. The spacious kitchen has a breakfast area which opens to the outside. There is also an "option room" which may serve as the guest quarters with a private bath, a private study or a children's den. Upstairs, the master suite has its own sitting area and an unusual vaulted ceiling. Two other bedrooms share a bath—a fourth has a private bath as well as nostalgic access to the second-floor porch. This home is designed with a basement foundation.

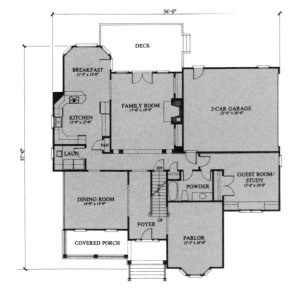

Design by
Design Traditions

113

Design EE3569
Square Footage: 1,981

● A graceful entry opens this impressive one-story design; the foyer introduces an open gathering room/dining room combination. A front-facing study could easily convert into a bedroom for guests—a full bath is directly accessible from the rear of the room. In the kitchen, such features as an island cooktop and a built-in desk add to livability. A corner bedroom takes advantage of front and side views. The master bedroom accesses the rear terrace and also sports a bath with dual lavatories and a whirlpool. Other special features of the house include multi-pane windows, a warming fireplace, a cozy covered dining porch and a two-car garage. Note the handy storage closet in the laundry area.

QUOTE ONE™
Cost to build? See page 232 to order complete cost estimate to build this house in your area!

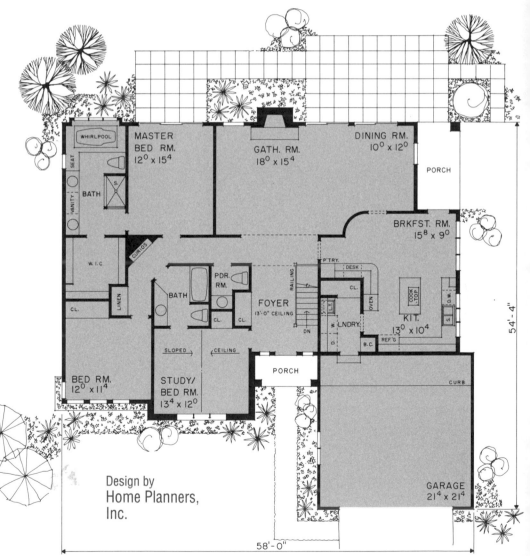

Design by
Home Planners, Inc.

Design EE3565

First Floor: 1,248 square feet
Second Floor: 1,012 square feet
Total: 2,260 square feet

● Every detail of this plan speaks of modern design. The exterior is simple yet elegant, while the interior floor plan is thorough and efficient. The formal living and dining rooms are to the left of the foyer, separated by columns. The living room features a wall of windows and a fireplace. The kitchen, with its island cooktop, is adjacent to the large family room with terrace access. A study with additional terrace access completes the first floor. The master bedroom features a balcony and a spectacular bath with a whirlpool tub, a shower with a seat, separate vanities and a walk-in closet. Two family bedrooms share a full bath. Also notice the three-car garage.

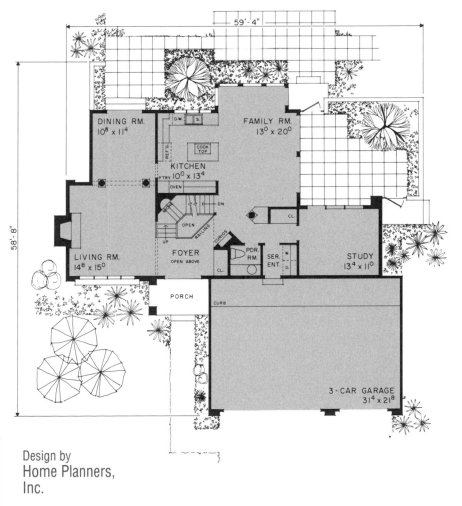

Design by
Home Planners,
Inc.

Design EE3559
Square Footage: 2,916

● Intricate details make the most of this lovely one-story: high, varied roof lines, circle and half-circle window detailing, multi-pane windows and a solid chimney stack. The floor plan caters to comfortable living. Besides the living room/dining room area to the rear, there is a large conversation area with a fireplace and plenty of windows. The kitchen is separated from living areas by an angled snack-bar counter. A media room to the front of the plan provides space for more private activities. Three bedrooms grace the right side of the plan. The master suite features a tray vaulted ceiling and sliding glass doors to the rear terrace. The dressing area is graced by His and Hers walk-in closets, a double-bowl lavatory and a compartmented commode. The shower area is highlighted with glass block and is sunken down one step. A garden whirlpool finishes off the area. For information on customizing this design, call 1-800-521-6797, ext. 800.

Design by
Home Planners,
Inc.

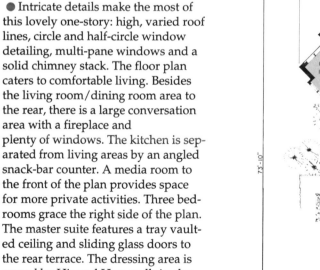

QUOTE ONE™
Cost to build? See page 232 to order complete cost estimate to build this house in your area!

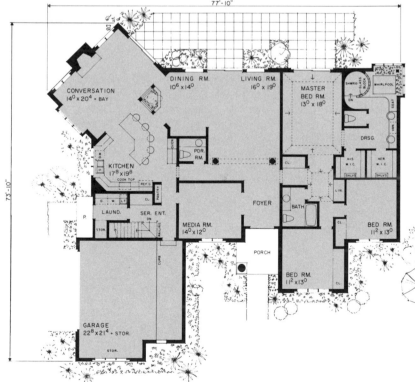

Design EE3558

First Floor: 2,328 square feet
Second Floor: 603 square feet
Total: 2,931 square feet

Design by
Home Planners,
Inc.

● This home will keep even the most active family from feeling cramped. A broad foyer opens to a living room that measures 24 feet across and features sliding glass doors to a rear terrace and a covered porch. Adjacent to the kitchen is a conversation area with additional access to the covered porch, a snack bar, fireplace and a window bay. A butler's pantry leads to the formal dining room. Placed conveniently on the first floor, the master suite features a roomy bath with a huge walk-in closet and dual vanities. Two large bedrooms are found on the second floor.

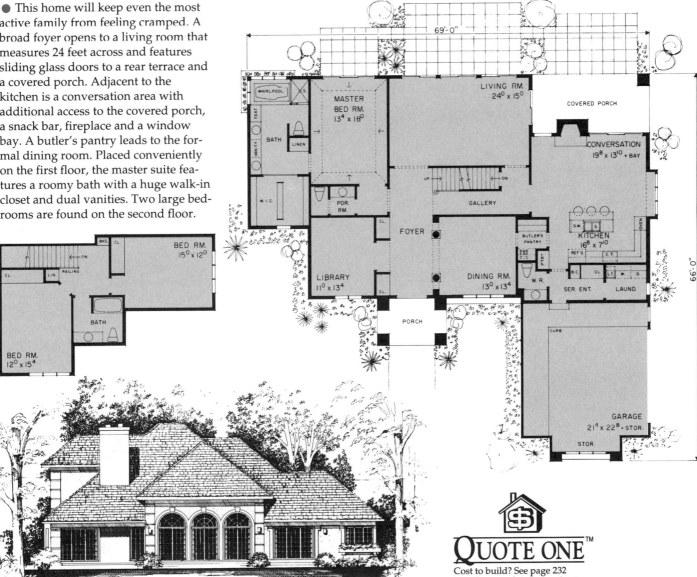

Quote One™

Cost to build? See page 232 to order complete cost estimate to build this house in your area!

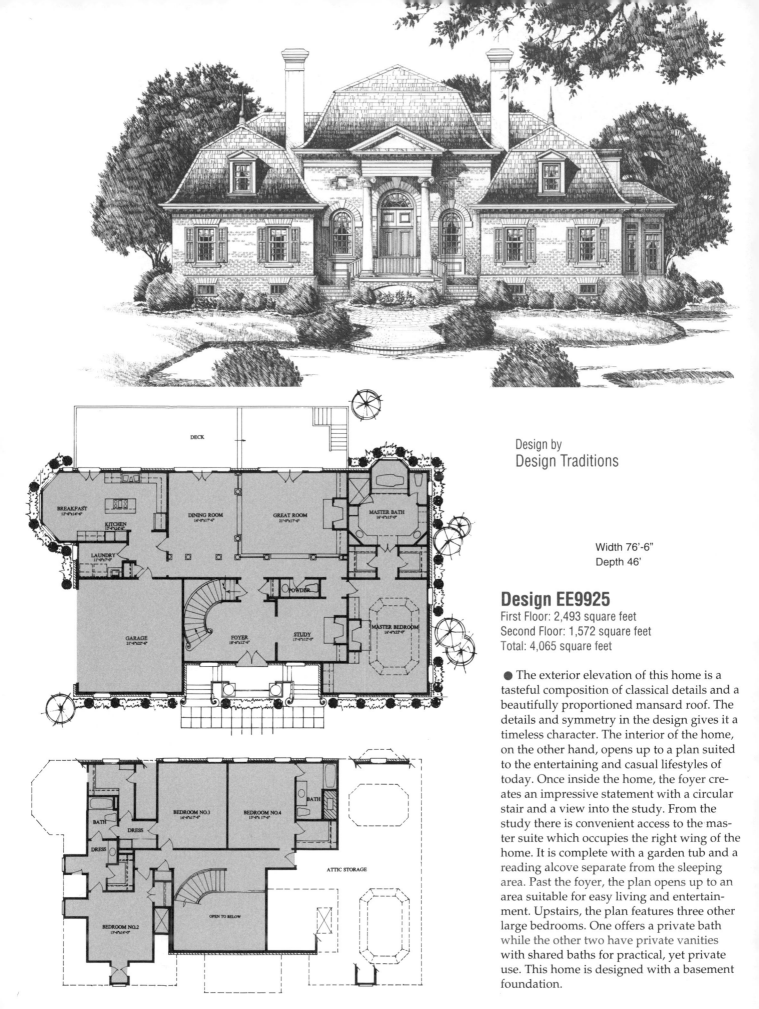

Design by
Design Traditions

Width 76'-6"
Depth 46'

Design EE9925
First Floor: 2,493 square feet
Second Floor: 1,572 square feet
Total: 4,065 square feet

● The exterior elevation of this home is a tasteful composition of classical details and a beautifully proportioned mansard roof. The details and symmetry in the design gives it a timeless character. The interior of the home, on the other hand, opens up to a plan suited to the entertaining and casual lifestyles of today. Once inside the home, the foyer creates an impressive statement with a circular stair and a view into the study. From the study there is convenient access to the master suite which occupies the right wing of the home. It is complete with a garden tub and a reading alcove separate from the sleeping area. Past the foyer, the plan opens up to an area suitable for easy living and entertainment. Upstairs, the plan features three other large bedrooms. One offers a private bath while the other two have private vanities with shared baths for practical, yet private use. This home is designed with a basement foundation.

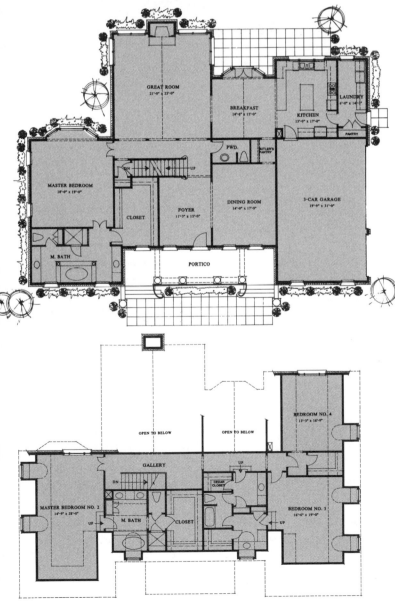

Design by
Design Traditions

Width 75'-10"
Depth 58'-4"

Design EE9926
First Floor: 2,530 square feet
Second Floor: 1,969 square feet
Total: 4,499 square feet

● This elegant home has many traditional architectural features that make it a classic. The wrought iron railings which skirt each of the front staircases, lead past expansive shuttered windows to the covered portico. The overdoor transom together with the windows gently light the foyer and formal dining room. Beyond the foyer, the vaulted great room, with its immense central fireplace, provides convenient access to the remainder of the house. Both the breakfast room and the great room are open to the second floor gallery. The functional master suite provides easy passage to all sections of the house, yet still maintains a private retreat with a view to the back. Completing the suite are a bath and a large walk-in closet. The large guest suite with its dormered windows could also serve as an upstairs master suite. The remaining two bedrooms share a common bath, with each having a private vanity and a walk-in closet. This home is designed with a basement foundation.

Open To Below

Attic Storage

Bedroom No. 4
15⁰x13⁰

Dn

Dn

Bedroom No. 2
18⁰x14⁰

Open To Below

Bedroom No. 3
14⁰x16⁶

Open To Below

Exercise/Sitting Room
13⁰x13⁰

Up

Keeping Room
15³x16⁰

Living Room
29⁰x19⁰

Breakfast
17⁹x9⁶

Dn

Master Bedroom
24⁶x16⁶

Kitchen
19⁰x13⁶

Study
18⁰x14⁰

Foyer
15⁰x14⁰

Dining Room
14⁰x16⁶

Up

Width 80'-3"
Depth 57'-6"

Design by
Design Traditions

Design EE9927

First Floor: 3,608 square feet
Second Floor: 1,442 square feet
Total: 5,050 square feet

● Classical brick and limestone accents on this brick home create the appearance of a stately English manor. Rich in detail, the home has a detached garage connected by a covered breezeway to continue the charm and stately grace of the design. Once inside the home, you will find a grand two-story foyer complete with a graceful curved staircase. Adjacent and open to the foyer are a banquet-sized dining room and formal study. A large entertaining living room, a vaulted den and a spacious breakfast room and kitchen make up the first-floor living areas. In the master suite, His and Hers amenities and a private exercise room set the pace. A second or back stair is conveniently located just off the living areas for easy access to the spacious bedrooms upstairs. Each has a private bath and a walk-in closet. This home is designed with a basement foundation.

Design by
Design Traditions

Design EE9928

First Floor: 2,959 square feet
Second Floor: 1,326 square feet
Total: 4,285 square feet

● The ornamental limestone and stucco detailing and the brick exterior provides much of the eclectic character of this home. The impressive two-story facade and raised front pediment give the home its stately image. Inside, the two-story foyer opens to an adjacent study and dining room. An open rail from the gallery above looks down on the foyer and living room below to give a very open appeal to the formal area of the home. The master suite—with its garden tub bath, large closets, convenient access to the study and sitting room—provides the perfect retreat. The kitchen is uniquely situated in a functional arrangement with the breakfast area and keeping room. All rooms at the rear of the home overlook the patio and back yard. Upstairs, three large bedrooms and an optional guest suite, maid's quarters or bonus room meet the needs of a growing family. This home is designed with a basement foundation.

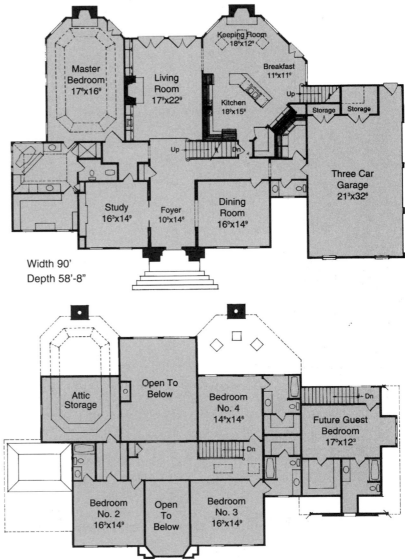

121

Bedroom
No. 3
14⁹x12⁰

Bedroom
No. 4
15⁶x12⁰

Attic
Storage

Dn

Bedroom
No. 2
15⁵x13⁶

Open To
Below

Bonus Room
13⁶x19³

Breakfast
9⁶x11⁰

Kitchen
18⁵x12⁰

Great Room
24⁶x15⁶

Keeping Room
16⁶x15⁶

Master
Bedroom
20⁶x15⁵

Up

Sewing/Hobby
Room
12⁵x9⁰

Dn

Dining
Room
15³x13⁶

Foyer
15⁶x11⁶

Study
15⁶x13⁶

Up

Two Car Garage
21³x21⁶

WIDTH 89'-3"
DEPTH 60'-10"

Design EE9922

First Floor: 3,030 square feet
Second Floor: 1,510 square feet
Total: 4,540 square feet
Bonus Room: 324 square feet

● Brick details, casement windows and large expanses of glass add an Old World touch of glamour to this gracious two-story home. Inside, asymmetrical shapes create an interesting twist to this functional floor plan. Sunlight floods the two-story foyer which is highlighted by the sweeping curves of the balustrade. For formal occasions, look to the spacious dining room, the inviting study and the vaulted great room The master suite provides a quiet retreat with access to the study through paneled pocket doors. Luxury abounds in the spacious master bedrooms nd sumptuous master bath complete with a relaxing garden tub, dual vanities and a huge walk-in closet. The kitchen, breakfast room and keeping room provide a well-designed family living area. Three private secondary bedrooms with full baths are contained on the second floor. A bonus room is also featured on the second floor, perfect for a children's den. This home is designed with a basement foundation.

Design by
Design Traditions

COPYRIGHT 1993 LARRY E. BELK

Design EE8044

First Floor: 1,897 square feet
Second Floor: 1,219 square feet
Total: 3,116 square feet

Design EE8045

First Floor: 1,844 square feet
Second Floor: 1,103 square feet
Total: 2,947 square feet

● A stucco finish and a front porch with a metal roof dress up a more traditional farmhouse in this home designed for the growing family. A large kitchen, breakfast room and family room are open and adjacent to one another to provide a big area for family gatherings. The family room features a corner fireplace with a raised hearth and provides access to the covered porch in the rear. The living and dining rooms are available for more formal entertaining. Visual impact is created at the front door by opening both rooms from the foyer. The master bedroom is located downstairs. The luxuriously appointed master bath includes His and Hers walk-in closets, a seating area at the double vanity, a separate shower and a corner whirlpool tub. Either a three- (Design EE8044) or four-bedroom (Design EE8045) upstairs is available. Please specify crawlspace or slab foundation when ordering.

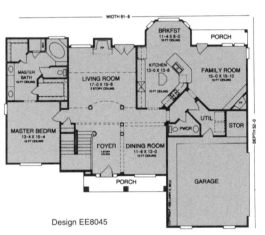

Design EE8045

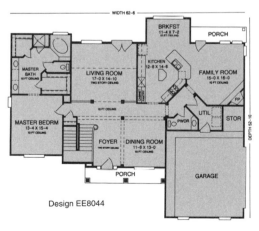

Design EE8044

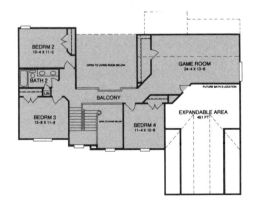

Design by
Larry E. Belk
Designs

123

Design EE8041

First Floor: 1,937 square feet
Second Floor: 1,215 square feet
Total: 3,152 square feet
Bonus Room: 451 square feet

● A massive, stacked-stone gable highlights the entrance to this magnificent European plan. The two-story foyer and the living room—coupled with ten-foot ceilings throughout the remainder of the first floor—provide an open and spacious feeling. The dining room is located to the right of the foyer and is open on two sides. An efficient kitchen with a work island is conveniently grouped with the breakfast room and the family room, sharing a warming fireplace and providing the ideal area for informal gatherings. An adjacent living room provides space for more formal entertaining. The first-floor master suite shares a luxurious master bath with dual vanities, His and Hers walk-in closets and a corner whirlpool tub. Upstairs are three bedrooms, a bath and an oversized game room. In addition, a large area over the garage is available for future expansion, making this a perfect plan for the growing family. This plan is available with either a crawlspace or slab foundation. Please specify when ordering.

Design by
Larry E. Belk
Designs

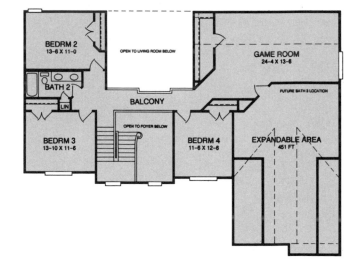

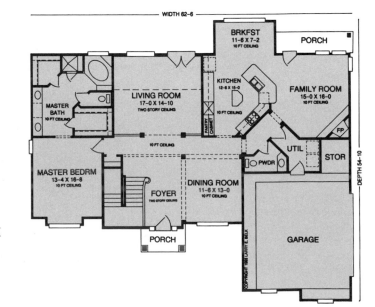

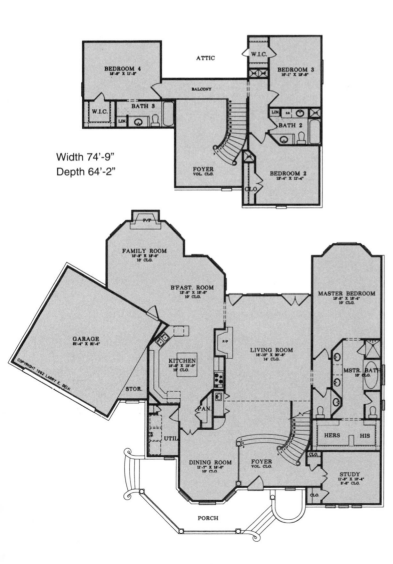

Width 74'-9"
Depth 64'-2"

Design by
Larry E. Belk
Designs

Design EE8024

First Floor: 2,263 square feet
Second Floor: 861 square feet
Total: 3,124 square feet

● The exterior of this home combines the ambience of the large, front porch with the sophistication of a stucco finish. The angled garage deflects attention and insures that the focus remains on the lovely porch area. On entering the home, a graceful, curved staircase rises through the two-story entry to draw your eye upward. Down three stairs, the living room features a complete window wall overlooking the rear. The kitchen, breakfast room and family room are all open to provide a gathering area for the family. The kitchen is replete with many cabinets, a large work island and a walk-in pantry. The master bedroom is large with a bayed sitting area overlooking the back. The master bath includes all the amenities as well as an enormous His and Hers walk-in closet. Also included on the first floor is a study. Upstairs, the home is completed with three bedrooms and two full baths.

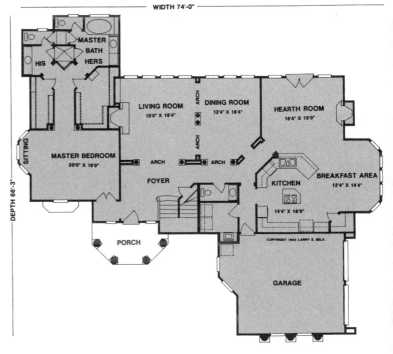

Design EE8031 First Floor: 2,287 square feet
Second Floor: 1,216 square feet; Total: 3,503 square feet

● A European flair distinguishes this lovely stucco home. The colonnade with graceful arches draws attention to the entry of the home and completes this beautiful picture. A two-story foyer, a living room, a dining room and ten-foot ceilings in the balance of the downstairs give this home an expansive feel. The living and dining rooms are entered through arches supported by columns. The detail is repeated above in arched plant ledges. The arch detail continues between the living and dining room, setting a mood of casual elegance. Windows across the back of both of these rooms provide a complete vista to the rear grounds beyond. The kitchen, breakfast area and hearth room are grouped to allow for informal entertaining and family gatherings. The master suite includes a bay sitting area and a His and Hers bath with separate dressing areas. Enormous walk-in closets are perfect for custom built-ins. Upstairs, the home includes three bedrooms, two baths and a large game room.

Design by
Larry E. Belk
Designs

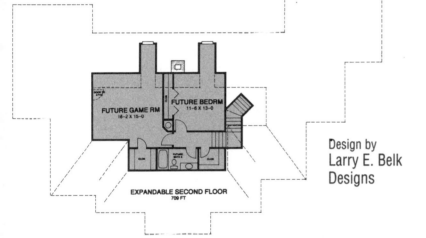

Design EE8013
Square Footage: 2,409

● The stately elegance of this lovely home is evident from first glance. The front door, flanked by four Ionic columns, welcomes all into the foyer. Upon entering the great room through two square columns, the focus is on a large masonry fireplace. Built-ins are included on one wall for entertainment equipment and books. Moving from the great room, Bedrooms 2 and 3 are located off the hallway. The master suite is located at the rear of the house with a luxury master bath that includes large, walk-in His and Hers closets. On the opposite side of the house, two square columns from the foyer to the dining room mirror the columned great room. The kitchen, equipped with an eating bar, a walk-in pantry and a desk, is well designed for the busy cook. A window located over the sink adds lots of natural light. The breakfast area offers a full view of the back yard with access to a spacious covered porch perfect for screening. A staircase from the kitchen area rises to an expandable second floor. This plan is available with either a crawlspace or slab foundation. Please specify when ordering. This plan is available with either a crawlspace or slab foundation. Please specify when ordering.

Design by
Larry E. Belk
Designs

FUTURE GAME RM
16-2 X 15-0

FUTURE BEDRM
11-6 X 13-0

EXPANDABLE SECOND FLOOR
709 FT

Width 85'-8"
Depth 68'-4"

STORAGE

DOUBLE GARAGE

BRICK STEPS

COVERED PORCH

MASTER BATH

MASTER BEDROOM
18-0 X 13-6
9 FT CEILING

BREAKFAST
10-0 X 11-6
9 FT CEILING

PWDR

BEDROOM 2
12-4 X 12-0
9 FT CEILING

GREAT ROOM
21-4 X 17-0
9 FT CEILING

UTIL

KITCHEN
14-6 X 16-0
9 FT CEILING

PAN

FOYER
9 FT CEILING

BATH 2

BEDROOM 3
13-0 X 11-6
9 FT CEILING

DINING ROOM
13-4 X 14-0
9 FT CEILING

PORCH

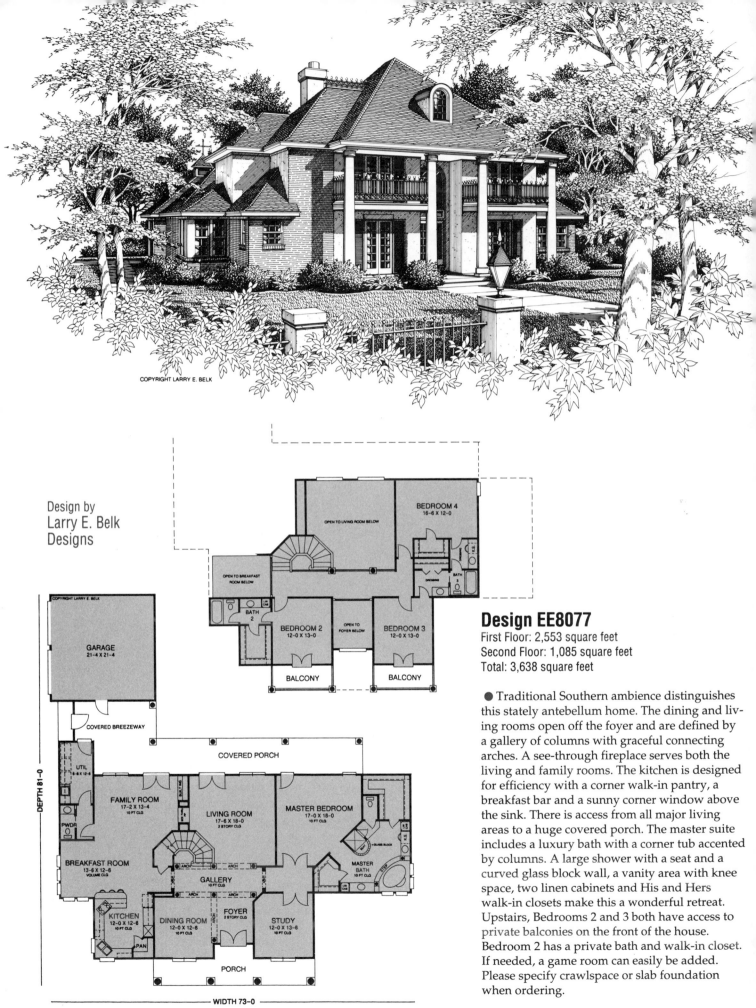

COPYRIGHT LARRY E. BELK

Design by
Larry E. Belk
Designs

BEDROOM 4
16-6 X 12-0

OPEN TO LIVING ROOM BELOW

OPEN TO BREAKFAST
ROOM BELOW

BATH
2

BEDROOM 2
12-0 X 13-0

OPEN TO
FOYER BELOW

BEDROOM 3
12-0 X 13-0

BATH
3

BALCONY

BALCONY

COPYRIGHT LARRY E. BELK

GARAGE
21-4 X 21-4

COVERED BREEZEWAY

UTIL
8-6 X 12-6

COVERED PORCH

FAMILY ROOM
17-2 X 13-4
10 FT CLG

LIVING ROOM
17-6 X 18-0
2 STORY CLG

MASTER BEDROOM
17-6 X 18-0
10 FT CLG

PWDR

BREAKFAST ROOM
13-6 X 12-6
VOLUME CLG

GALLERY
10 FT CLG

MASTER
BATH
10 FT CLG

KITCHEN
12-0 X 12-6
10 FT CLG

DINING ROOM
12-0 X 12-8
10 FT CLG

FOYER
2 STORY CLG

STUDY
12-0 X 13-6
10 FT CLG

PAN

PORCH

DEPTH 81-0

WIDTH 73-0

Design EE8077

First Floor: 2,553 square feet
Second Floor: 1,085 square feet
Total: 3,638 square feet

● Traditional Southern ambience distinguishes this stately antebellum home. The dining and living rooms open off the foyer and are defined by a gallery of columns with graceful connecting arches. A see-through fireplace serves both the living and family rooms. The kitchen is designed for efficiency with a corner walk-in pantry, a breakfast bar and a sunny corner window above the sink. There is access from all major living areas to a huge covered porch. The master suite includes a luxury bath with a corner tub accented by columns. A large shower with a seat and a curved glass block wall, a vanity area with knee space, two linen cabinets and His and Hers walk-in closets make this a wonderful retreat. Upstairs, Bedrooms 2 and 3 both have access to private balconies on the front of the house. Bedroom 2 has a private bath and walk-in closet. If needed, a game room can easily be added. Please specify crawlspace or slab foundation when ordering.

Tennessee Traditional & Memphis Homes

Rich in traditional charm, the homes in this section fit a variety of building sites in both city and country. And no where is this more exemplified than among the rolling landscapes of Tennessee. Incorporated in these structures: European — specifically French — roof lines and exterior materials such as stucco; Gothic columns; and favorite "all-American" building attributes such as the use of brick, siding and dormer windows. Palladian windows to let in sunlight and cupolas for quaintness further the hill-country feel of these comfortable designs.

Ranch-like in demeanor, EE8063 upholds its Tennessee Style. A combination of brick and siding creates a pleasing exterior offset by a columned porch that facilitates outdoor livability. A Palladian window set in a front-facing gable offers an elegant viewpoint, while dormer windows and a cupola set off a multi-faceted roof line.

An American bungalow — EE9898 — takes off with additional design features: a shingled exterior; a front porch defined by arches; and a French-inspired roof line. A projecting gable with vertical siding provides an extra measure of interest. All in all, this charming design will complement a lush landscape or a neighborhood setting with ease.

Naturally, as seen in previous sections, the farmhouse exhibits universal appeal. This is no more apparent than in this section of Tennessee Traditionals. In Design EE9018 — a French Country adaptation — farmhouse appeal comes through with definite distinction. A highly pitched roof highlights a brick and stucco exterior. Shutters flank multi-pane windows. At the side of the house, columns define an arbor — perfect for enjoying country mornings. Inside, livability takes a very modern turn with everything from built-ins to a divine master bedroom suite.

With all this and more to choose from, let a little bit of Tennessee into your heart and home!

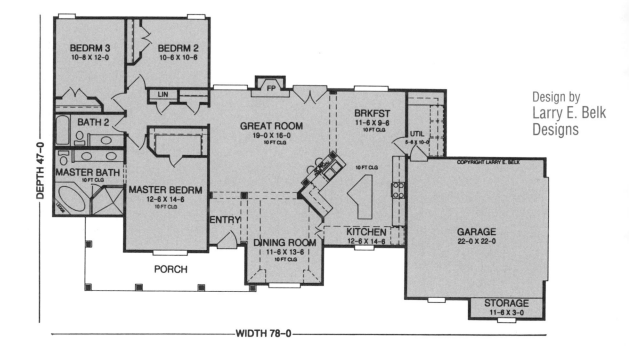

COPYRIGHT LARRY E. BELK

Design by
Larry E. Belk
Designs

BEDRM 3
10-8 X 12-0

BEDRM 2
10-6 X 10-6

LIN

BATH 2

MASTER BATH
10 FT CLG

MASTER BEDRM
12-6 X 14-6
10 FT CLG

FP

GREAT ROOM
19-0 X 16-0
10 FT CLG

BRKFST
11-6 X 9-6
10 FT CLG

UTIL
5-6 X 10-0

10 FT CLG

COPYRIGHT LARRY E. BELK

GARAGE
22-0 X 22-0

ENTRY

DINING ROOM
11-6 X 13-6
10 FT CLG

KITCHEN
12-6 X 14-6

PORCH

STORAGE
11-6 X 3-0

DEPTH 47-0

WIDTH 78-0

Design EE8063

Square Footage: 1,789

● A traditional brick and siding elevation with a lovely wraparound porch sets the stage for a plan that incorporates features demanded by today's lifestyle. The entry opens to the great room and dining room. The use of square columns to define the areas gives the plan the look and feel of a much larger home. The kitchen features loads of counter space and a large work island. The sink is angled toward the great room and features a 42" pass-through bar

above. Washer, dryer and freezer space are available in the utility room along with cabinets for storage and countertops for work area. The master bedroom includes a walk-in closet with ample space for two. The master bath features all the amenities: a corner whirlpool, a shower and His and Hers vanities. Bedrooms 2 and 3 are located nearby and complete the plan. Please specify slab or crawlspace when ordering.

Design EE8070
Square Footage: 2,561

Design by
**Larry E. Belk
Designs**

● This split bedroom plan is loaded with impact at the front door. An angled foyer steps down into the living room and directs the eye to an arched opening flanked with columns. Built-in display shelving on either side gives plenty of room for collectibles or books. Another step down leads to the formal dining room. The kitchen features a breakfast room with a bay window and a coffered ceiling treatment. The family room and kitchen are conveniently grouped with the breakfast room to provide a large area for family gatherings and informal entertaining. The master suite is entered through angled double doors. The eye is drawn to the master bath visible through French doors. Columns mounted on pedestals flank the entry. Inside, a luxury bath awaits with a whirlpool tub as the centerpiece. His and Hers vanities, a shower and two large walk-in closets are standard. On the opposite side of the home two additional bedrooms with large walk-in closets and a roomy bath complete this best-selling plan. Please specify crawlspace or slab foundation when ordering.

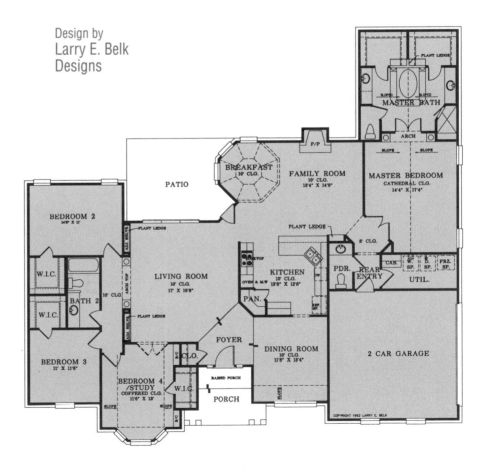

Width 70'
Depth 65'-6"

131

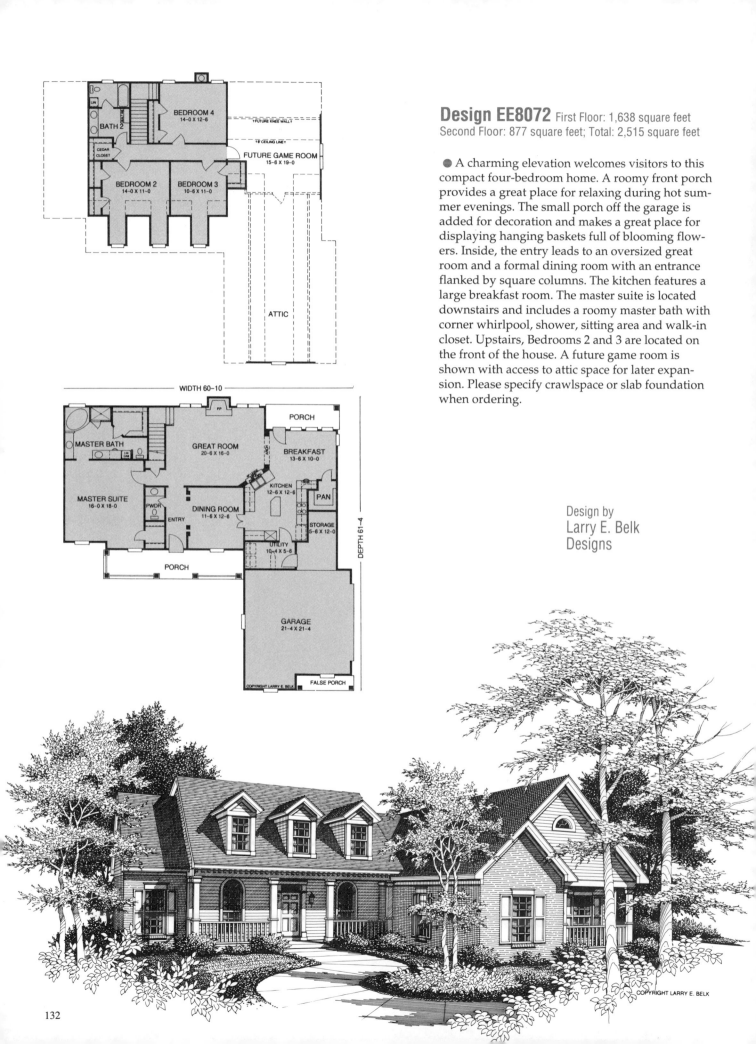

Design EE8072 First Floor: 1,638 square feet
Second Floor: 877 square feet; Total: 2,515 square feet

● A charming elevation welcomes visitors to this compact four-bedroom home. A roomy front porch provides a great place for relaxing during hot summer evenings. The small porch off the garage is added for decoration and makes a great place for displaying hanging baskets full of blooming flowers. Inside, the entry leads to an oversized great room and a formal dining room with an entrance flanked by square columns. The kitchen features a large breakfast room. The master suite is located downstairs and includes a roomy master bath with corner whirlpool, shower, sitting area and walk-in closet. Upstairs, Bedrooms 2 and 3 are located on the front of the house. A future game room is shown with access to attic space for later expansion. Please specify crawlspace or slab foundation when ordering.

Design by
Larry E. Belk
Designs

BEDROOM 4 14-0 X 12-6
BATH 2
LIN
CEDAR CLOSET
† FUTURE KNEE WALL †
† 8' CEILING LINE †
FUTURE GAME ROOM 15-6 X 19-0
BEDROOM 2 14-0 X 11-0
BEDROOM 3 10-6 X 11-0
ATTIC

WIDTH 60-10

MASTER BATH
GREAT ROOM 20-6 X 16-0
FP
PORCH
BREAKFAST 13-6 X 10-0
MASTER SUITE 16-0 X 18-0
PWDR
ENTRY
DINING ROOM 11-6 X 12-6
KITCHEN 12-6 X 12-6
PAN
STORAGE 5-6 X 12-0
UTILITY 10-4 X 5-6
PORCH
DEPTH 61-4
GARAGE 21-4 X 21-4
COPYRIGHT LARRY E. BELK
FALSE PORCH

COPYRIGHT LARRY E. BELK

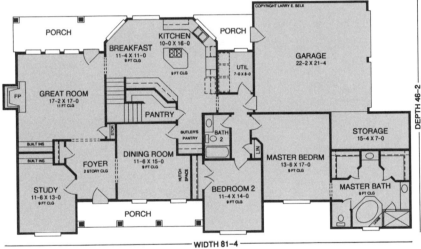

PORCH

KITCHEN
10-0 X 16-0

BREAKFAST
11-4 X 11-0
9 FT CLG

PORCH

COPYRIGHT LARRY E. BELK

GARAGE
22-2 X 21-4

GREAT ROOM
17-2 X 17-0
11 FT CLG

FP

PANTRY

UTIL
7-0 X 8-0

BUILT INS

BUILT INS

FOYER
2 STORY CLG

DINING ROOM
11-6 X 15-0
9 FT CLG

BUTLER'S
PANTRY

BATH
2

LIN

STORAGE
15-4 X 7-0

MASTER BEDRM
13-6 X 17-0
9 FT CLG

STUDY
11-6 X 13-0
9 FT CLG

BEDROOM 2
11-4 X 14-0
9 FT CLG

MASTER BATH
9 FT CLG

PORCH

DEPTH 46-2

WIDTH 81-4

Design EE8074

First Floor: 2,255 square feet
Second Floor: 986 square feet
Total: 3,241 square feet

● Pleasing to the eye in every way, this
lovely home evokes the timeless appeal of
the Southern traditional style. The great
room with an eleven-foot ceiling and a
study open off the two-story foyer. A large,
formal dining room features a built-in nook
for that special china cabinet or server. The
kitchen features loads of counter space and
an oversized work island with a built-in
cook top. Both a walk-in pantry and a butler's pantry are accessed from the dining
room. The master suite includes a luxury
bath with an angled whirlpool tub, a shower
and His and Hers vanities and walk-in clo-
ets. Upstairs is highlighted by an enormous
game room perfect for both children and
adults. Two additional bedrooms and a bath
complete the plan. A large walk-in attic provides area for expansion at a later date.
Please specify crawlspace or slab foundation
when ordering.

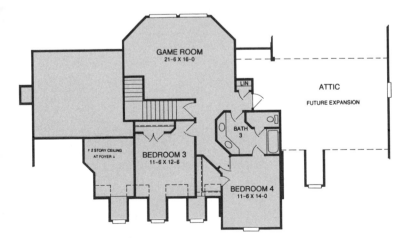

GAME ROOM
21-6 X 16-0

ATTIC

FUTURE EXPANSION

LIN

↑ 2 STORY CEILING
AT FOYER ↓

BATH
3

BEDROOM 3
11-6 X 12-6

BEDROOM 4
11-6 X 14-0

Design by
Larry E. Belk
Designs

Quote One™

Cost to build? See page 232
to order complete cost estimate
to build this house in your area!

Design EE3600

Square Footage: 2,258

●This unique one-story plan
seems tailor-made for a small family
or for empty-nesters. Formal areas are
situated well for entertaining—living
room to the right and formal dining
room to the left. A large family room
is found to the rear. It has access to a
rear wood deck and is warmed in the
cold months by a welcoming hearth.
The U-shaped kitchen features an
attached morning room for casual
meals. It is near the laundry room and
a wash room. Bedrooms are split. The
master suite sits to the right of the
plan and has a walk-in closet and a
fine bath. A nearby study has a private porch. One family bedroom is
on the other side of the home and
also has a private bath. If needed
the plan can also be built with a third
bedroom sharing the bath. For information on customizing this design,
call 1-800-521-6797, ext. 800.

Design by
Home Planners,
Inc.

Design EE3327
Square Footage: 2,881

● The high, massive hipped roof of this home creates an imposing facade while varying roof planes and projecting gables enhance appeal. A central, high-ceilinged foyer routes traffic efficiently to the sleeping, formal and informal zones of the house. Note the sliding glass doors that provide access to outdoor living facilities. A built-in china cabinet and planter unit are fine decor features. In the angular kitchen, a high ceiling and efficient work patterning set the pace. The conversation room may act as a multi-purpose room. For TV time, a media room caters to audio-visual activities. Sleeping quarters take off with the spacious master bedroom; here you'll find a tray ceiling and sliding doors to the rear yard. An abundance of wall space for effective and flexible furniture arrangement further characterizes the room. Two sizable bedrooms serve the children. For information on customizing this design, call 1-800-521-6797, ext. 800.

Width 77'-11"
Depth 73'-11"

Design by
Home Planners,
Inc.

QUOTE ONE™
Cost to build? See page 232
to order complete cost estimate
to build this house in your area!

Design EE8910

First Floor: 1,163 square feet
Second Floor: 540 square feet
Total: 1,703 square feet

● With a brick and wood siding exterior, this home takes on a comfortable, traditional air. The family will love the breakfast room and its front-yard views; the kitchen, open to this area, boasts a corner sink with dual windows overlooking the side yard. A plant shelf graces the dining and living rooms as well as the tiled entry. The living room offers a fireplace and a vaulted ceiling—a sophisticated feature for modern living. To round out the first floor, a grand master suite with a ten-foot vaulted ceiling offers a private bath with dual lavatories and a compartmented toilet. With a walk-in closet, this bedroom can't be beat. Upstairs, two family bedrooms each sport a walk-in closet. A loft or game area facilitates family fun.

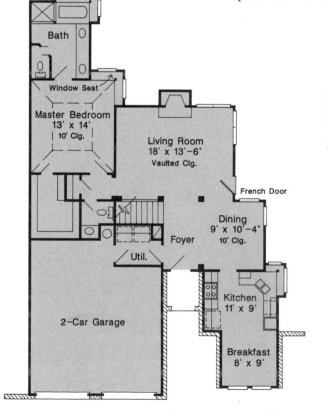

Design by
Larry W.
Garnett &
Associates, Inc.

Width 46'-8"
Depth 61'-2"

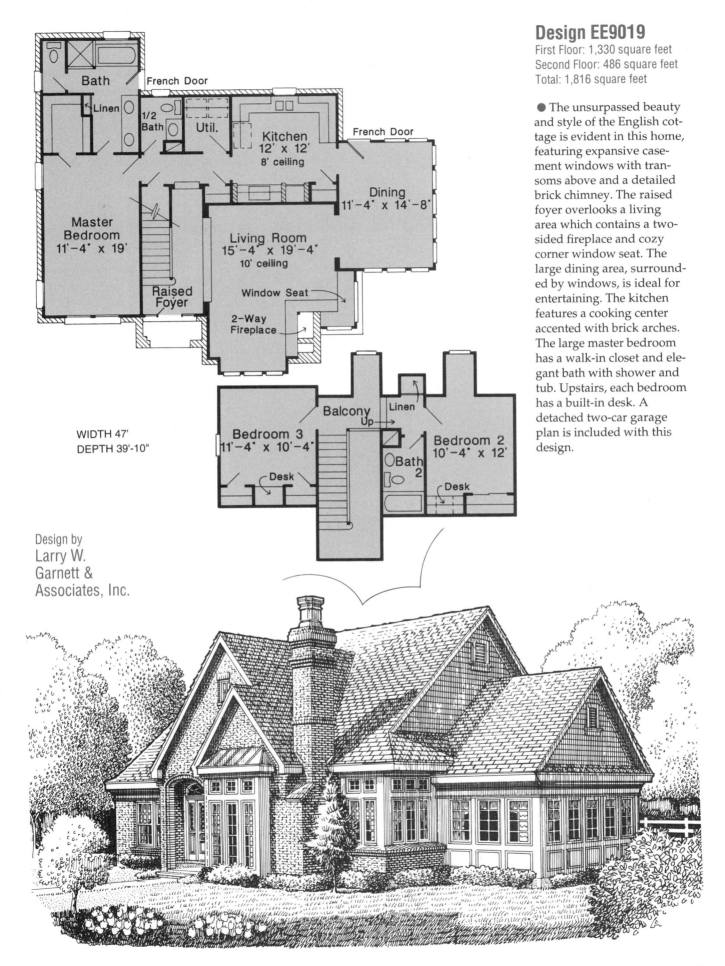

Design EE9019

First Floor: 1,330 square feet
Second Floor: 486 square feet
Total: 1,816 square feet

● The unsurpassed beauty and style of the English cottage is evident in this home, featuring expansive casement windows with transoms above and a detailed brick chimney. The raised foyer overlooks a living area which contains a two-sided fireplace and cozy corner window seat. The large dining area, surrounded by windows, is ideal for entertaining. The kitchen features a cooking center accented with brick arches. The large master bedroom has a walk-in closet and elegant bath with shower and tub. Upstairs, each bedroom has a built-in desk. A detached two-car garage plan is included with this design.

Bath

Linen

1/2 Bath

Util.

Kitchen
12' x 12'
8' ceiling

French Door

French Door

Dining
11'-4" x 14'-8"

Master Bedroom
11'-4" x 19'

Living Room
15'-4" x 19'-4"
10' ceiling

Raised Foyer

Window Seat

2-Way Fireplace

WIDTH 47'
DEPTH 39'-10"

Balcony

Linen

Up

Bedroom 3
11'-4" x 10'-4"

Desk

Bath 2

Bedroom 2
10'-4" x 12'

Desk

Design by
Larry W.
Garnett &
Associates, Inc.

137

● Brick and stucco combine to create a home reminiscent of the French countryside. A detailed brick archway leads to the front entry with a glass transom above an elegant front door with sidelights. Inside, the living room features a massive fireplace, flanked by built-in bookcases and a media center. The study, with its expansive windows and a forty-two-inch high bookcase is a delightful area for reading or relaxing. Opening directly to the light-filled breakfast/sunroom, the conveniently located kitchen also serves the living area. Adjacent to the two-car garage is a large utility room, with plenty of counter and cabinet space, along with a deep sink. Upstairs, three bedrooms, each with walk-in closets, share a bathroom. The lavish master bedroom steps down to His and Hers dressing areas. The garden tub and shower utilize glass-block walls. In addition to a large walk-in closet, there is also an exercise area with plenty of natural light.

Design by
Larry W. Garnett & Associates, Inc.

Design EE9018

First Floor: 1,341 square feet
Second Floor: 1,377 square feet
Total: 2,718 square feet

Width 41'
Depth 60' - 6"

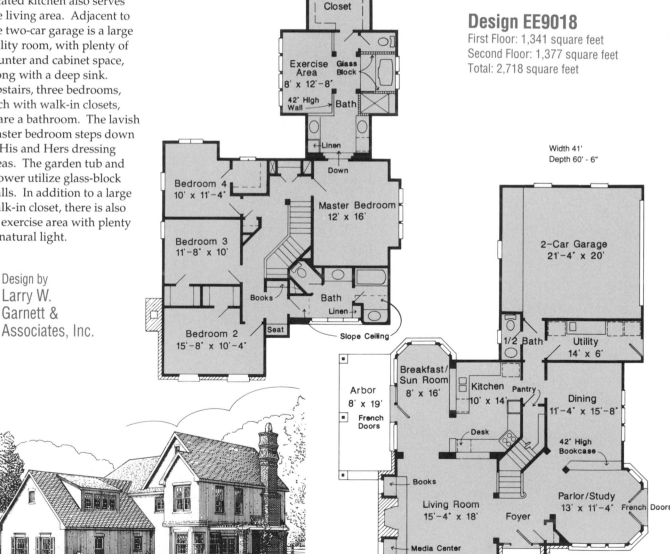

Closet

Exercise Area
8' x 12'-8"

Glass Block

42" High Wall

Bath

Linen

Down

Bedroom 4
10' x 11'-4"

Master Bedroom
12' x 16'

Bedroom 3
11'-8" x 10'

Books

Bath

Linen

Bedroom 2
15'-8" x 10'-4"

Seat

Slope Ceiling

2-Car Garage
21'-4" x 20'

1/2 Bath

Utility
14' x 6'

Arbor
8' x 19'

French Doors

Breakfast/ Sun Room
8' x 16'

Kitchen
10' x 14'

Pantry

Desk

Dining
11'-4" x 15'-8"

42" High Bookcase

Books

Living Room
15'-4" x 18'

Foyer

Parlor/Study
13' x 11'-4"

French Doors

Media Center

Design by
Larry W.
Garnett &
Associates, Inc.

Width 52'-8"
Depth 41'

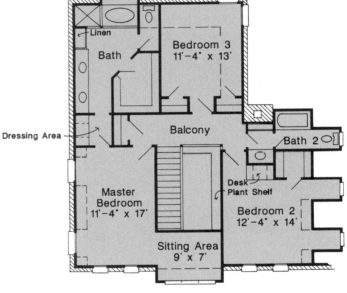

Linen

Bath

Bedroom 3
11'-4" x 13'

Dressing Area

Balcony

Bath 2

Master
Bedroom
11'-4" x 17'

Desk
Plant Shelf

Bedroom 2
12'-4" x 14'

Sitting Area
9' x 7'

Design EE8929

First Floor: 1,305 square feet
Second Floor: 1,111 square feet
Total: 2,416 square feet

● A wraparound terrace with columns sets the stage for this lovely volume home. The foyer presents a formal dining room to the left and a living room with two sets of French doors and a fireplace to the right. Straight ahead, the casual areas of the home open with a family room that features a media center and a pass-through to the kitchen. A brightly lit breakfast area bumps out from the kitchen and will make mornings that much more delightful. Upstairs, three bedrooms accommodate the family well. A large master suite sports a sitting area, a dressing area and a bath with a walk-in closet and a whirlpool tub.

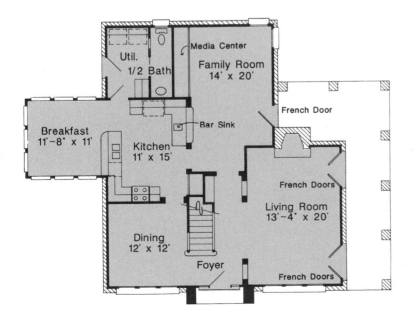

Util.
1/2 Bath

Media Center
Family Room
14' x 20'

French Door

Breakfast
11'-8" x 11'

Bar Sink

Kitchen
11' x 15'

French Doors

Dining
12' x 12'

Living Room
13'-4" x 20'

Foyer

French Doors

COPYRIGHT 1992 LARRY E. BELK

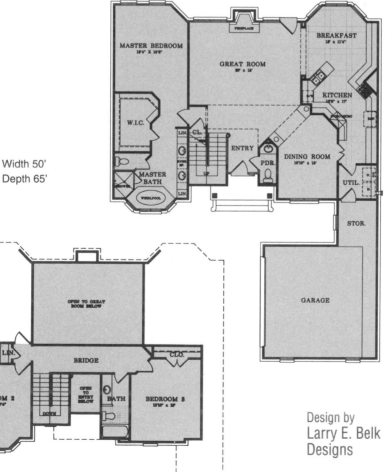

Width 50'
Depth 65'

Design EE8008

First Floor: 1,700 square feet
Second Floor: 668 square feet
Total: 2,368 square feet

● Designed for a narrow, golf-course lot, this home mixes wood shingles, brick and a swoop roof to achieve a bungalow look. The garage location can be moved to the right to open up the elevation and make the home appear larger from the curb. Ten-foot ceilings downstairs and the use of glass across the rear make this home feel open and spacious. The large master suite on the left of the home includes an enormous walk-in closet perfect for built-ins. Upstairs, two bedrooms and a bath complete the plan. This plan is available with either a crawlspace or slab foundation. Please specify when ordering.

Design by
Larry E. Belk
Designs

Design EE8011

First Floor: 1,934 square feet
Second Floor: 528 square feet
Total: 2,462 square feet

● This charming cottage-style home featuring a swoop roof is a real charmer. Inside, a two-story foyer opens through a large arch to the living room with a ten-foot coffered ceiling. Another arch defines the dining room. A see-through fireplace is located between the living room and the breakfast area featuring a bay window and a coffered ceiling. A large kitchen, a utility room and a walk-in pantry complete the area. The master bedroom, with ten-foot ceiling, a sitting area and a luxury master bath, is located on the opposite side of the home. Bedroom 2 and Bath 2 are located nearby. Bedrooms 3 and 4 are located upstairs along with an expandable game room.

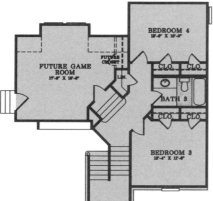

Design by
Larry E. Belk
Designs

Width 64'-10"
Depth 59'-8"

Width 57'-6"
Depth 54'

Design by
Design Traditions

Design EE9898

First Floor: 2,070 square feet
Second Floor: 790 square feet
Total: 2,860 square feet

● Wood shingles add a cozy touch to the exterior of this home; the arched covered front porch adds its own bit of warmth. Interior rooms include a great room with a bay window and a fireplace, a formal dining room and a study with another fireplace. A guest room on the first floor contains a full bath and a walk-in closet. The relaxing master suite is also on the first floor and features a pampering master bath with His and Hers walk-in closets, dual vanities, a separate shower and a whirlpool tub just waiting to soothe and rejuvenate. The second floor holds two additional bedrooms, a loft area and a gallery which overlooks the central hall. This home is designed with a basement foundation.

Design EE9908 First Floor: 1,944 square feet
Second Floor: 1,055 square feet; Total: 2,999 square feet

● Interesting rooflincs, multi-level eaves and a two-story double-bay window create a unique cottage farmhouse appearance for this charming home. A combination of columns and stone create a cozy and inviting porch. The grand foyer leads to the formal dining room and large great room, both graced with columns. The great room features a cozy fireplace and opens to the deck through French door. The breakfast room, divided from the great room by an open stair-case, shares space with an efficient L-shaped kitchen and nearby laundry room, making domestic endeavors easy to accomplish. The right wing is devoted to a sumptuous, amenity-filled master suite with convenient access to the study for after-hours research or quiet reading. The second floor contains three secondary bedrooms and two baths for family and guests. This home is designed with a basement foundation.

Width 51'-6"
Depth 72'

Design by
Design Traditions

Design EE8012 First Floor: 1,768 square feet
Second Floor: 632 square feet; Total: 2,400 square feet

Design by
Larry E. Belk
Designs

● This country charmer mixes brick and siding to come up with a look that is inviting to all. A volume ceiling in the foyer and family room opens up the plan and gives the impression of a home much larger. A display niche adds detail in the foyer and a fireplace and a built-in entertainment center are featured in the family room. An eating bar, walk-in pantry and a work island add to the efficiency of the kitchen. A highlight of the master bedroom is a sitting area which opens onto a covered porch. The master bath adds pampering touches with a large walk-in closet, a luxurious corner tub and a separate shower. Two additional bedrooms and a bath are included upstairs. This plan is available with either a crawlspace or slab foundation. Please specify when ordering.

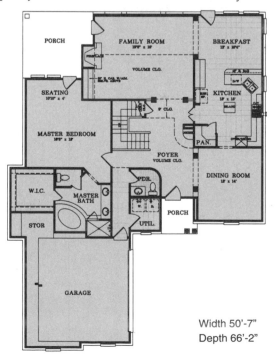

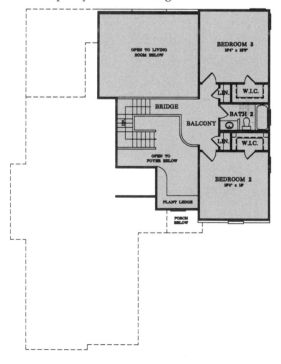

Width 50'-7"
Depth 66'-2"

Design EE9869

First Floor: 1,475 square feet
Second Floor: 1,460 square feet; Total: 2,935 square feet

● This country home of stucco and stone features elliptical keystone detailing and a covered entranceway. Through the columned entry, the two-story foyer opens to the living room with a wet bar. The media room features a fireplace and is accessed from both the main hall and great room. A hall powder room and coat closet are located to the rear of the foyer. The two-story great room with a fireplace is open to the breakfast area, kitchen and rear staircase, making entertaining a pleasure. The kitchen design is ideal with a breakfast bar and a preparation island and is conveniently located near the laundry room. The dining room with its elliptical window is ideal for formal entertaining. The upper level begins with the balcony landing overlooking the great room. The master bedroom features a bay-windowed sitting area and a tray ceiling. The master bath has dual vanities, a corner garden tub, a separate shower, a large walk-in closet and an optional secret room. Across the balcony, Bedrooms 2 and 3 share a bath. Bedroom 4 in the front of the home has a private bath. This home is designed with a basement foundation.

Design by
Design Traditions

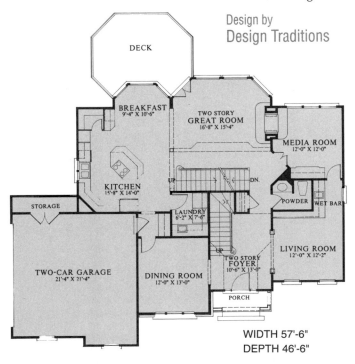

WIDTH 57'-6"
DEPTH 46'-6"

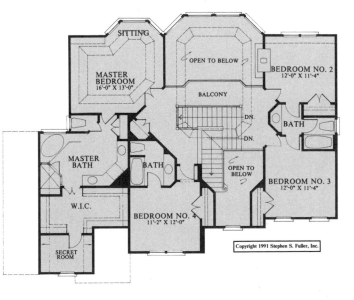

COPYRIGHT 1993

Design EE8037 First Floor: 1,930 square feet
Second Floor: 791 square feet; Total: 2,721 square feet

● A delightful elevation with a swoop roof captures the eye and provides just the right touch for this inviting home. Inside, an angled foyer with a volume ceiling directs attention to the enormous great room. The dining room is detailed with massive round columns connected by arches and shares a see-through fireplace with the great room. The master suite includes an upscale master bath and access to a private covered porch. Bedroom 2 is located nearby and is perfect for a nursery or a home office/study. The kitchen features a large cooktop island and a walk-in pantry. The second floor is dominated by an oversized game room. Two family bedrooms, each with a walk-in closet, a bath and a linen closet complete the upstairs.

Design by
Larry E. Belk
Designs

COPYRIGHT 1991 LARRY E. BELK

Width 64'-4"
Depth 62'

Design EE8005 First Floor: 2,238 square feet
Second Floor: 617 square feet; Total: 2,855 square feet

● This stately traditional home is distinguished by a two-story brick gable accented with brick quoins. Inside, the vaulted-ceiling foyer is accented by a curved wall backing the staircase. The dining room, with a nine-foot ceiling, is separated from the living room by an arched opening supported by double columns on pedestals. The kitchen and family room have ten-foot ceilings and continue the open theme of this home with an angled eating bar separating the kitchen and family areas. The kitchen also sports a large work island and a tremendous walk-in pantry. The bay window is a highlight of the breakfast area. The master bedroom, with a luxury bath, is located downstairs. The bedroom has ten-foot ceilings with triple French doors opening to the rear. The second bedroom downstairs can also be used as a study and features nine-foot ceilings. The curved staircase leads upstairs to two bedrooms, each with a walk-in closet. Please specify crawlspace or slab foundation when ordering.

Width 68'-8"
Depth 77'-8"

Design by
Larry E. Belk
Designs

COPYRIGHT LARRY E. BELK

WIDTH 67-8

MASTER BATH

COVERED PORCH

BRKFST
12-6 X 10-6

FAMILY ROOM
15-0 X 19-0

FP

MASTER BEDRM
16-0 X 15-4

LIVING ROOM
19-0 X 15-4
VAULTED TO 2 STORY

KIT
12-6 X 15-4

BATH 2

UTIL

STOR

PWDR

BEDRM 2/STUDY
13-8 X 12-4

FOYER
2 STORY CLG

DINING ROOM
10-8 X 12-8

DEPTH 74-2

PORCH

3 CAR GARAGE

COPYRIGHT LARRY E. BELK

Design by
Larry E. Belk
Designs

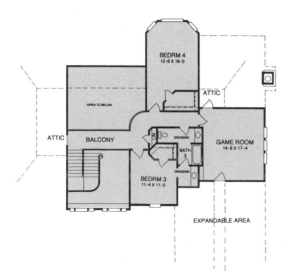

BEDRM 4
12-6 X 16-0

ATTIC

OPEN TO BELOW

ATTIC

BALCONY

DRESSING

GAME ROOM
14-6 X 17-4

BATH

BEDRM 3
11-4 X 11-0

DRESSING

EXPANDABLE AREA

Design EE8075 First Floor: 2,469 square feet
Second Floor: 1,013 square feet; Total: 3,482 square feet

● The texture created by the use of stacked stone, siding and brick makes this home a stand out from the curb. Inside, the two-story foyer opens to the vaulted living room and covered porch beyond. The dining room carries a formal flair with square columns defining one wall. The kitchen, with a large work island, the breakfast room and the family room are all conveniently grouped and provide a large area for informal entertaining. The master suite includes a master bath replete with all the amenities including a whirlpool tub, a shower, His and Hers vanities with knee space and His and Hers walk-in closets. A second bedroom is located nearby and is perfect for a nursery, a guest bedroom or a study. Upstairs, two additional bedrooms share a bath designed with a private vanity area for each bedroom. A large game room completes this lovely home. Expandable area is available over the three-car garage and provides a great opportunity to add that in-home office, exercise room or hobby room. Please specify crawlspace or slab foundation when ordering.

COPYRIGHT 1992 LARRY E. BELK

PORCH

GREAT ROOM
20' X 18'
13' CLG.

HERS
PLANT LEDGE
7'-4" HT.
8' CLG.

HIS

MASTER
BATH
10' CLG.

PORCH

BREAKFAST
14' X 10'
10' CLG.

F.P.
FLUSH HEARTH

KITCHEN
13' X 16'
10' CLG.

FOYER
VOL. CLG.

MASTER BEDROOM
17' X 18'
9' CLG.

DINING RM.
14' X 11'
10' CLG.

UTIL.

PANTRY

PORCH

LOW CABINET
LINEN

PLANT LEDGE
7'-4" HT.

BATH 2

BEDROOM 2
11'-6" X 12'-4"
9' CLG.

GARAGE
21' X 21'

COPYRIGHT 1991 LARRY E. BELK

Width 64'-4"
Depth 62'

BEDROOM 3
15'-4" X 11'-4"

W.I.C.

GAME ROOM
16'-8" X 18'-3"

FOYER

OVERLOOK
BELOW

BATH 3

SLOPE

LIN.

PLANT LEDGE

BEDROOM 4
11'-4" X 12'-6"

Design by
Larry E. Belk
Designs

Design EE8003 First Floor: 1,961 square feet
Second Floor: 791 square feet; Total: 2,752 square feet

● The combination of stacked stone, brick and siding add warmth to this eye-catching elevation. Inside, the large, angled foyer provides unobstructed views into the great room and dining room. A see-through fireplace between the great room and dining room adds elegance and completes a stunning dining room separated from the foyer by large arches supported by round columns. The kitchen includes a bay window and continues with the ten-foot ceilings found throughout the kitchen area. The home is designed with two bedrooms downstairs. The second bedroom is multi-functional and can be used as a nursery or office/study. All bedrooms downstairs have nine-foot ceilings. Upstairs features two bedrooms and a large game room. Please specify crawlspace or slab foundation when ordering.

149

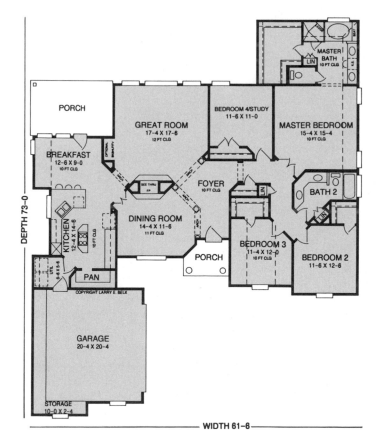

Design EE8067
Square Footage: 2,247

● A traditional elevation is made elegant with a simple swoop roof and an accent of stucco. Inside the home, the angled foyer—with a ten-foot ceiling—immediately draws attention to the great room beyond. A series of arches and decorative columns gives the interior a stately feel. The dining room and great room share a see-through fireplace. The kitchen features a cook top island, a large walk-in pantry and an eating bar. The master suite is entered through angled double doors. A whirlpool tub, a shower, His and Hers vanities with knee space, a linen closet and an enormous walk-in closet are standard. Bedrooms 2 and 3 both feature large walk-in closets. Bedroom 4 can be used as a study or office. Please specify crawlspace or slab foundation when ordering.

Design by
Larry E. Belk
Designs

Texas Brick & Mansion Styles

*I*n the spirit of new places and open spaces, the home designs from Texas exhibit a whole new fashion. Stunning, grandiose—not unlike the landscape encompassed by the state's borders—the homes of Texas take the best of the South and the "New Frontier" to create a lasting impression.

With facades of brick and mortar, many of these homes recall French styling with an extra amount of charisma. For instance, corner quoins and curved roof lines combine with traditional bay windows and Texas "volume" construction to define a new look. And it doesn't end there as Victorian traditions appear with renewed vigor. All in all, styles reflect a philosophy of uniting old and new — and bigger and better — to arrive at Americana, Texas-style.

The designs in this section take livability from around 1,700 square feet to over 4,000. Whether one-story French-inspired or two-story magnificent mansion, a certain framework exists to guarantee comfort. For example, the prevailing use of brick, a practical building material, creates beautiful exteriors. Also common, open floor plans match open views. In both these instances, Design EE9086 excels. Its entry reveals a free-flowing living pattern. Indoor/outdoor relationships also appear in this design, thus furthering its Southern appeal.

With Southern grace, EE8004 opens with a two-story foyer and a curving staircase. Showcasing Victorian influences, this design also incorporates a turret — made more enchanting by housing two charming bedrooms. A rear porch meets outdoor enthusiasts at both the breakfast and great rooms.

In rare form, Design EE8038 makes a sensational home-building choice. Drawing on French influences with a raised roof and corner quoins, this home delights with its raised porch and circle-head windows. Large proportions give way to an elegant interior that emphasizes integrated living patterns and luxury. As far as Texas traditions go, this home — like many in this section — takes them to new heights.

No matter what you set your sights on, this collection of Texas finery aims to please!

Design by
Larry W.
Garnett &
Associates, Inc.

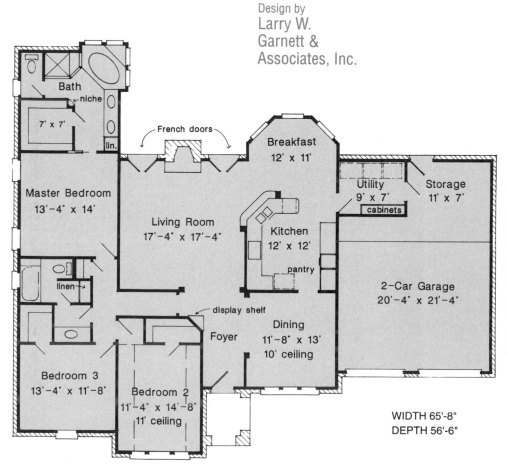

Bath

niche

7' x 7'

lin.

French doors

Master Bedroom
13'-4" x 14'

Living Room
17'-4" x 17'-4"

linen

Breakfast
12' x 11'

Utility
9' x 7'

Storage
11' x 7'

cabinets

Kitchen
12' x 12'

pantry

2-Car Garage
20'-4" x 21'-4"

display shelf

Foyer

Dining
11'-8" x 13'
10' ceiling

Bedroom 3
13'-4" x 11'-8"

Bedroom 2
11'-4" x 14'-8"
11' ceiling

WIDTH 65'-8"
DEPTH 56'-6"

Design EE9088
Square Footage: 1,994

● This charming budget-conscious design provides an abundance of living space. Radiating around the roomy kitchen are the dining room with ten-foot ceiling and living room with French doors and fireplace. A glass-surrounded breakfast area near the kitchen provides space for casual eating. Three bedrooms, all with walk-in closets, dominate the left wing of the home. Bedroom 2 has an eleven-foot sloped ceiling. The master suite features a corner tub and a glass-enclosed shower with seat. Note the large utility room and storage space in the garage.

Design EE9089
Square Footage: 1,849

Design by
Larry W. Garnett & Associates, Inc.

● A wonderful floor plan is found on the interior of this cozy one-story plan. The large living room and conveniently placed dining room both open from the raised foyer. In between is the galley kitchen with huge pantry and attached breakfast area. French doors flanking the fireplace in the living room open to the rear yard. To the right of the plan is the master bedroom with walk-in closet and double lavatories. To the left of the plan are two family bedrooms sharing a full bath in between.

WIDTH 60'
DEPTH 57'-4"

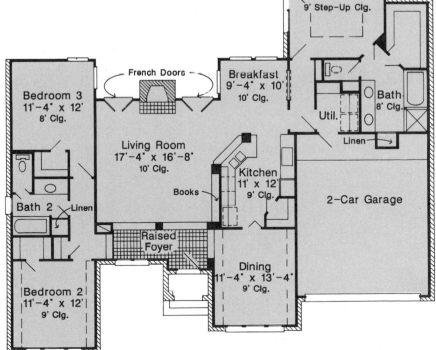

Design by
Larry W.
Garnett &
Associates, Inc.

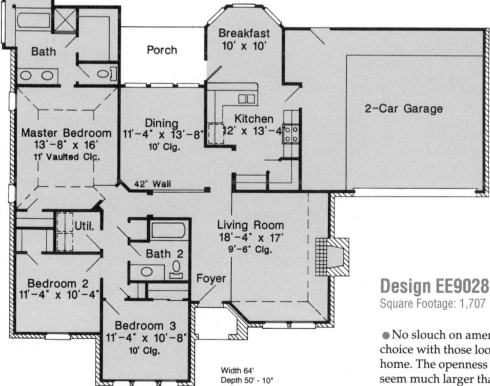

Bath

Porch

Breakfast
10' x 10'

2-Car Garage

Master Bedroom
13'-8" x 16'
11' Vaulted Clg.

Dining
11'-4" x 13'-8"
10' Clg.

Kitchen
12' x 13'-4"

42" Wall

Util.

Living Room
18'-4" x 17'
9'-6" Clg.

Bath 2

Foyer

Bedroom 2
11'-4" x 10'-4"

Bedroom 3
11'-4" x 10'-8"
10' Clg.

Width 64'
Depth 50' - 10"

Design EE9028
Square Footage: 1,707

● No slouch on amenities, this plan is a popular choice with those looking for a smaller sized home. The openness of the floor plan makes it seem much larger than it really is. Note, for example the high ceilings in the living room and master bedroom and the short front wall defining the dining area. A bay-windowed breakfast room opens the kitchen area (don't miss the attached porch for outdoor dining). Three bedrooms include a large master suite. The laundry area is conveniently located near the bedrooms and shared bath.

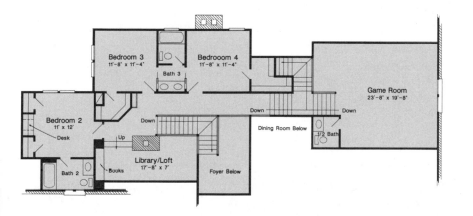

Bedroom 3
11'-8" x 11'-4"

Bath 3

Bedroooom 4
11'-8" x 11'-4"

Game Room
23'-8" x 19'-8"

Bedroom 2
11' x 12'

Desk

Down

Down

Dining Room Below

Down

1/2 Bath

Up

Library/Loft
17'-8" x 7'

Foyer Below

Books

Bath 2

Design EE9152

First Floor: 2,272 square feet
Second Floor: 988 square feet
Optional Gameroom: 465 square feet
Total: 3,725 square feet

● Beautiful style reigns both inside and out for this gracious two-story design. The facade was influenced by Tudor homes of the 1930s. The foyer opens to a formal living room with a fireplace and a built-in bookcase. The formal dining room has a sloped ceiling with a balcony above. The kitchen has an island cooktop and shares a fireplace with the bay-windowed breakfast area. The master suite features French doors and a luxurious master bath with a raised area for a whirlpool tub. The second floor holds three secondary bedrooms and an optional gameroom.

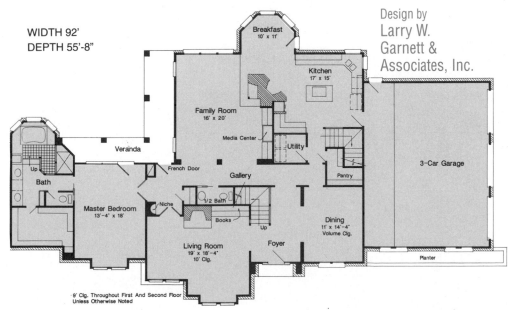

WIDTH 92'
DEPTH 55'-8"

Design by
Larry W.
Garnett &
Associates, Inc.

Breakfast
10' x 11'

Kitchen
17' x 15'

Family Room
16' x 20'

Media Center

Utility

3-Car Garage

Veranda

French Door

Gallery

Pantry

Up

Bath

Niche

1/2 Bath

Books

Master Bedroom
13'-4" x 18'

Up

Dining
11' x 14'-4"
Volume Clg.

Living Room
19' x 18'-4"
10' Clg.

Foyer

Planter

9' Clg. Throughout First And Second Floor
Unless Otherwise Noted

Design EE9027

Square Footage: 1,822

● This is a beautiful one-story plan and one that will adequately serve family needs in a limited amount of space. A central living area with fireplace acts as the hub of the plan, opening up from the front foyer. Close by are the efficient kitchen and dining area. Three bedrooms are grouped together to the left side of the plan. The master suite demands close attention to its many amenities: fireplace, French doors to a rear terrace, and a luxurious bath with oversized shower. A two-car garage features utility room space and a storage area.

Design by
Larry W.
Garnett &
Associates, Inc.

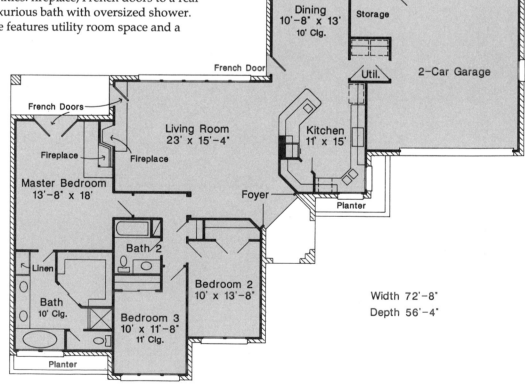

Dining
10'-8" x 13'
10' Clg.

Storage

Util.

2-Car Garage

French Door

French Doors

Living Room
23' x 15'-4"

Kitchen
11' x 15'

Fireplace

Fireplace

Master Bedroom
13'-8" x 18'

Foyer

Planter

Bath 2

Linen

Bath
10' Clg.

Bedroom 2
10' x 13'-8"

Bedroom 3
10' x 11'-8"
11' Clg.

Width 72'-8"
Depth 56'-4"

Planter

Design EE9086 Square Footage: 2,093

● Besides being an eye-catching one-story, this plan provides a practical and livable floor plan. From the entry foyer, go to the right to the formal dining room and to the left to the living room with fireplace and ten-foot ceiling. The L-shaped kitchen has an adjacent breakfast area that overlooks the large covered porch. This porch could be enclosed—either screened or glassed. The hallway to the bedrooms features an eleven-foot ceiling with plant ledges recessed above the adjacent closets.

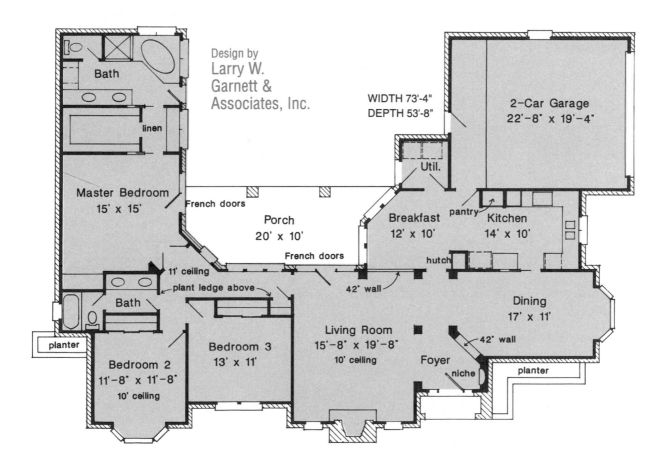

Design by
Larry W.
Garnett &
Associates, Inc.

WIDTH 73'-4"
DEPTH 53'-8"

Bath

linen

Master Bedroom
15' x 15'

French doors

11' ceiling

plant ledge above

Bath

planter

Bedroom 2
11'-8" x 11'-8"
10' ceiling

Bedroom 3
13' x 11'

Porch
20' x 10'

French doors

Living Room
15'-8" x 19'-8"
10' ceiling

42" wall

Util.

Breakfast
12' x 10'

pantry

hutch

42" wall

Foyer

niche

2-Car Garage
22'-8" x 19'-4"

Kitchen
14' x 10'

Dining
17' x 11'

42" wall

planter

Width 79'-8"
Depth 63'

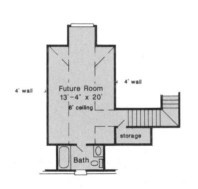

4' wall

Future Room
13'-4" x 20'

8' ceiling

4' wall

storage

Bath

Storage
21'-4" x 7'-8"

Breakfast
10' x 11'

2-Car Garage
21'-4" x 21'-4"

French door

Covered Porch
29' x 13'

Util.

Kitchen

French doors

up

12' x 12'

French doors

32' high wall

Living Room
15'-8" x 24'

11' ceiling

Master Bedroom
16' x 18'

Dining
12'-4" x 15'-8"

media center

9' ceiling

10' ceiling

display niche

linen

Bath 2

linen

Bath

books

linen

Bedroom 3
11'-4" x 14'-4"

books

Bedroom 2
12'-4" x 11'

Design EE9184

Square Footage: 2,325
Future Room: 377 square feet

● For fine traditional living, look no
further than this delightful one-story
home. The front entry opens with an elegant view to the dining room and living
room. Half walls, a tiered ceiling, a fireplace and French doors opening to a rear
covered porch all add distinction to the
latter. In the kitchen, efficient planning
includes an island work space and a
pass-through to the breakfast area. A utility area leads to the two-car garage with
storage. Three bedrooms include two secondary bedrooms with walk-in closets
and bookshelves. The master bedroom is
sure to please with its fireplace and private bath. There's also room to grow with
a future room located over the garage. It
provides a full bath and lots of privacy.

Design by
Larry W.
Garnett &
Associates, Inc.

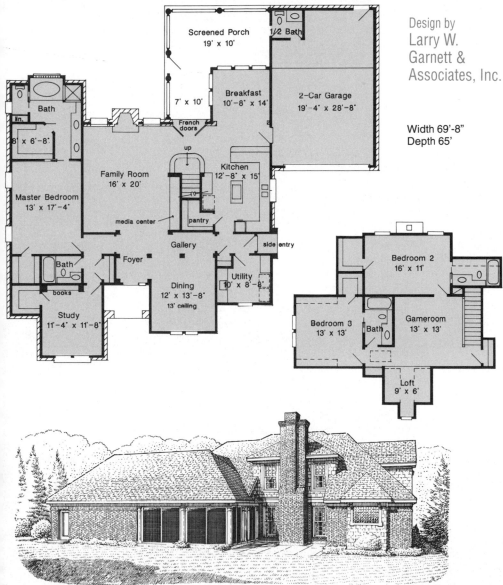

Design by
Larry W.
Garnett &
Associates, Inc.

Width 69'-8"
Depth 65'

Design EE9183

First Floor: 2,138 square feet
Second Floor: 842 square feet
Total: 2,980 square feet

● This plan abounds with all the amenities, starting with a columned foyer that leads to a spacious dining room and an even bigger family room. A study located at the front of the house will convert to the ideal guest room with its walk-in closet and nearby full bath. In the kitchen, an island cooktop sets the pace—along with an immense walk-in pantry. Off the breakfast area, a screened porch wraps around to the back of the house and even gains access to a wash room that connects to the garage. A utility room enjoys its own sunny spot as well as a helpful countertop. Three bedrooms include a first-floor master suite with two walk-in closets and a fabulous private bath. The secondary bedrooms on the second floor each feature walk-in closets and their own full bathrooms. A game room on this floor further enhances the plan.

COPYRIGHT 1993 LARRY E. BELK

Design EE8029 Square Footage: 3,461

Design by
Larry E. Belk
Designs

● This home provides a commanding entry with an octagonal shaped porch supported by large columns. This home is a sure winner for the corner or pie-shaped lot. Through the foyer is a large living room which opens to a covered porch. Flanking the foyer are the dining room and study. The gourmet kitchen includes a small bay window over the sink and an adjacent breakfast area including a small service sink. The master bedroom and bath are spacious and provide ample His and Hers closet space. A fourth bedroom and a full bath are privately located off the kitchen area. The permanent staircase is included to provide easy access to floored attic space above.

Width 87'
Depth 77'-4"

160

Design EE8004

First Floor: 2,154 square feet
Second Floor: 845 square feet
Total: 2,999 square feet

● The stacked bay window creates a turret effect and adds drama to this charming home. As you enter, the curved staircase and open view to the great room with its twelve-foot ceiling provide a stunning view. A see-through fireplace is featured between the great room and dining room. The dining room is distinguished by a ten-foot ceiling and arches with round column supports between the two-story foyer and the dining area. The kitchen combines a large walk-in pantry, a cooktop island and a breakfast area with a bay window. Two bedrooms are located downstairs with the master bedroom featuring a curved wall. A dressing area off the master bedroom includes spacious His and Hers walk-in closets. The second bedroom downstairs features a bay window and can be used as an office or nursery. Upstairs are two bedrooms (one with a bay window) and a large game room. This plan is available with either a crawl-space or slab foundation. Please specify when ordering.

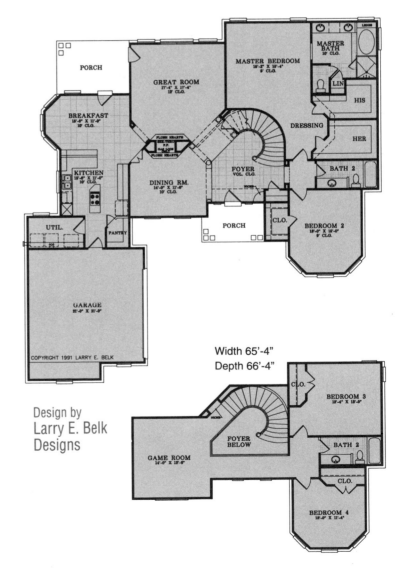

Design by
Larry E. Belk
Designs

Width 65'-4"
Depth 66'-4"

COPYRIGHT 1993 LARRY E. BELK

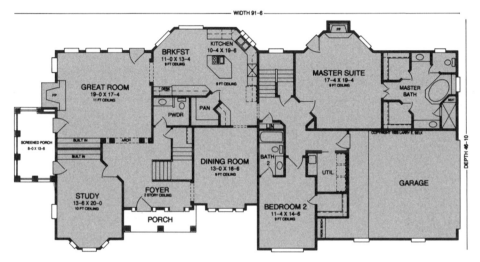

WIDTH 91-6

DEPTH 46-10

GREAT ROOM
19-0 X 17-4
11 FT CEILING

FP

BRKFST
11-0 X 13-4
9 FT CEILING

KITCHEN
10-4 X 19-6

DESK

PAN

PWDR

9 FT CEILING

MASTER SUITE
17-4 X 19-4
9 FT CEILING

FP

MASTER BATH

SEAT

COPYRIGHT 1993 LARRY E. BELK

SCREENED PORCH
8-0 X 13-6

BUILT IN

BUILT IN

DINING ROOM
13-0 X 16-6
9 FT CEILING

LIN

BATH 2

UTIL

GARAGE

STUDY
13-6 X 20-0
10 FT CEILING

FOYER
2 STORY CEILING

PORCH

BEDROOM 2
11-4 X 14-6
9 FT CEILING

WORK BENCH

Design by
Larry E. Belk
Designs

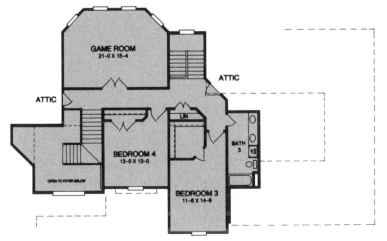

GAME ROOM
21-0 X 15-4

ATTIC

ATTIC

LIN

BATH 3

BEDROOM 4
13-0 X 13-0

OPEN TO FOYER BELOW

BEDROOM 3
11-6 X 14-6

Design EE8078
First Floor: 2,648 square feet
Second Floor: 1,102 square feet
Total: 3,750 square feet

● Put a little luxury into your life with this fine brick traditional. A front porch welcomes all inside. A great room with a fireplace and expansive windows provides the perfect spot for gatherings of all sorts. A large study nearby creates a quiet environment for working at home. In the kitchen, a large work island includes a cooktop. A walk-in pantry facilitates the storage of food stuffs. In the dining room, bumped-out windows shed light on entertainments. On the first floor, the master suite has its own fireplace and a pampering bath. A second bedroom with a private bath is nearby. Upstairs, two more bedrooms and an expansive great room will house family members comfortably.

Design by
Larry E. Belk Designs

Width 69'-5"
Depth 81'-1"

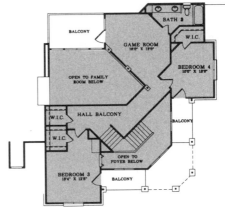

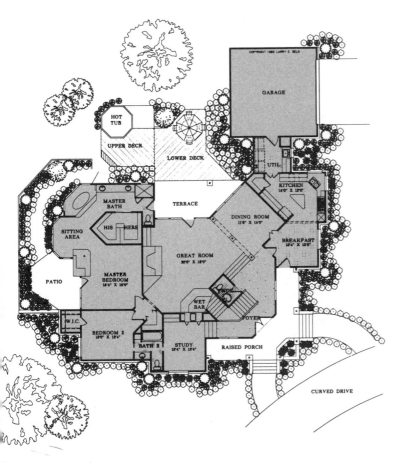

Design EE8038

First Floor: 2,515 square feet
Second Floor: 978 square feet
Total: 3,493 square feet

● This gorgeous home is tailor-made for the corner or pie-shaped lot. Featuring mirror-image gables on both sides this elevation is stunning from any direction. A two-story entry and great room command attention upon entering the home. The master suite includes a masonry fireplace situated between the sitting area and the master bedroom. An owner's study conveniently located off the foyer can be used as a bedroom. A gourmet kitchen with a triangular work island, a corner sink and a large pantry is located on the opposite side of the home. The dining room, accented by columns, overlooks the great room. Upstairs, one bedroom with a private outside balcony is ideal for an office. A game room, a bath and another bedroom with a private outside balcony provide the finishing touch to this elegant home.

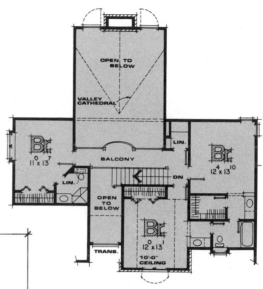

Design by
**Design
Basics,
Inc.**

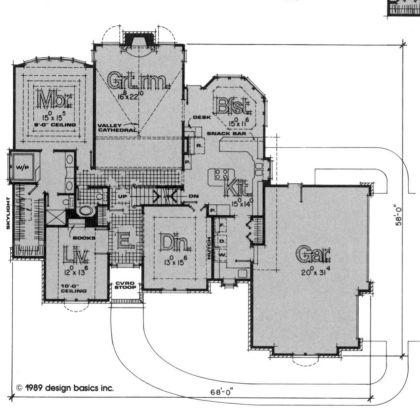

© 1989 design basics inc.

Design EE9244

First Floor: 1,972 square feet
Second Floor: 893 square feet
Total: 2,865 square feet

● Natural light floods the hard-surfaced entry area of this home—an area flanked by the formal living room and dining room. The massive great room to the rear of the plan boasts a valley cathedral ceiling and fireplace framed by windows to the rear yard. A grand gourmet island kitchen has two pantries and overlooks the gazebo dinette. Split-bedroom planning puts the master suite on the first floor. Besides its bow window and tiered ceiling, this retreat features a whirlpool tub, His and Hers vanities, skylit walk-in closet and compartmented stool and shower. Upstairs bedrooms include two with a Hollywood bath and one with its own three-quarter bath.

Design EE9211

First Floor: 2,355 square feet
Second Floor: 1,135 square feet
Total: 3,490 square feet

● Brick, stone quoins, hipped roof and unusual window treatments lend a European air to this striking home. Inside is a gracious floor plan to match. A two-story entry, flanked by a formal dining room with detailed ceiling and a den with fireplace, leads to the enormous great room with columned doorway. Nearby is an ample kitchen with an octagonal breakfast room. Also on this level, the master suite features a huge walk-in closet, access to the den, and a large bath with dressing area and whirlpool. Upstairs are three good-sized bedrooms and two baths.

Design by

**Design
Basics,
Inc.**

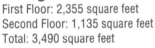

© 1988 design basics inc.

Design EE9228

First Floor: 1,733 square feet
Second Floor: 1,586 square feet
Total: 3,319 square feet

● The creator of this gracious plan seems to have thought of everything. The two-story entry opens into the formal dining room with detailed ceiling and living room. Note the interesting window treatments. Double doors lead from the living room to the beamed-ceiling family room with fireplace and built-in bookshelves. One step down is a cheery sun room with wet bar and pass-through to the kitchen. The kitchen's work area is well-planned with island work center, built-ins and pantry. The sunny bayed windows in the breakfast area overlook the rear yard. The spacious upstairs features three secondary bedrooms and an enormous master suite which includes a sitting area with fireplace, walk-in closet and whirlpool bath.

Design by
Design
Basics,
Inc.

© 1987 design basics inc.

Design by
**Design
Basics,
Inc.**

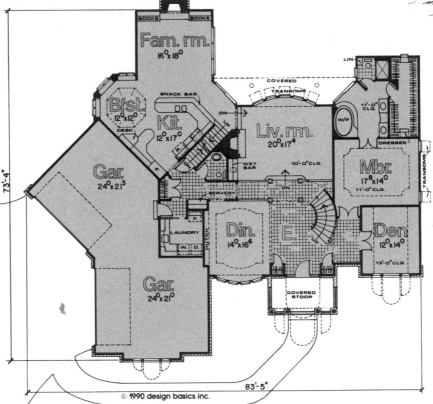

Design EE9346

First Floor: 2,617 square feet
Second Floor: 1,072 square feet
Total: 3,689 square feet

● A spectacular volume entry with a curving staircase features columns to the formal areas of this home. The living room contains a fireplace, bowed window and a wet bar. The formal dining room contains hutch space and a nearby servery. All main-level rooms have nine-foot ceilings. To the rear of the plan is the family room. It has bookcases surrounding a fireplace. French doors lead into the den with a stunning window. The master suite is located on the first floor and has a most elegant bath and a huge walk-in closet. Second-floor bedrooms also have walk-in closets and private baths.

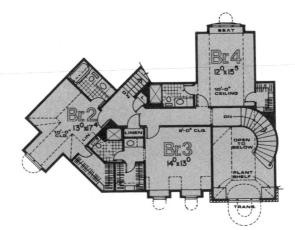

© 1990 design basics inc.

Design EE9151

First Floor: 2,230 square feet
Second Floor: 1,899 square feet
Total: 4,129 square feet

● Rich with traditional detail, this elegant home will be treasured for a lifetime. The side-lit entry leads to a beautiful raised foyer from which the first floor unfolds. To the left is a bay-windowed music alcove and gallery with living room beyond. The formal dining area is to the right. At the center of the plan is an L-shaped island kitchen with corner sinks and large walk-in pantry. A glass enhanced breakfast room contains French doors to a covered porch. A bedroom with full bath and study complete this floor. Upstairs are three additional bedrooms, each with its own bath, and a large gameroom. The master suite has double walk-in closets.

Design by
Larry W.
Garnett &
Associates, Inc.

Width 82'
Depth 46'-2"

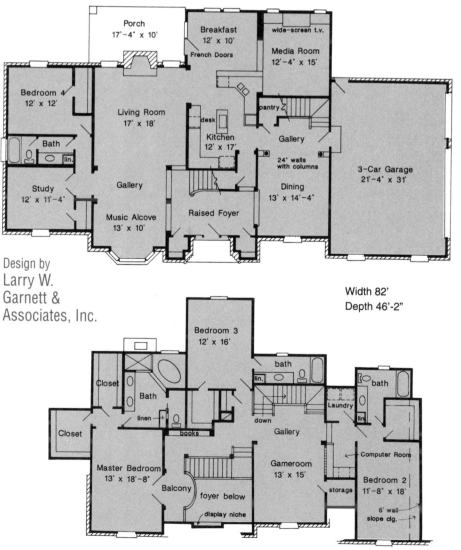

Florida, Spanish & Mediterranean Designs

et the sun shine in with one of the designs in this section; each one will provide a successful home-building experience. With Floridian, Spanish and Mediterranean roots, many — if not all — will complement a variety of building sites. First brought over from the Mediterranean during times of exploration, these homes are now decked out in contemporary fashion, with sleek lines, commodious living patterns and a great deal of indoor/outdoor relationships. These stuccoed beauties feature verandas, patios, lanais and walled gardens. Glorious windows and bright open spaces provide maximum enjoyment of the outdoors from the comfort of the indoors. Family living areas abound with combined kitchen/family or leisure rooms often culminating in open-air areas a step away.

Design EE3475 exhibits the essence of these styles with its earthy facade done in stucco and its tiled roof. Its volume look functions in practical terms, too, by allowing warm air to rise and cool air to circulate through living areas. Privacy walls allow garden areas directly outside windows. In the rear of the house, a covered terrace yields outdoor enjoyment. And true to the style's heritage, this design would work well seaside or hillside.

Upholding Spanish traditions, Design EE9082 sits well on a relatively narrow lot, perfect for today's highly priced — and highly prized — parcels of land. Stucco, a tiled roof and intricate interior spaces function as common denominators of this housing style. To further livability in warm-weather areas, this design incorporates a cool covered porch offset by a tiled courtyard and a fountain.

The homes in this section — each featuring a sunny disposition — will no doubt live up to your highest expectations!

© The Sater Group, Inc.

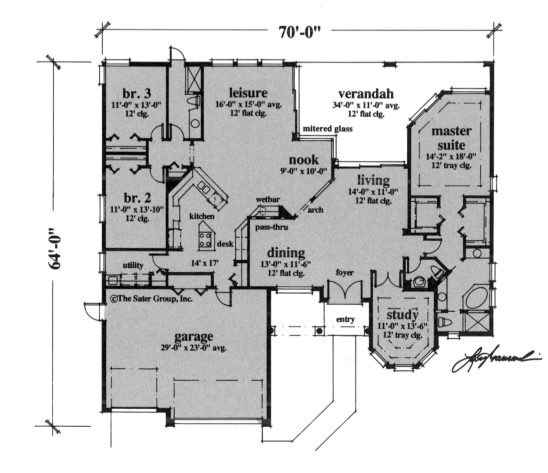

br. 3
11'-0" x 13'-0"
12' clg.

leisure
16'-0" x 15'-0" avg.
12' flat clg.

verandah
34'-0" x 11'-0" avg.
12' flat clg.

mitered glass

nook
9'-0" x 10'-0"

living
14'-0" x 11'-0"
12' flat clg.

master suite
14'-2" x 18'-0"
12' tray clg.

br. 2
11'-0" x 13'-10"
12' clg.

wetbar

kitchen

pass-thru

arch

desk

dining
13'-0" x 11'-6"
12' flat clg.

14' x 17'

utility

©The Sater Group, Inc.

foyer

garage
29'-0" x 23'-0" avg.

entry

study
11'-0" x 13'-6"
12' tray clg.

70'-0"

64'-0"

Design EE6628
Square Footage: 2,582

● With three bedrooms and a study, there's plenty of room for the whole family in this stunning Floridian home. Living areas display openness and elegance by design. A study opens through double doors and will provide plenty of peace and quiet for more studious pursuits. In the master bedroom, a tiered ceiling, His and Hers closets and a super bath offer the best accommodations. There's even private access to the veranda. The other two bedrooms are located off the kitchen and leisure room. A full bath leads outside to provide perfect pool facilities. In the garage, a third-car stall leaves room for a visitor's car or additional storage.

Design by
The Sater
Design Collection

© The Sater Group, Inc.

Jenkins & hinshaw

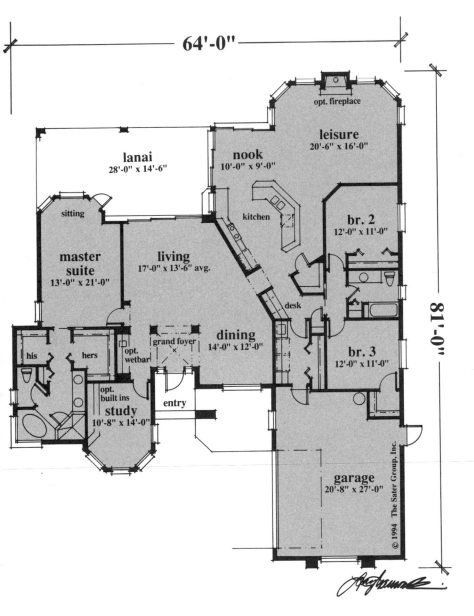

64'-0"

81'-0"

opt. fireplace

lanai
28'-0" x 14'-6"

nook
10'-0" x 9'-0"

leisure
20'-6" x 16'-0"

sitting

kitchen

br. 2
12'-0" x 11'-0"

master suite
13'-0" x 21'-0"

living
17'-0" x 13'-6" avg.

desk

his   hers

opt. wetbar

dining
14'-0" x 12'-0"

grand foyer

br. 3
12'-0" x 11'-0"

opt. built ins

study
10'-8" x 14'-0"

entry

garage
20'-8" x 27'-0"

© 1994 The Sater Group, Inc.

Design by
The Sater
Design Collection

Design EE6626 Square Footage: 2,589

● A grand foyer opens up this delightful one-story home. A living room/dining room combination facilitates everything from parties to relaxing with the Sunday paper. A nearby lanai allows outdoor enjoyments. In the kitchen, convenience begins with a curving work island equipped with a sink and a dishwasher. The breakfast nook lends light and air to the area. A leisure room with an optional fireplace enhances this casual gathering center. Two bedrooms are close by and share a hall bath. At the left side of the home, the master bedroom suite delights with a bayed sitting area, His and Hers closets and a stylish bath. For quieter pursuits, a study with optional built-ins is reached through a corridor with a wet bar.

© The Sater Group, Inc.

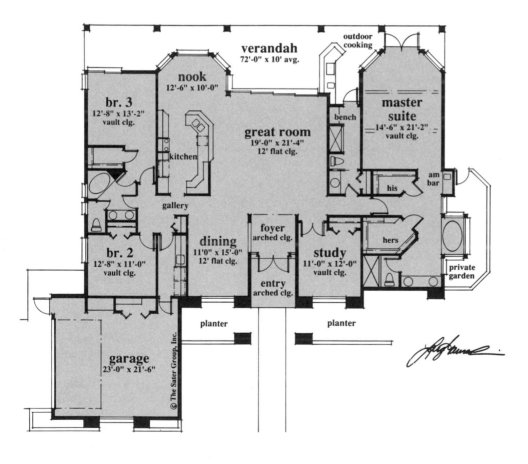

verandah
72'-0" x 10' avg.

outdoor cooking

nook
12'-6" x 10'-0"

br. 3
12'-8" x 13'-2"
vault clg.

kitchen

great room
19'-0" x 21'-4"
12' flat clg.

bench

master suite
14'-6" x 21'-2"
vault clg.

his

am bar

gallery

hers

br. 2
12'-8" x 11'-0"
vault clg.

dining
11'0" x 15'-0"
12' flat clg.

foyer
arched clg.

study
11'-0" x 12'-0"
vault clg.

private garden

entry
arched clg.

planter

planter

garage
23'-0" x 21'-6"

© The Sater Group, Inc.

Design by
The Sater
Design Collection

WIDTH 76'
DEPTH 73'

Design EE6627
Square Footage: 2,648

● For something delightfully different, try this warm-weather winner. The foyer grants a spectacular view of the great room and the dining room. The kitchen easily services the bayed breakfast nook. A veranda stretches across the rear of the house and offers an outdoor kitchen and direct access to a full bath for summertime fun and sun. The master suite opens to this open-air living area by way of double doors. Otherwise, it also excels in livability with a morning bar, dual walk-in closets, a whirlpool tub in a bumped-out nook and a double-bowl vanity. In the study, a closet offers additional storage space. Two secondary bedrooms share a bath with a corner tub and a compartmented toilet.

© The Sater Group, Inc.

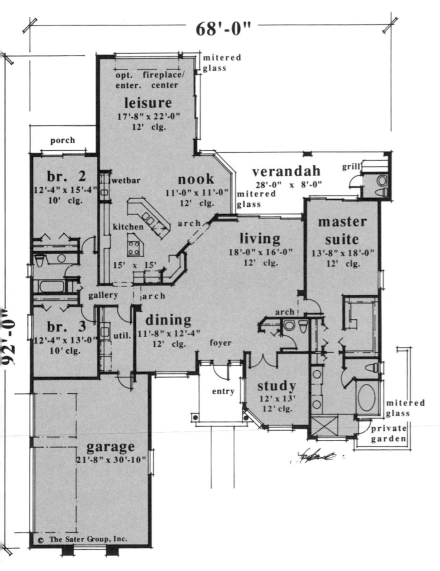

68'-0"

mitered glass

opt. fireplace/ enter. center

leisure
17'-8" x 22'-0"
12' clg.

porch

br. 2
12'-4" x 15'-4"
10' clg.

wetbar

nook
11'-0" x 11'-0"
12' clg.

verandah
28'-0" x 8'-0"
mitered glass

grill

kitchen

arch

master suite
13'-8" x 18'-0"
12' clg.

15' x 15'

living
18'-0" x 16'-0"
12' clg.

gallery

arch

br. 3
12'-4" x 13'-0"
10' clg.

util.

dining
11'-8" x 12'-4"
12' clg.

foyer

arch

92'-0"

garage
21'-8" x 30'-10"

entry

study
12' x 13'
12' clg.

mitered glass

private garden

© The Sater Group, Inc.

Design EE6606
Square Footage: 2,984

● Glass surrounds the entry of this appealing stucco home. Arched doorways lead from the formal living and dining rooms to the sleeping zones and the informal living area. The study is situated to the right of the entry and will make a wonderful home office. Ideally suited for informal entertaining, the gourmet kitchen shares space with a sunny breakfast nook and a spacious leisure room which offers access to the rear grounds and a covered veranda. The leisure room provides optional space for a fireplace and entertainment center. The master suite sports two closets: an oversized walk-in closet and a smaller closet nearby. Treat yourself to a relaxing soak in the garden tub or enter the private garden through an adjacent door. A separate shower, dual vanities and a compartmented toilet complete the master sleeping quarters. On the opposite side of the plan, two secondary bedrooms share a full bath.

Design by
**The Sater
Design Collection**

173

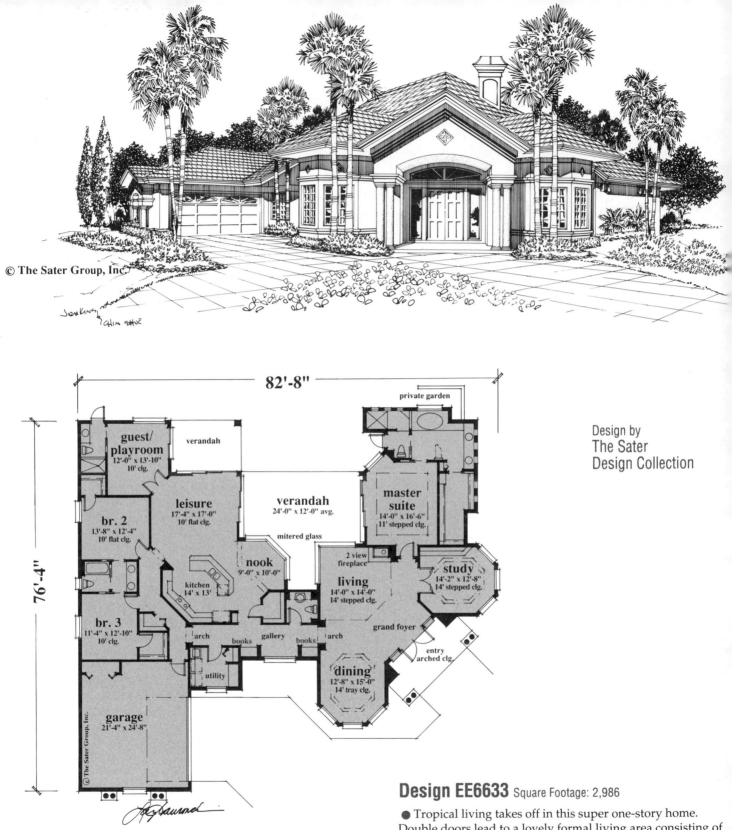

© The Sater Group, Inc

82'-8"

private garden

Design by
The Sater
Design Collection

guest/
playroom
12'-0" x 13'-10"
10' clg.

verandah

master
suite
14'-0" x 16'-6"
11' stepped clg.

leisure
17'-4" x 17'-0"
10' flat clg.

76'-4"

verandah
24'-0" x 12'-0" avg.

br. 2
13'-8" x 12'-4"
10' flat clg.

mitered glass

nook
9'-0" x 10'-0"

2 view
fireplace

study
14'-2" x 12'-8"
14' stepped clg.

kitchen
14' x 13'

living
14'-0" x 14'-0"
14' stepped clg.

br. 3
11'-4" x 12'-10"
10' clg.

arch

books

gallery

books

arch

grand foyer

entry
arched clg.

utility

dining
12'-8" x 15'-0"
14' tray clg.

garage
21'-4" x 24'-8"

© The Sater Group, Inc.

Design EE6633 Square Footage: 2,986

● Tropical living takes off in this super one-story home.
Double doors lead to a lovely formal living area consisting of
a living room, dining room and study. Through an archway,
a gallery adds an air of distinction. The kitchen is open to a
sunny nook and a bright leisure area for delightful dining
and relaxing. A play room opens off this area and is sure to
please the kids of the house. A full bath here leads outside.
Two bedrooms nearby each sport a walk-in closet and utilize
a full bath in between. The master bedroom suite enjoys a
private bath with a whirlpool tub, dual lavs, a large walk-in
closet and a compartmented toilet and shower.

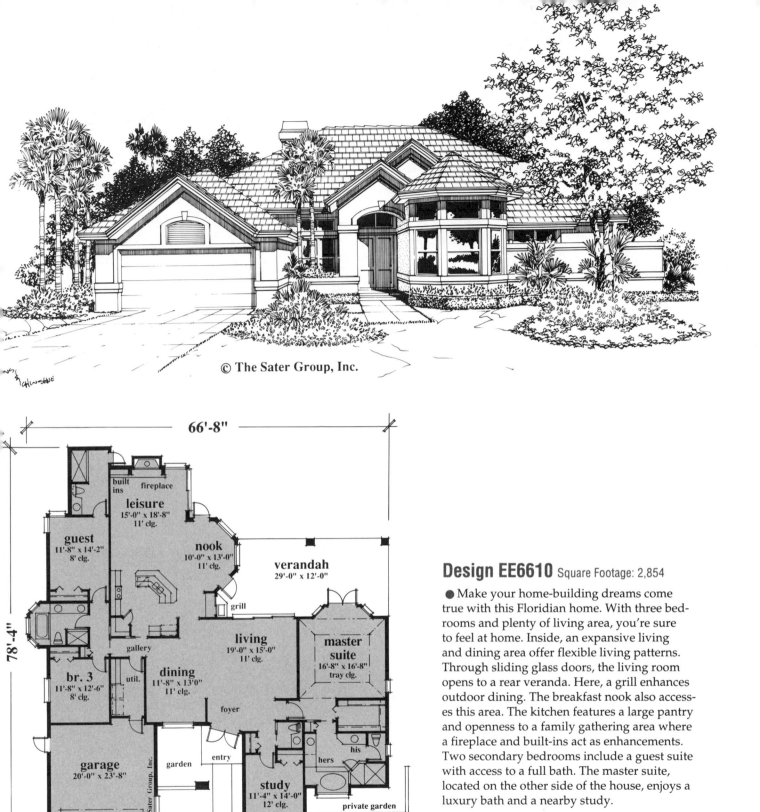

© The Sater Group, Inc.

66'-8"

78'-4"

guest
11'-8" x 14'-2"
8' clg.

leisure
15'-0" x 18'-8"
11' clg.

built ins

fireplace

nook
10'-0" x 13'-0"
11' clg.

verandah
29'-0" x 12'-0"

grill

gallery

br. 3
11'-8" x 12'-6"
8' clg.

util.

dining
11'-8" x 13'0"
11' clg.

living
19'-0" x 15'-0"
11' clg.

master suite
16'-8" x 16'-8"
tray clg.

foyer

hers

his

garage
20'-0" x 23'-8"

garden

entry

study
11'-4" x 14'-0"
12' clg.

private garden

© The Sater Group, Inc.

Design EE6610 Square Footage: 2,854

● Make your home-building dreams come true with this Floridian home. With three bedrooms and plenty of living area, you're sure to feel at home. Inside, an expansive living and dining area offer flexible living patterns. Through sliding glass doors, the living room opens to a rear veranda. Here, a grill enhances outdoor dining. The breakfast nook also accesses this area. The kitchen features a large pantry and openness to a family gathering area where a fireplace and built-ins act as enhancements. Two secondary bedrooms include a guest suite with access to a full bath. The master suite, located on the other side of the house, enjoys a luxury bath and a nearby study.

Design by
The Sater
Design Collection

© The Sater Group, Inc.

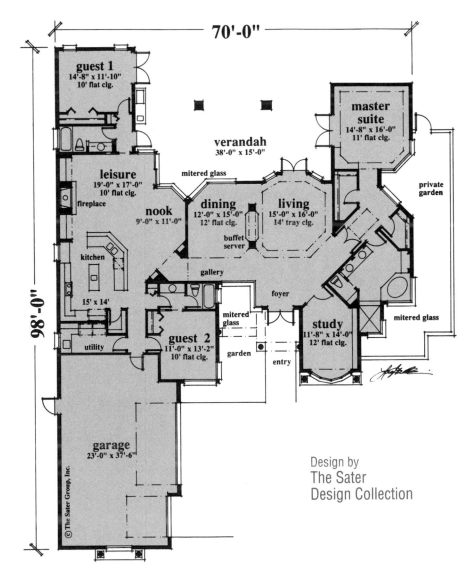

70'-0"

98'-0"

guest 1
14'-8" x 11'-10"
10' flat clg.

leisure
19'-0" x 17'-0"
10' flat clg.

fireplace

nook
9'-0" x 11'-0"

verandah
38'-0" x 15'-0"

mitered glass

dining
12'-0" x 15'-0"
12' flat clg.

buffet server

living
15'-0" x 16'-0"
14' tray clg.

master suite
14'-8" x 16'-0"
11' flat clg.

private garden

kitchen

15' x 14'

gallery

guest 2
11'-0" x 13'-2"
10' flat clg.

utility

mitered glass

garden

foyer

entry

study
11'-8" x 14'-0"
12' flat clg.

mitered glass

garage
23'-0" x 37'-6"

© The Sater Group, Inc.

Design by
The Sater
Design Collection

Design EE6602
Square Footage: 2,794

● Classic columns, circle-head windows and a bay-windowed study give this stucco home a wonderful street presence. The foyer leads into the formal living and dining areas. An arched buffet server separates these rooms and contributes an open feeling. The kitchen, nook and leisure room are grouped for informal living. A desk/message center in the island kitchen, art niches in the nook and a fireplace with an entertainment center and shelves add custom touches. Two secondary suites have guest baths and offer full privacy from the master wing. The master suite hosts a private garden area, while the master bath features a walk-in shower that overlooks the garden, and a water closet room with space for books or a television. Large His and Hers walk-in closets complete these private quarters.

patio

DINING
13-4 x 12-6

GREAT RM.
15-4 x 22-4

MASTER
BED RM.
15-4 x 16-8

KIT.
13-4 x 10-10

fireplace

(cathedral ceiling)

lin.

master
bath

UTIL.
7-4 x 7-4

walk-in
closet

skylight

d w

cl

cl

FOYER
7-0 x 9-0

BED RM./
STUDY
11-8 x 11-0

bath

GARAGE
22-0 x 23-0

covered
porch

BED RM.
11-8 x 12-0

closet

5-4

55-0

60-0

Design EE9740
Square Footage: 1,838

● This three-bedroom South-western design is enhanced by the use of arched windows and a dramatic arched entrance. An expansive great room features a cathedral ceiling and a fireplace with direct access to the patio and the dining room. An efficient U-shaped kitchen has plenty of counter space and easily serves both the dining and great rooms. A private master suite features a large walk-in closet and skylit bath with double vanity, whirlpool tub, and separate shower. Two additional bedrooms have generous closet space and share a full bath with double vanity.

Design by
Donald A.
Gardner,
Architects, Inc.

Design EE3344
Square Footage: 3,054

QUOTE ONE™
Cost to build? See page 232
to order complete cost estimate
to build this house in your area!

QUIET TERRACE

MASTER BEDROOM
13⁰ x 17⁴

WHIRLPOOL

HER BATH

HIS BATH

DRESSING RM

HER WALK-IN CLOSET

HIS WALK-IN CLOSET

BEDROOM
10¹⁰ x 11⁰

BEDROOM
10¹⁰ x 14⁴

LINEN

BATH

CL

BEDROOM
11⁸ x 12⁰

FLOWER PORCH
13⁰ x 11⁸

SKYLIGHTS ABOVE

SLOPED CEILING

SKYLIGHT

LIVING RM
13⁰ x 19⁴

FOYER

DN

TRELLIS ABOVE

COURTYARD

DINING RM
13⁰ x 11⁰

KITCHEN
10⁰ x 11⁴

BRKFST RM
8⁴ x 11⁴

DESK

COOK TOP

REF'G

OVEN

S

PLAY TERRACE

FAMILY RM
15⁴ x 19⁶

RAISED HEARTH

PDR RM

BC

PANTRY

S BAR CL

STUDY
13⁰ x 11⁰

CL

BAR
S

LAUNDRY
7¹⁰ x 10⁰

LT W D

CL

P

GARAGE
21⁴ x 21⁴

70'-2"

85'-8"

Design by
Home Planners,
Inc.

● This home features interior planning for today's active family. Living areas include a living room with fireplace, a cozy study and family room with wet bar. Convenient to the kitchen is the formal dining room with attractive bay window overlooking the back yard. The four-bedroom sleeping area contains a sumptuous master suite. Also notice the cheerful flower porch with access from the master suite, living room and dining room.

Design EE3480
Square Footage: 1,845

● The inviting facade of this sun-country home introduces a most livable floor plan. Beyond the grand entry, a comfortable gathering room, with a central fireplace, shares sweeping, open spaces with the dining room. Sliding glass doors lead to a rear terrace. An efficiently patterned kitchen makes use of a large, walk-in pantry and a breakfast room. A snack bar offers a third mealtime eating option. Nearby, a full laundry room rounds out the modern livability of this utilitarian area. Away from the hustle and bustle of the day, the sleeping wing offers a study with a wide opening off the foyer. If desired as a bedroom, the size and location of the doorway could be moved to the bedroom hallway to afford the proper amount of privacy. Note the large closets in both secondary bedrooms. In the master bedroom, look for double closets and a pampering bath with double lavs, a vanity and a whirlpool bath. For information on customizing this design, call 1-800-521-6797, ext. 800.

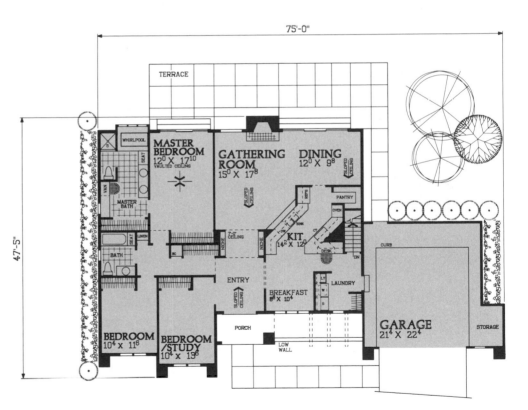

QUOTE ONE™
Cost to build? See page 232
to order complete cost estimate
to build this house in your area!

Design by
Home Planners,
Inc.

Design EE3602
Square Footage: 2,312

● This unique one-story plan seems tailor-made for a small family or for empty-nesters. Formal areas are situated well for entertaining—living room to the right and formal dining room to the left. A large family room is found to the rear. It has access to a rear wood deck and is warmed in the cold months by a welcoming hearth. The U-shaped kitchen features an attached morning room for casual meals. It is near the laundry room and a wash room. Bedrooms are split. The master suite sits to the right of the plan and has a walk-in closet and a fine bath. A nearby study has a private porch. Two family bedrooms on the other side of the home share a private bath. For information on customizing this design, call 1-800-521-6797, ext. 800.

Design by
Home Planners,
Inc.

Design EE3475
Square Footage: 3,286

● The colorful, tiled hipped roof with varying roof planes and wide overhangs sets off this Spanish design. Projecting gabled roofs create added interest. Meanwhile, the sheltered front entrance is both dramatic and inviting with double doors opening to the central foyer. Here, a long plant shelf serves as a nice introduction. In the sunken living room, a curved, raised-hearth fireplace acts as a focal point. Double glass doors lead to a covered terrace. The U-shaped kitchen is efficient with its island work surface, breakfast bar, pantry and broom closet. An informal nook delights with its projecting bay and high ceiling. This generous, open area extends to include the family room and will cater to many of the family's informal living activities. Opposite the more formal living room is the separate dining room. Its expanse of glass looks out on the garden court. A major floor-planning feature of this design is found in the sleeping arrangements; notice the complete separation of the parents' and children's bedroom facilities. For information on customizing this design, call 1-800-521-6797, ext. 800.

Quote One™

Cost to build? See page 232 to order complete cost estimate to build this house in your area!

Design by
Home Planners, Inc.

Design EE9082
Square Footage: 2,360

● Reminiscent of the homes built long ago, this Spanish adaptation has many components to draw attention to it. Note the long entry porch leading to an angled foyer flanked by a huge living room with a cathedral ceiling and a dining room with a sloped ceiling. Across the gallery is a long porch with skylights that overlooks the tiled courtyard. The kitchen features plenty of counter space and a large pantry. To the rear, in privacy, is the master bedroom suite. It has a tub area with a raised gazebo ceiling and transom windows. There are also two family bedrooms sharing a full bath with double vanities.

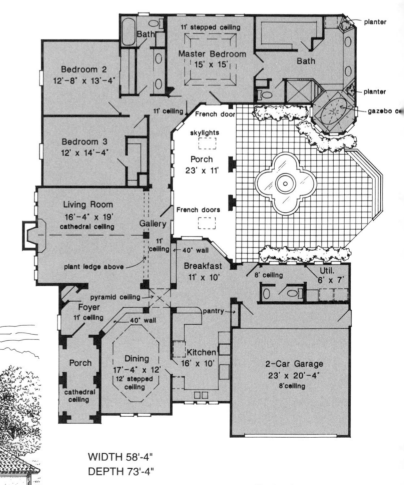

WIDTH 58'-4"
DEPTH 73'-4"

Design by
Larry W.
Garnett &
Associates, Inc.

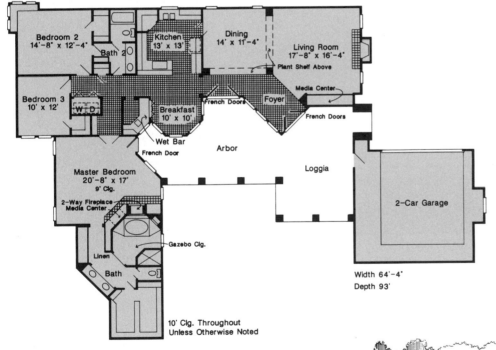

Bedroom 2
14'-8" x 12'-4"

Bath 2

Bedroom 3
10' x 12'

W D

Kitchen
13' x 13'

Breakfast
10' x 10'

Wet Bar

French Door

Dining
14' x 11'-4"

Plant Shelf Above

French Doors

Living Room
17'-8" x 16'-4"

Media Center

Foyer

French Doors

Arbor

Loggia

2-Car Garage

Master Bedroom
20'-8" x 17'
9' Clg.

2-Way Fireplace
Media Center

Gazebo Clg.

Linen

Bath

10' Clg. Throughout
Unless Otherwise Noted

Width 64'-4"
Depth 93'

Design by
Larry W.
Garnett &
Associates, Inc.

Design EE9083
Square Footage: 2,176

● This grand design caters to outdoor lifestyles with areas that invite visitation. The front entry opens to a beautiful and characteristic Spanish courtyard with a loggia, an arbor and a spa area. The foyer runs the length of the home and leads from open living and dining areas to a convenient kitchen and breakfast nook, then back to the sleeping quarters. The master suite is especially notable with its luxurious bath and ample closet space. Note the many extras in the plan: a fireplace and a media center in the living room and in the master bedroom, a wet bar at the breakfast nook, and an oversized pantry in the kitchen.

Quote One™

Cost to build? See page 232
to order complete cost estimate
to build this house in your area!

Design by
**Home Planners,
Inc.**

Design EE3436
Square Footage: 2,573

● This dashing Spanish home, with its captivating front courtyard, presents a delightful introduction to the inside living spaces. These excel with a central living room/dining room combination. A wet bar here makes entertaining easy. In the kitchen, a huge pantry and interesting angles are sure to please the house gourmet. A breakfast nook with a corner fireplace further enhances this area. The master bedroom makes room for a private bath with a whirlpool tub and dual lavatories; a walk-in closet adds to the modern amenities here. Two additional bedrooms make use of a Hollywood bath. Each bedroom is highlighted by a spacious walk-in closet. For information on customizing this design, call 1-800-521-6797, ext. 800.

Design by
Home Planners,
Inc.

Design EE2922
Square Footage: 3,505

● Loaded with custom features, this plan seems to have everything imaginable. There's an enormous sunken gathering room and cozy study. The country-style kitchen contains an efficient work area, as well as space for relaxing in the morning and sitting rooms. Two nice-sized bedrooms and a luxurious master suite round out the plan.

© The Sater Group, Inc.

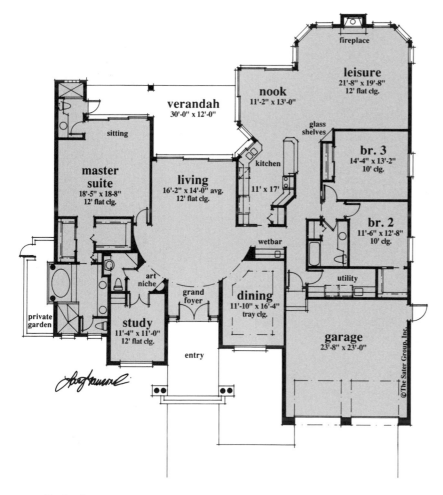

fireplace

leisure
21'-8" x 19'-8"
12' flat clg.

verandah
30'-0" x 12'-0"

nook
11'-2" x 13'-0"

glass shelves

br. 3
14'-4" x 13'-2"
10' clg.

sitting

master suite
18'-5" x 18'-8"
12' flat clg.

living
16'-2" x 14'-0" avg.
12' flat clg.

kitchen

11' x 17'

br. 2
11'-6" x 12'-8"
10' clg.

wetbar

art niche

grand foyer

dining
11'-10" x 16'-4"
tray clg.

utility

private garden

study
11'-4" x 11'-0"
12' flat clg.

entry

garage
23'-8" x 23'-0"

© The Sater Group, Inc.

Design EE6625
Square Footage: 3,273

● For elegant entertainments, this house is in a class all its own. The entry gives way to an impressive living room with a dining room and study radiating off it. The rear wall offers passage to a rear porch, making outdoor enjoyments possible. The master bedroom suite rests to one side of the plan and includes His and Hers walk-in closets and a luxury bath. Another full bath located here leads to the outdoors. At the other side of the house, informal living areas open with a kitchen, a breakfast nook and a family gathering area. Two bedrooms here share a full bath and will provide ample space for children or guests.

Design by
**The Sater
Design Collection**

Width 71'-4"
Depth 77'

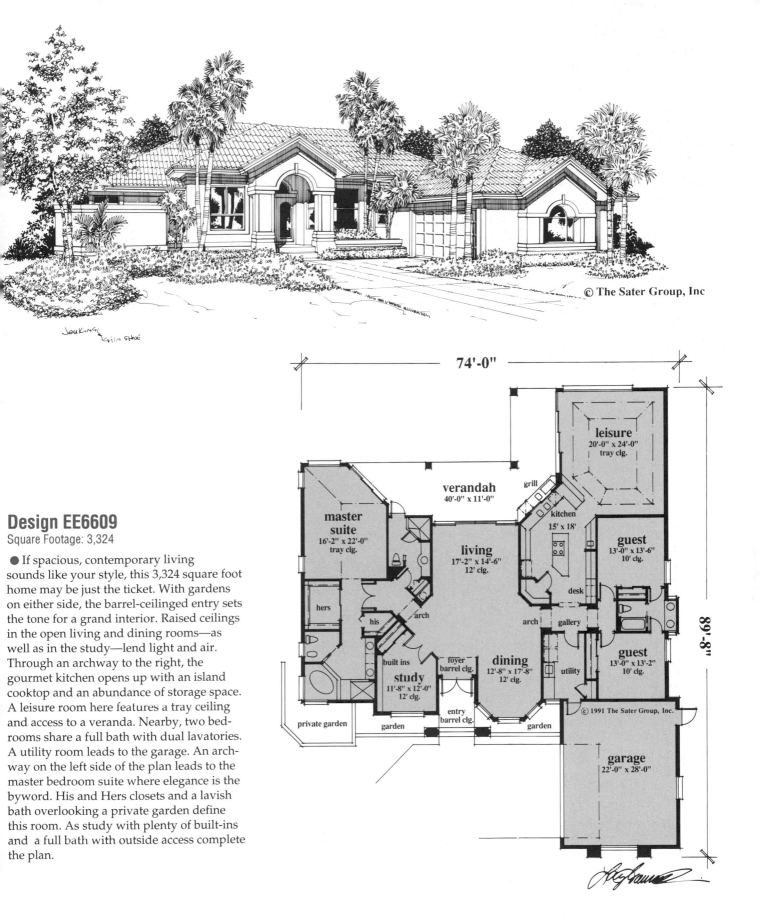

© The Sater Group, Inc

Design EE6609
Square Footage: 3,324

● If spacious, contemporary living sounds like your style, this 3,324 square foot home may be just the ticket. With gardens on either side, the barrel-ceilinged entry sets the tone for a grand interior. Raised ceilings in the open living and dining rooms—as well as in the study—lend light and air. Through an archway to the right, the gourmet kitchen opens up with an island cooktop and an abundance of storage space. A leisure room here features a tray ceiling and access to a veranda. Nearby, two bedrooms share a full bath with dual lavatories. A utility room leads to the garage. An archway on the left side of the plan leads to the master bedroom suite where elegance is the byword. His and Hers closets and a lavish bath overlooking a private garden define this room. As study with plenty of built-ins and a full bath with outside access complete the plan.

74'-0"

89'-8"

leisure 20'-0" x 24'-0" tray clg.

verandah 40'-0" x 11'-0"

grill

kitchen 15' x 18'

master suite 16'-2" x 22'-0" tray clg.

living 17'-2" x 14'-6" 12' clg.

guest 13'-0" x 13'-6" 10' clg.

hers

his

arch

desk

built ins

arch

gallery

guest 13'-0" x 13'-2" 10' clg.

study 11'-8" x 12'-0" 12' clg.

foyer barrel clg.

dining 12'-8" x 17'-8" 12' clg.

utility

private garden

garden

entry barrel clg.

garden

© 1991 The Sater Group, Inc.

garage 22'-0" x 28'-0"

Design by
The Sater
Design Collection

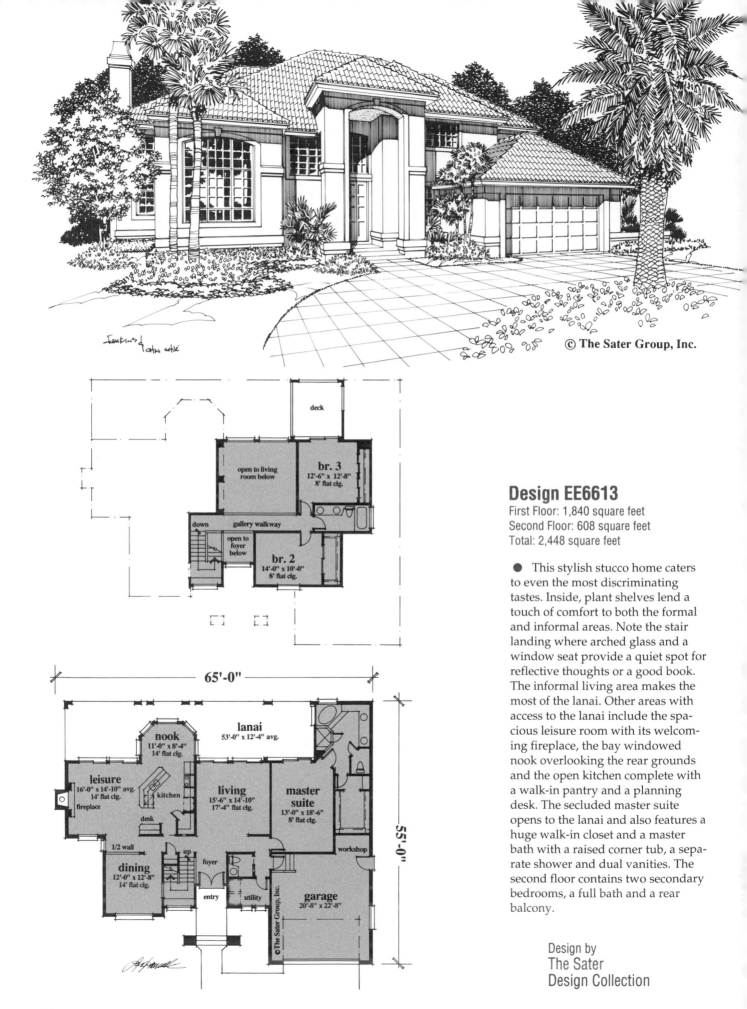

deck

open to living room below

br. 3
12'-6" x 12'-8"
8' flat clg.

down

gallery walkway

open to foyer below

br. 2
14'-0" x 10'-0"
8' flat clg.

© The Sater Group, Inc.

← 65'-0" →

nook
11'-0" x 8'-4"
14' flat clg.

lanai
53'-0" x 12'-4" avg.

leisure
16'-0" x 14'-10" avg.
14' flat clg.

fireplace

kitchen

living
15'-6" x 14'-10"
17'-4" flat clg.

master suite
13'-0" x 18'-6"
8' flat clg.

desk

1/2 wall

up

workshop

dining
12'-0" x 12'-8"
14' flat clg.

foyer

entry

utility

garage
20'-8" x 22'-8"

55'-0"

© The Sater Group, Inc.

Design EE6613

First Floor: 1,840 square feet
Second Floor: 608 square feet
Total: 2,448 square feet

● This stylish stucco home caters to even the most discriminating tastes. Inside, plant shelves lend a touch of comfort to both the formal and informal areas. Note the stair landing where arched glass and a window seat provide a quiet spot for reflective thoughts or a good book. The informal living area makes the most of the lanai. Other areas with access to the lanai include the spacious leisure room with its welcoming fireplace, the bay windowed nook overlooking the rear grounds and the open kitchen complete with a walk-in pantry and a planning desk. The secluded master suite opens to the lanai and also features a huge walk-in closet and a master bath with a raised corner tub, a separate shower and dual vanities. The second floor contains two secondary bedrooms, a full bath and a rear balcony.

Design by
The Sater
Design Collection

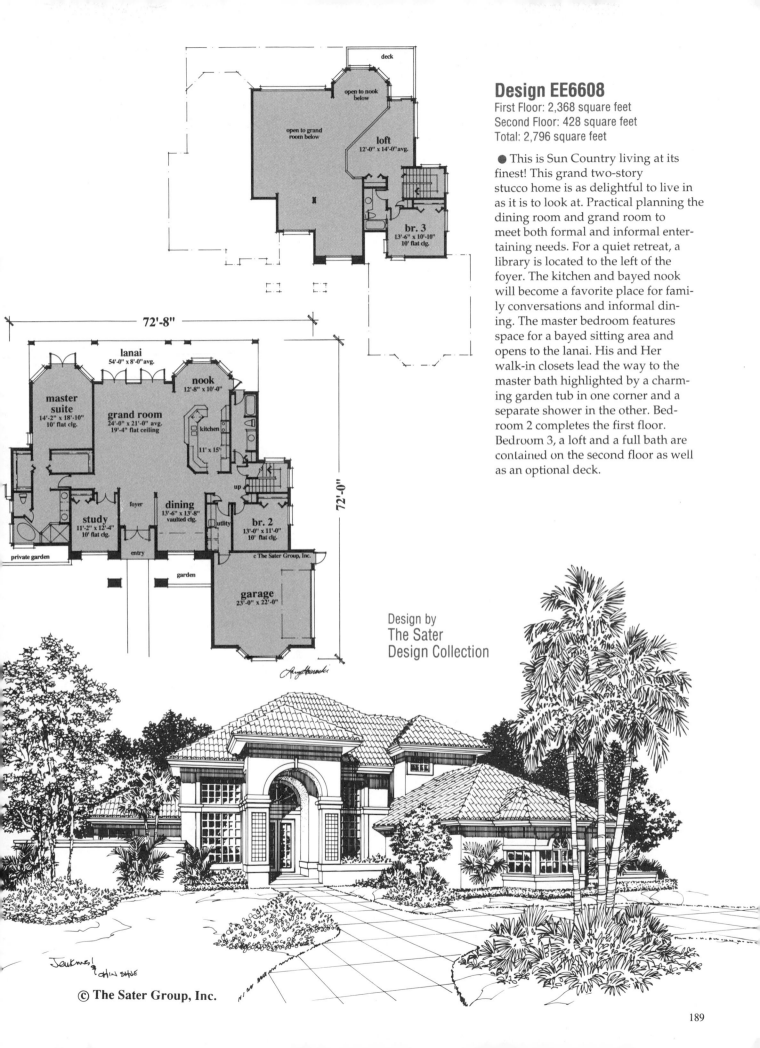

deck

open to nook below

open to grand room below

loft
12'-0" x 14'-0" avg.

br. 3
13'-6" x 10'-10"
10' flat clg.

Design EE6608
First Floor: 2,368 square feet
Second Floor: 428 square feet
Total: 2,796 square feet

● This is Sun Country living at its finest! This grand two-story stucco home is as delightful to live in as it is to look at. Practical planning the dining room and grand room to meet both formal and informal entertaining needs. For a quiet retreat, a library is located to the left of the foyer. The kitchen and bayed nook will become a favorite place for family conversations and informal dining. The master bedroom features space for a bayed sitting area and opens to the lanai. His and Her walk-in closets lead the way to the master bath highlighted by a charming garden tub in one corner and a separate shower in the other. Bedroom 2 completes the first floor. Bedroom 3, a loft and a full bath are contained on the second floor as well as an optional deck.

72'-8"

lanai
54'-0" x 8'-0" avg.

master suite
14'-2" x 18'-10"
10' flat clg.

grand room
24'-0" x 21'-0" avg.
19'-4" flat ceiling

nook
12'-8" x 10'-0"

kitchen

11' x 15'

up

72'-0"

foyer

study
11'-2" x 12'-4"
10' flat clg.

dining
13'-6" x 13'-8"
vaulted clg.

utility

br. 2
13'-0" x 11'-0"
10' flat clg.

private garden

entry

garden

c The Sater Group, Inc.

garage
23'-0" x 22'-0"

Design by
The Sater
Design Collection

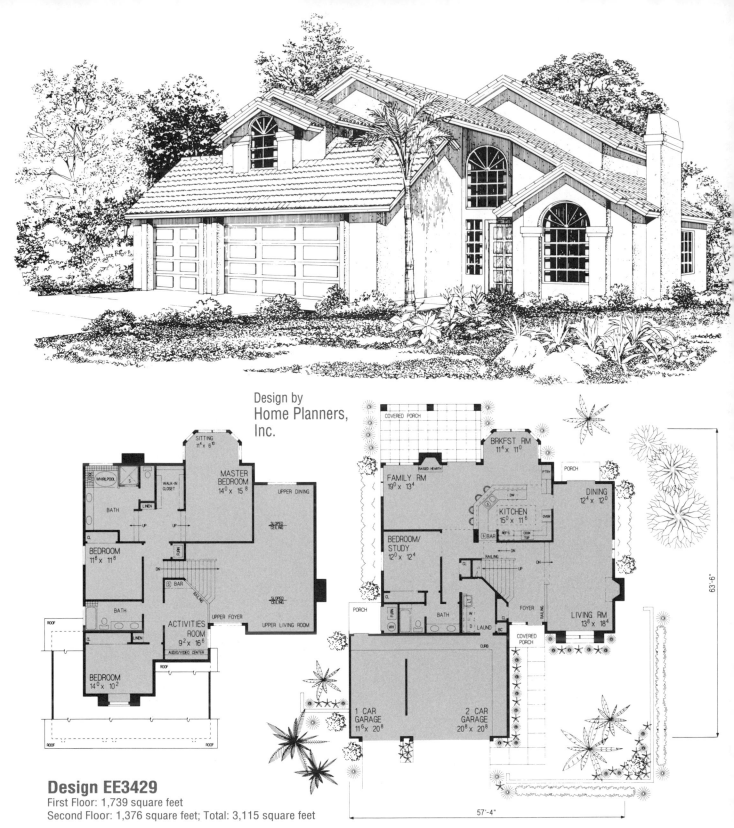

Design by
Home Planners,
Inc.

Design EE3429

First Floor: 1,739 square feet
Second Floor: 1,376 square feet; Total: 3,115 square feet

● From the dramatic open entry to the covered back porch, this home delivers a full measure of livability in Spanish design. Formal living areas (living room and dining room) have a counterpoint in the family room and glassed-in breakfast room. The kitchen is a hub for both areas. Notice that the first-floor study has an adjacent bath, making it a fine guest room when needed. On the second floor, the activities room serves two family bedrooms and a grand master suite. For information on customizing this design, call 1-800-521-6797, ext. 800.

Coastal, Tidewater & Island Designs

In this section, fanciful living takes flight with homes designed for tropical climes. Though drawing on traditional elements such as shuttered windows, Palladian windows and siding, many of these stuccoed homes lend themselves to a sleek contemporary look. All utilize outdoor spaces effectively; porches and verandas often greet visitors and take them straight through to rear, open-air living centers. Raised roof lines add modern flair and allow warm air to rise up and away from interior spaces.

With unmistakable appeal, designs such as EE9188 extol the virtues of Bungalow style. Appropriate for exclusive beach property — or nearby neighborhood property — this little house packs a powerful punch. Living areas open up right off the front porch and entry. Ample proportions define bedrooms, making visits and year-round living most comfortable.

Along the coasts or along the tidewaters, an "Old Florida" building style makes the most of the surroundings. To escape high waters, main floors lie above the foundation on piles; break-away lattice-door panels underneath hide anything in storage. Interesting entries are abundant and metal roofs further define this unique style. Design EE6615 serves as a good example. Inside, living areas expand to a veranda in the back and a sun deck off one side of the great room. The second-floor master suite opens up to a private deck. In an expanded interpretation, EE6620 offers details such as built-ins and an elevator.

Whether on the Gulf or in the Virgin Islands, and no matter what the temperature or tide, the homes in this section will provide years of comfortable living.

Design by
Larry W.
Garnett &
Associates, Inc.

Width 51'
Depth 44'-8"

Design EE9181
Square Footage: 1,370

● With wood siding and a wrapping veranda, this three-bedroom home will take on tropical climes with traditional flair. A French door opens to the foyer with a nearby closet. The living room rises with a ten-foot ceiling. French doors here lead to the veranda and open to balmy summer breezes. The dining room shares an open, columned space with the living room as well as the kitchen. A U-shaped layout in the kitchen provides an efficient work space for the resident cook. French doors also open off the dining room and provide passage to a pleasant rear terrace. Each secondary bedroom extends ample closet space while the master bedroom enjoys an enormous walk-in closet. In the master bath, a double-bowl vanity, dressing table and compartmented toilet guarantee modern convenience.

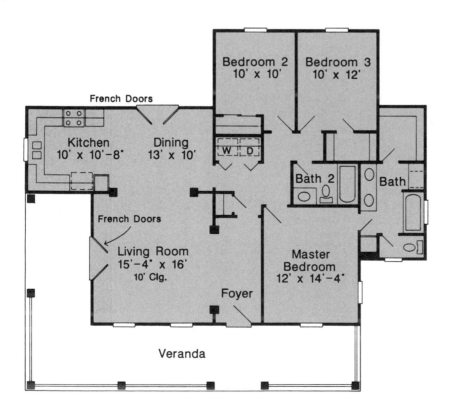

French Doors

Kitchen
10' x 10'-8"

Dining
13' x 10'

Bedroom 2
10' x 10'

Bedroom 3
10' x 12'

W | D

Bath 2

Bath

French Doors

Living Room
15'-4" x 16'
10' Clg.

Master
Bedroom
12' x 14'-4"

Foyer

Veranda

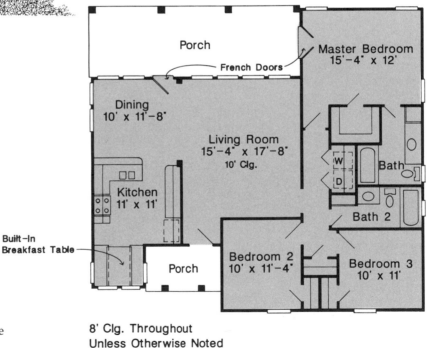

Porch

French Doors

Master Bedroom
15'-4" x 12'

Dining
10' x 11'-8"

Living Room
15'-4" x 17'-8"
10' Clg.

W
D

Bath

Kitchen
11' x 11'

Bath 2

Built-In
Breakfast Table

Porch

Bedroom 2
10' x 11'-4"

Bedroom 3
10' x 11'

Design EE9188 Square Footage: 1,334

● Beachside or otherwise, this little home packs powerful appeal. Living areas encompass a living/dining room combination where a French door leads to a porch. The kitchen, which extends livability through a built-in nook table, is open to the dining room. Three bedrooms include two secondary bedrooms, each of ample proportions. A full bath is situated nearby. In the master bedroom, a walk-in closet and a private bath are appreciated enhancements. French doors open to the porch outside. For added outdoor livability, a terrace radiates from the back of the house.

8' Clg. Throughout
Unless Otherwise Noted

Design by
Larry W.
Garnett &
Associates, Inc.

Width 43'-4"
Depth 38'-8"

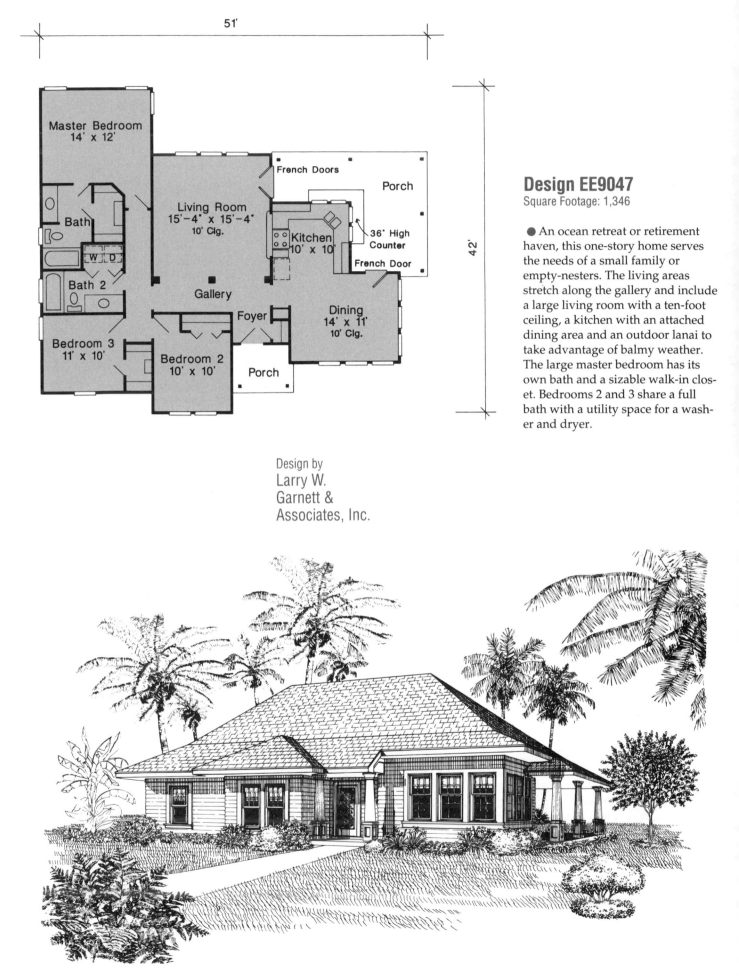

51'

Master Bedroom
14' x 12'

Bath

Bath 2

W D

Living Room
15'-4" x 15'-4"
10' Clg.

Gallery

French Doors

Porch

Kitchen
10' x 10'

36" High
Counter

French Door

42'

Bedroom 3
11' x 10'

Bedroom 2
10' x 10'

Foyer

Porch

Dining
14' x 11'
10' Clg.

Design EE9047
Square Footage: 1,346

● An ocean retreat or retirement haven, this one-story home serves the needs of a small family or empty-nesters. The living areas stretch along the gallery and include a large living room with a ten-foot ceiling, a kitchen with an attached dining area and an outdoor lanai to take advantage of balmy weather. The large master bedroom has its own bath and a sizable walk-in closet. Bedrooms 2 and 3 share a full bath with a utility space for a washer and dryer.

Design by
Larry W.
Garnett &
Associates, Inc.

Quote One™

Cost to build? See page 232
to order complete cost estimate
to build this house in your area!

Design EE3375

Square Footage: 1,378

● Prepare for warmer climes with this two- or three-bedroom home. A covered porch with columns leads to the interior where a breakfast room sits to the left and a media room (or use this room as a bedroom) sits to the right. In the living room, a fireplace and a sloped ceiling lend definition. The dining room is open to this area and features sliding glass doors to a rear terrace. In the kitchen, a U-shape assures efficiency. Two bedrooms include a master suite with a private bath and a walk-in closet.

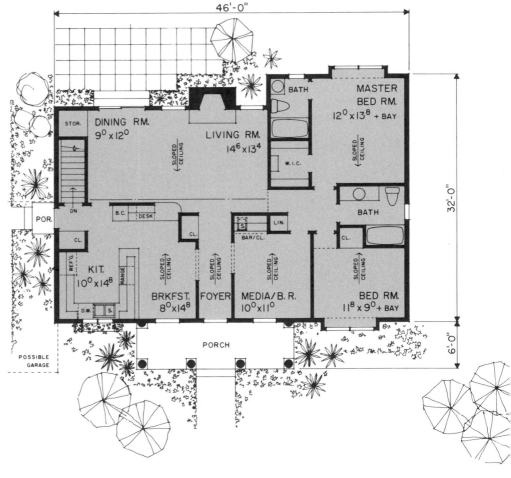

Design by
Home Planners,
Inc.

© The Sater Group, Inc.

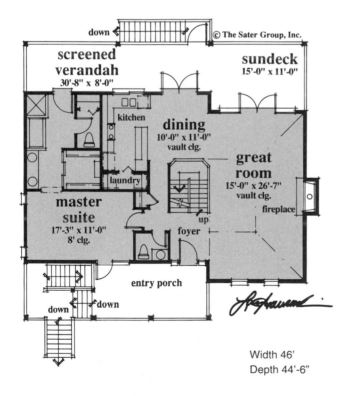

screened verandah
30'-8" x 8'-0"

sundeck
15'-0" x 11'-0"

down

kitchen

dining
10'-0" x 11'-0"
vault clg.

great room
15'-0" x 26'-7"
vault clg.

fireplace

laundry

up

master suite
17'-3" x 11'-0"
8' clg.

foyer

entry porch

down   down

down

Width 46'
Depth 44'-6"

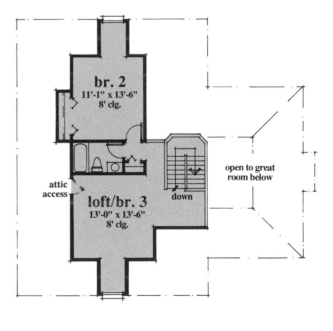

br. 2
11'-1" x 13'-6"
8' clg.

attic access

loft/br. 3
13'-0" x 13'-6"
8' clg.

down

open to great room below

Design by
The Sater
Design Collection

Design EE6617 First Floor: 1,189 square feet
Second Floor: 575 square feet; Total: 1,764 square feet

● An abundance of porches and a deck encourage year-round indoor outdoor relationships in this classic two-story home. The spacious living room with its cozy fireplace and the adjacent dining room—both with access to the screened porch/deck area—are perfect for formal or informal entertaining. An efficient kitchen and a nearby laundry room make chores easy. The private master suite offers access to the screened porch and leads into a relaxing master bath complete with a walk-in closet, a tub and separate shower, double-bowl lavs and a compartmented toilet. Bedroom 2 shares the second floor with a full bath and a loft which may be used as a third bedroom.

Design EE6616 First Floor: 1,136 square feet
Second Floor: 636 square feet; Total: 1,772 square feet

● This two-story coastal design is sure to please with its warm character and decorative windows walk. The covered entry—with its dramatic transom window—leads to a spacious living room highlighted by a warming fireplace. To the right, the dining room and kitchen combine to provide a delightful place for mealtimes inside or out, with access to a side deck through double doors. A study, a bedroom and a full bath complete the first floor. The luxurious master suite is located on the second floor for privacy and features an oversized walk-in closet and a separate dressing area. The pampering master bath enjoys a relaxing whirlpool tub, a double-bowl vanity and a compartmented toilet.

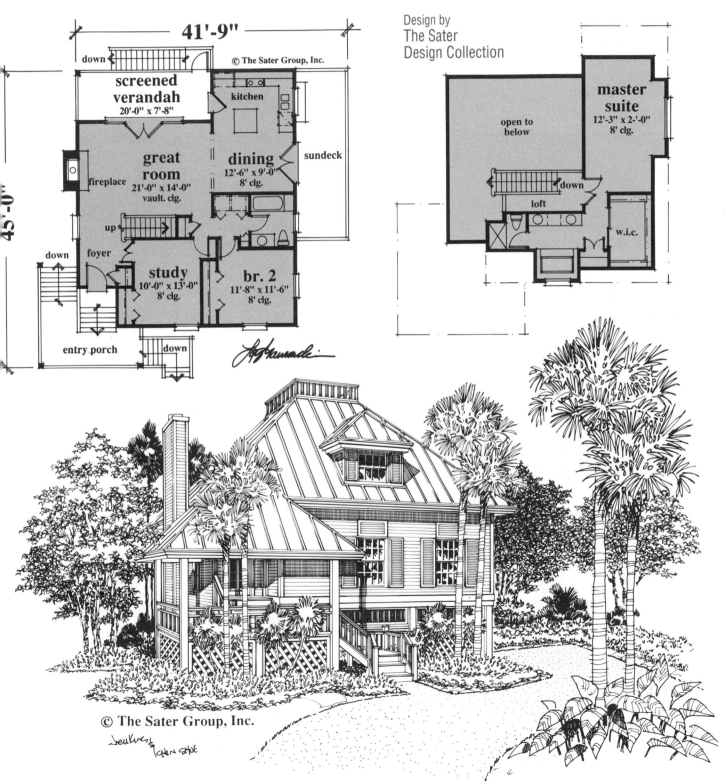

41'-9"

down

screened verandah
20'-0" x 7'-8"

© The Sater Group, Inc.

kitchen

great room
21'-0" x 14'-0"
vault. clg.

dining
12'-6" x 9'-0"
8' clg.

sundeck

fireplace

45'-0"

up

down

foyer

study
10'-0" x 13'-0"
8' clg.

br. 2
11'-8" x 11'-6"
8' clg.

entry porch

down

Design by
The Sater
Design Collection

open to below

master suite
12'-3" x 2'-0"
8' clg.

down

loft

w.i.c.

© The Sater Group, Inc.

197

Design EE8001

First Floor: 1,309 square feet
Second Floor: 1,343 square feet
Total: 2,652 square feet

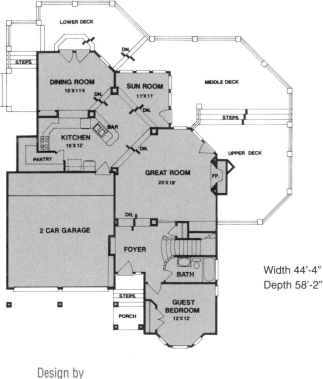

Width 44'-4"
Depth 58'-2"

Design by
Larry E. Belk
Designs

● Clean, contemporary lines set this home apart and make it a stand-out in any location. The metal roof and roof-top cupola rotated on a 45-degree angle add interest. Stunning is the word when the front door opens on this home. Remote control transoms in the cupola open automatically to increase ventilation. The great room, sun room, dining room and kitchen are all adjacent to provide areas for entertaining. Originally designed for a sloping site, the home incorporates multiple levels inside. Additionally, there is access to a series of multi-level outside decks from the dining room, sun room and great room. All these areas have at least one glass wall overlooking the rear. The master bedroom and bath upstairs are bridged by a pipe rail balcony that provides access to a rear outside deck. The master suite includes a huge master closet. Additional storage and closet area is located off the hallway to the office. The open, spacious layout and emphasis on the views to the rear make this home a winner for harbor/marina, golf course, lake or wooded sites.

COPYRIGHT 1993 LARRY E. BELK

STEPS

PORCH

SITTING

MASTER BEDROOM
20' X 16'

REF.

RANGE

KITCHEN

UTIL.

K'S

WP TUB

BUTLERS PANTRY

POWDER

SHOWER SEAT

D/W

P.

OPEN BAR

ARCH

UP

DINING ROOM
15' X 11'

WET BAR

ARCH   ARCH

LIVING ROOM
18' X 15'

FP

2 CAR GARAGE

PORCH

DECK

BEDROOM 2
12' X 13'

BATH 2

BEDROOM 3
12' X 13'

BUILT-IN BOOK SHELVES

DOWN

LOFT

MECH. RM.

BONUS AREA
17' X 20'

VOL. CEILING

BALCONY

DECK

Width 40'
Depth 66'

Design by
Larry E. Belk
Designs

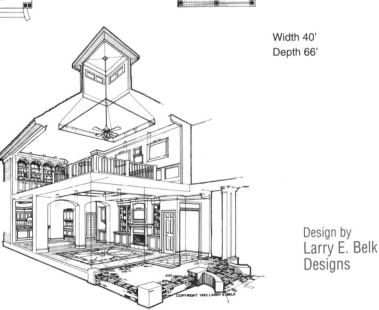

COPYRIGHT 1993 LARRY E. BELK

Design EE8002

First Floor: 1,530 square feet
Second Floor: 968 square feet
Total: 2,498 square feet

● The timeless influence of the French Quarter is exemplified in this home designed for river-front living. The double French-door entry opens into a large living room/dining room area separated by a double archway. The living room ceiling opens up through two stories to the cupola above. A railed balcony with loft on the second floor overlooks the living room. A pass-through between the kitchen and dining room also provides seating at a bar for informal dining. The spacious master bedroom at the rear includes a sitting area and a roomy master bath with a large walk-in closet. Two additional bedrooms, a bath and a bonus area for an office or game room are located upstairs. With ten-foot ceilings downstairs and nine-foot ceilings upstairs, there is a feeling of spaciousness. The inclusion of fabulous decks on the front and back of the second story make this home perfect for entertaining.

© The Sater Group, Inc.

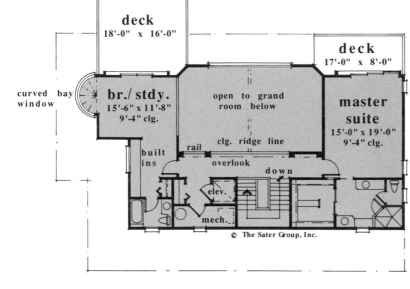

deck
18'-0" x 16'-0"

deck
17'-0" x 8'-0"

curved bay
window

br./stdy.
15'-6" x 11'-8"
9'-4" clg.

open to grand
room below

**master
suite**
15'-0" x 19'-0"
9'-4" clg.

clg. ridge line

built
ins

rail

overlook

down

elev.

mech.

© The Sater Group, Inc.

Design by
**The Sater
Design Collection**

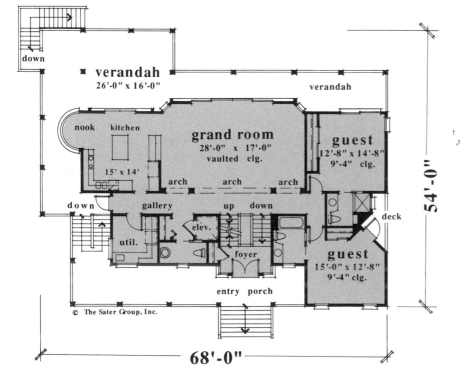

down

verandah
26'-0" x 16'-0"

verandah

nook   kitchen

grand room
28'-0" x 17'-0"
vaulted clg.

guest
12'-8" x 14'-8"
9'-4" clg.

15' x 14'

arch   arch   arch

down

gallery   up   down

elev.

util.

deck

foyer

guest
15'-0" x 12'-8"
9'-4" clg.

entry porch

© The Sater Group, Inc.

54'-0"

68'-0"

Design EE6618

First Floor: 1,944 square feet
Second Floor: 1,196 square feet
Lower Level: 195 square feet
Total: 3,335 square feet

● In the grand room of this home, family and friends will enjoy the ambience created by arches and access to a veranda. Two guest rooms flank a full bath—one of the guest rooms also sports a private deck. The kitchen services a circular breakfast nook. Upstairs, a balcony overlook furthers the drama of the great room. The master suite, with a deck and a private bath opening through a pocket door, will be a pleasure to occupy. Another bedroom—or use this room for a study—sits at the other side of this floor. It has a curved bay window, an expansive deck, built-ins and a full bath.

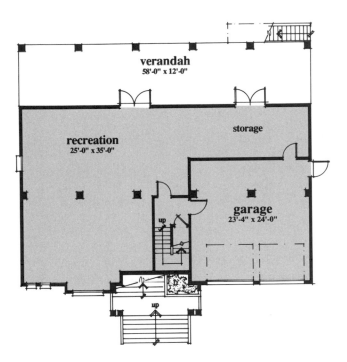

verandah
58'-0" x 12'-0"

recreation
25'-0" x 35'-0"

storage

garage
23'-4" x 24'-0"

up

up

Width 58'
Depth 54'

Design by
The Sater
Design Collection

Design EE6622 Square Footage: 2,190

● A dramatic set of stairs leads to the entry of this home. The foyer leads to an expansive living room with a fireplace and built-in bookshelves. A lanai opens off this area and will assure outdoor enjoyments. For formal meals, a front-facing dining room offers a bumped-out bay. The kitchen serves this area easily as well as the breakfast room. A study and three bedrooms make up the rest of the floor plan. Two secondary bedrooms share a full hall bath. A utility area is also nearby. In the master suite, two walk-in closets and a full bath are appreciated features. In the bedroom, a set of French doors offers passage to the lanai.

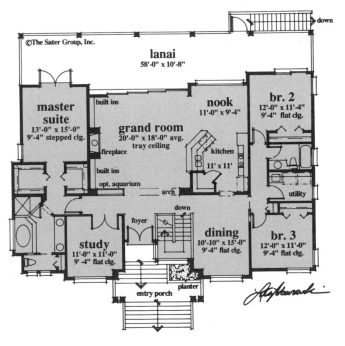

©The Sater Group, Inc.

down

lanai
58'-0" x 10'-8"

master suite
13'-0" x 15'-0"
9'-4" stepped clg.

built ins

fireplace

built ins

opt. aquarium

arch

nook
11'-0" x 9'-4"

grand room
20'-0" x 18'-0" avg.
tray ceiling

kitchen
11' x 11'

br. 2
12'-0" x 11'-4"
9'-4" flat clg.

utility

br. 3
12'-0" x 11'-0"
9'-4" flat clg.

foyer

down

dining
10'-10" x 15'-0"
9'-4" flat clg.

study
11'-0" x 11'-0"
9'-4" flat clg.

entry porch   planter

© The Sater Group, Inc.

Design by
**The Sater
Design Collection**

Design EE6615

First Floor: 1,736 square feet; Second Floor: 640 square feet
Lower Level: 840 square feet; Total: 3,216 square feet

● Lattice panels, shutters, a balustrade and a metal roof add character to this delightful coastal home. Double doors flanking a fireplace open to the sun deck from the spacious great room sporting a vaulted ceiling. Access to the veranda is provided from this room also. An adjacent dining room provides views of the rear grounds and space for formal and informal entertaining. The glassed-in nook shares space with the L-shaped kitchen and a center work island. Bedrooms 2 and 3, a full bath and a utility room complete this floor. Upstairs, a sumptuous master suite awaits. Double doors extend to a private deck from the master bedroom. His and Hers walk-in closets lead the way to a grand master bath featuring an arched whirlpool tub, a double-bowl vanity and a separate shower.

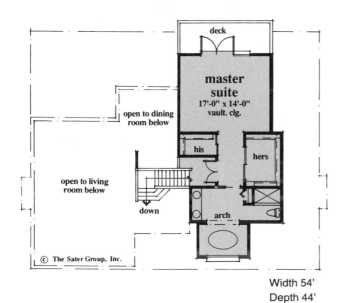

Width 54'
Depth 44'

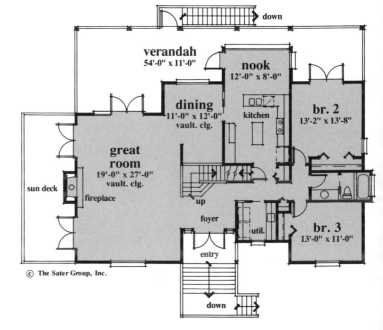

© 1990 The Sater Group, Inc.

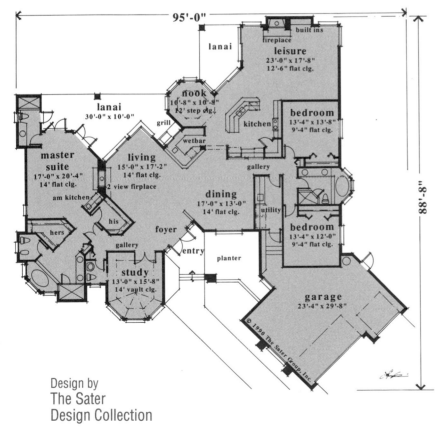

95'-0"

built ins
fireplace
lanai

leisure
23'-0" x 17'-8"
12'-6" flat clg.

nook
10'-8" x 10'-8"
12' step clg.

lanai
30'-0" x 10'-0"

grill

kitchen

bedroom
13'-4" x 13'-8"
9'-4" flat clg.

wetbar

master
suite
17'-0" x 20'-4"
14' flat clg.

living
15'-0" x 17'-2"
14' flat clg.

gallery

am kitchen

2 view firplace

dining
17'-0" x 13'-0"
14' flat clg.

utility

his

hers

foyer

bedroom
13'-4" x 12'-0"
9'-4" flat clg.

gallery

entry

planter

88'-8"

study
13'-0" x 15'-8"
14' vault clg.

garage
23'-4" x 29'-8"

© 1990 The Sater Group, Inc.

Design by
The Sater
Design Collection

Design EE6634 Square Footage: 3,477

● Make dreams come true with this fine sunny
design. An octagonal study provides a nice focal
point both inside and outside. The living areas
remain open to each other and access outdoor
areas. A wet bar makes entertaining a breeze,
especially with a window pass-through to a grill
area on the lanai. The kitchen enjoys shared
space with a lovely breakfast nook and a bright
leisure room. Two bedrooms are located near
family living centers. They share a dapper hall
bath that includes a separate shower, a double-
bowl vanity and a bumped-out whirlpool tub. In
the master bedroom suite, luxury abounds with
a two-way fireplace, a morning kitchen, two
walk-in closets and a compartmented bath.
Another full bath accommodates a pool area.

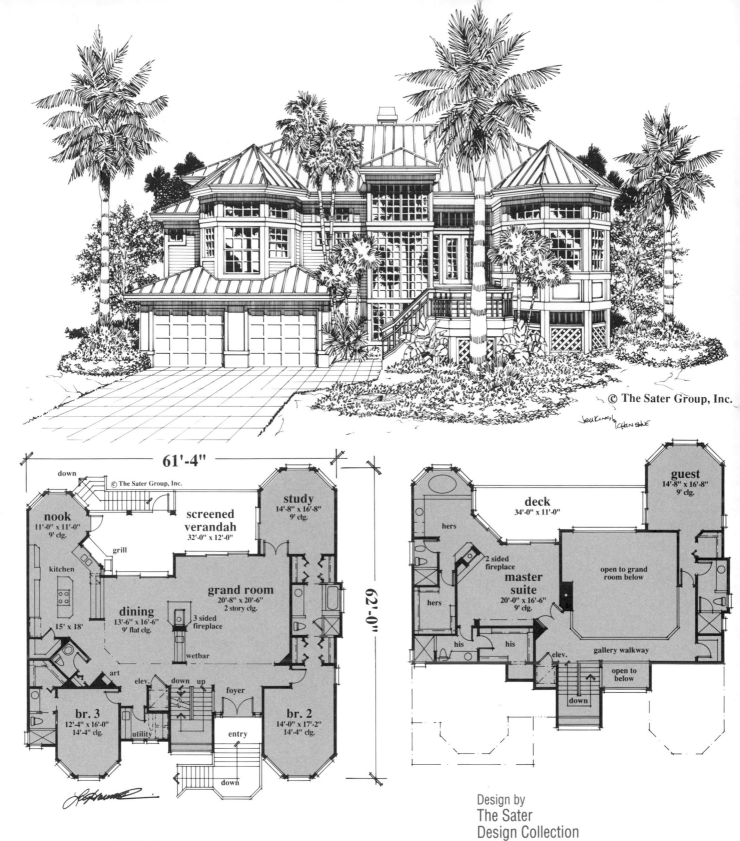

© The Sater Group, Inc.

Design by
The Sater
Design Collection

Design EE6619 First Floor: 2,725 square feet
Second Floor: 1,418 square feet; Total: 4,143 square feet

● Florida living takes off in this grand design. A grand room gains attention as a superb entertaining area. A see-through fireplace here connects this room to the dining room. Sets of sliding glass doors offer passage to an expansive rear deck. In the study, quiet time is assured—or slip out the doors and onto the deck for a breather. A full bath connects the study and Bedroom 2. Bedroom 3 sits on the opposite side of the house and enjoys its own bath. The opposite side of the house and enjoys its own bath. The kitchen is fully functional with a large work island and a connecting breakfast nook. Upstairs, the master bedroom suite is something to behold. His and Hers baths, a see-through fireplace and access to an upper deck characterize this room. A guest bedroom suite is located on the other side of the upper floor and will make visits a real pleasure.

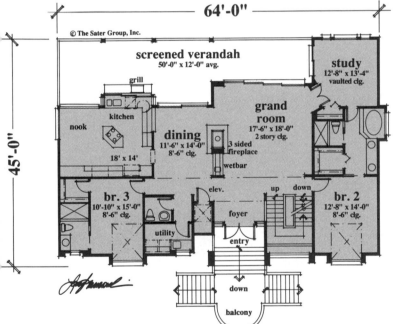

64'-0"

© The Sater Group, Inc.

screened verandah
50'-0" x 12'-0" avg.

grill

study
12'-8" x 13'-4"
vaulted clg.

kitchen

nook

18' x 14'

grand room
17'-6" x 18'-0"
2 story clg.

dining
11'-6" x 14'-0"
8'-6" clg.

3 sided fireplace

wetbar

45'-0"

br. 3
10'-10" x 15'-0"
8'-6" clg.

elev.

up   down

br. 2
12'-8" x 14'-0"
8'-6" clg.

foyer

utility

entry

down

balcony

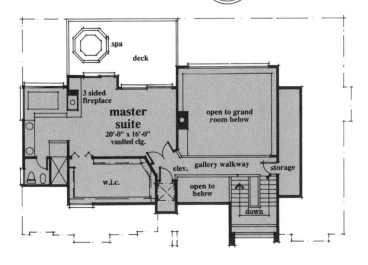

spa

deck

3 sided fireplace

master suite
20'-0" x 16'-0"
vaulted clg.

open to grand room below

w.i.c.

elev.

gallery walkway

storage

open to below

down

Design by
**The Sater
Design Collection**

Design EE6620

First Floor: 2,066 square feet
Lower Level: 1,260 square feet
Second Floor: 810 square feet
Total: 4,136 square feet

● If entertaining's your passion, then this is the design for you. With a large, open floor plan and an array of amenities, every gathering will be a success. The foyer embraces living areas accented by a glass fireplace and a wet bar. The living and dining rooms each access a screened entertainment center for outside enjoyments. The gourmet kitchen delights with its openness to the rest of the house. A morning room here also adds a nice touch. Two bedrooms and a den radiate from the first-floor living areas. Upstairs—or use the elevator—is a masterful master suite. It contains a huge walk-in closet, a whirlpool tub and a private sun deck.

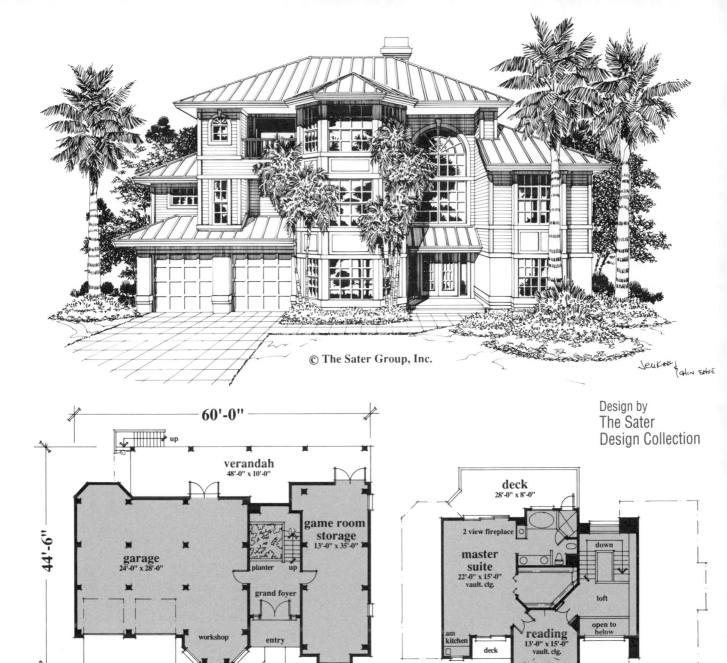

© The Sater Group, Inc.

Design by
**The Sater
Design Collection**

60'-0"

44'-6"

up

verandah
48'-0" x 10'-0"

**game room
storage**
13'-0" x 35'-0"

garage
24'-0" x 28'-0"

planter up

workshop

grand foyer

entry

deck
28'-0" x 8'-0"

2 view fireplace

down

**master
suite**
22'-0" x 15'-0"
vault. clg.

loft

am kitchen

deck

reading
13'-0" x 15'-0"
vault. clg.

open to
below

down

deck
48'-0" x 9'-0"

© The Sater Group, Inc.

nook
12'-0" x 9'-0"
9' clg.

kitchen

grand room
21'-0" x 15'-4"
9' clg.

fireplace

br. 2
13'-0" x 11'-8"
9' clg.

14' x 12'

gallery

down up

skylight
above

utility

dining
13'-0" x 14'-0"
9' clg.

open to
below

br. 3
13'-0" x 12'-0"
9' clg.

Design EE6621 Main Floor: 1,642 square feet
Upper Floor: 927 square feet; Total: 2,569 square feet

● Luxury abounds in this Floridian home. Upon
entry, a recreation room gains attention. Up the
stairs, livability takes off with an open living room, a
bayed dining room and a veranda that stretches
across the back of the plan. Two bedrooms occupy
the right side of this level and share a full hall bath
with dual lavs and a separate tub and shower. The
master retreat on the upper level pleases with
its own library, a morning kitchen, a large walk-in
closet and a pampering bath with a double-bowl vanity, a compartmented toilet and bidet, a whirlpool
tub and a shower that opens outside. A private deck
allows outdoor enjoyments.

Sun-Country Retirement Homes & Vacation Cottages

Thinking of making the move to that much-dreamed-about vacation or retirement home? In true Southern style, the houses in this section help make that move a definite reality. Whether Victorian or Floridian, one or two stories, the livability in these homes remains casual. Split-bedroom arrangements, combined living areas and ample outdoor living space all combine to present floor plans fit for full-scale enjoyment.

As far as living in the sun, Design EE6603 meets, if not exceeds, all expectations. A handsome stucco facade incorporates multi-pane windows, a dramatic entry and a raised roof line. Family and friends will feel right at home inside. For formal dinners and socializing, the living and dining rooms share open spaces. A lanai spans the rear of the house. Other features, such as a combined informal living area and luxurious baths, guarantee a royal retirement cottage, a super second home or a very fine vacation retreat.

The ultimate vacation cottage, Design EE4061 capitalizes on lake-side, mountain-side or curb-side appeal — all with extra measures of charm. A front covered porch echoes Southern traditions and provides the perfect vantage point for enjoying sunsets. Inside, a focal-point fireplace and efficient living patterns promote relaxed lifestyles.

With the fine selection of homes in this section, today is the perfect time to plan for tomorrow's relaxed and recreational lifestyles!

© The Sater Group, Inc.

Design EE6612

Square Footage: 1,487

● Here's an offer too good to pass up! Two elevations and a wealth of modern livability is presented in this compact one-story home. Inside, a great room with a vaulted ceiling opens to the lanai, offering wonderful options for either formal or informal entertaining. Step out onto the lanai and savor the outdoors from the delightful kitchen with its bay-windowed breakfast nook. Two secondary bedrooms (each with its own walk-in closet) share a full bath. Finally, enjoy the lanai from the calming master suite and pampering bath featuring a corner tub, a separate shower and a large walk-in closet.

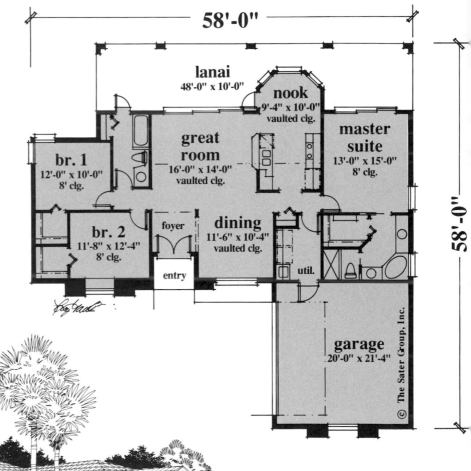

58'-0"

58'-0"

lanai 48'-0" x 10'-0"

nook 9'-4" x 10'-0" vaulted clg.

master suite 13'-0" x 15'-0" 8' clg.

br. 1 12'-0" x 10'-0" 8' clg.

great room 16'-0" x 14'-0" vaulted clg.

br. 2 11'-8" x 12'-4" 8' clg.

foyer

dining 11'-6" x 10'-4" vaulted clg.

util.

entry

garage 20'-0" x 21'-4"

© The Sater Group, Inc.

Design by
The Sater
Design Collection

© The Sater Group, Inc.

208

ter Group, Inc.

ⓒ

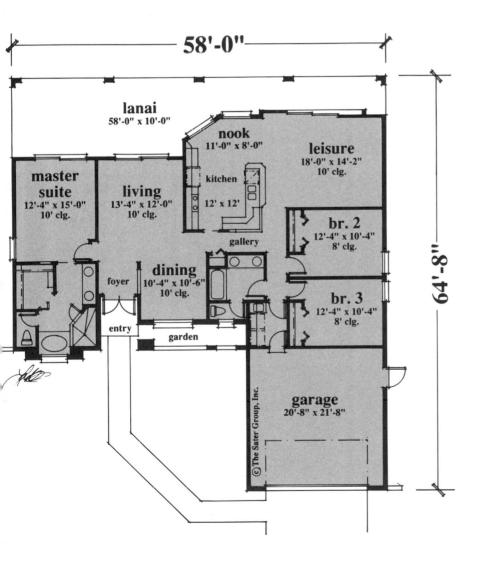

58'-0"

64'-8"

lanai
58'-0" x 10'-0"

nook
11'-0" x 8'-0"

leisure
18'-0" x 14'-2"
10' clg.

kitchen
12' x 12'

master
suite
12'-4" x 15'-0"
10' clg.

living
13'-4" x 12'-0"
10' clg.

br. 2
12'-4" x 10'-4"
8' clg.

gallery

dining
10'-4" x 10'-6"
10' clg.

foyer

br. 3
12'-4" x 10'-4"
8' clg.

entry

garden

© The Sater Group, Inc.

garage
20'-8" x 21'-8"

Design EE6603

Square Footage: 1,784

● This one-story stucco home is
filled with amenities. A raised entry
features double doors that lead to the
grand foyer. From the formal living
room, large sliding glass doors open to
the lanai, providing natural light and
outdoor views. The dining room is
separated from the foyer and living
area by a half-wall and a column. The
large kitchen, breakfast nook and
leisure room round out the informal
gathering areas. The secondary bedrooms are split from the master wing.
The cozy master suite sports a large
walk-in closet, a walk-in shower, a
whirlpool tub and a private water
closet.

Design by
**The Sater
Design Collection**

209

Design EE6632

Square Footage: 2,562

● Design excellence is apparent in this one-story home. With open living and dining rooms, and a covered veranda, gatherings of all sorts are a breeze. The kitchen combines with a leisure room to provide a super casual living space. It is enhanced by an optional fireplace and T.V. niche. Two bedrooms—with ample closet space in each—are separated by a full hall bath. Right off the tiled foyer, a den meets work and school needs. In the master bedroom suite, plenty of wall space affords a variety of furniture arrangements. The master bath pleases with a double-bowl vanity, a compartmented toilet, a corner whirlpool tub and a large shower. A walk-in closet is also nearby.

Design by
**The Sater
Design Collection**

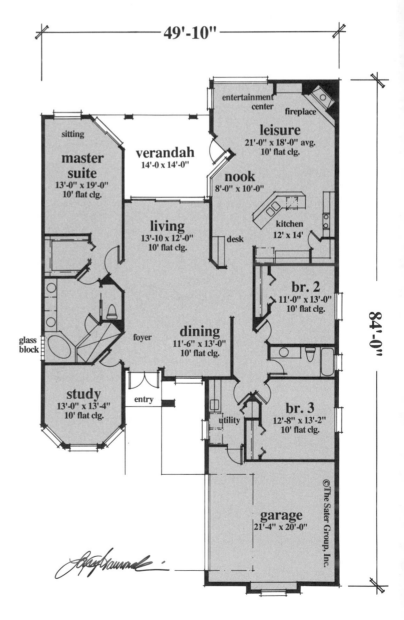

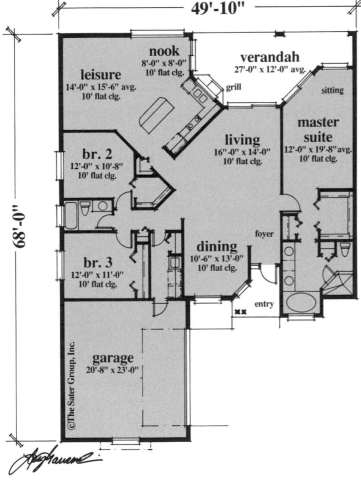

49'-10"

68'-0"

nook
8'-0" x 8'-0"
10' flat clg.

verandah
27'-0" x 12'-0" avg.

leisure
14'-0" x 15'-6" avg.
10' flat clg.

grill

sitting

**master
suite**
12'-0" x 19'-8"avg.
10' flat clg.

br. 2
12'-0" x 10'-8"
10' flat clg.

living
16'-0" x 14'-0"
10' flat clg.

foyer

br. 3
12'-0" x 11'-0"
10' flat clg.

dining
10'-6" x 13'-0"
10' flat clg.

entry

©The Sater Group, Inc.

garage
20'-8" x 23'-0"

Design EE6630 Square Footage: 1,953

● A clever floor plan distinguishes this three-bedroom stucco Floridian. It features formal living and dining rooms, plus an ample family room with adjacent breakfast nook. The angled kitchen over-looks this casual gathering area and contains a pass-through window to a patio counter. Secondary bedrooms are split from the master suite. They share a full bath. The master contains patio access and features a grand bath with corner shower, whirlpool tub and dual sinks. A handy utility room connects the living space to the two-car garage.

Design by
The Sater
Design Collection

© The Sater Group, Inc.

Design EE6607
Square Footage: 2,200

● A joyful marriage of indoor outdoor living relationships endures in
this spirited home. An abundance of
windows to the front of the plan allows
bright, warming sunlight to flood the
rooms. All rooms to the rear offer access
to a full-length veranda and a sunning
deck. An airy, open feeling is created
by the combination of the formal dining
room (divided from the foyer by a half-
wall), the spacious great room and the
charming kitchen. The latter is complete with a walk-in pantry and a bayed
breakfast nook. Split sleeping quarters
contain the master wing to the left and
two secondary bedrooms to the right.
The secluded master suite is highlighted
by a double walk-in closet, a relaxing
garden tub with a privacy wall, a separate shower and a double-bowl vanity.

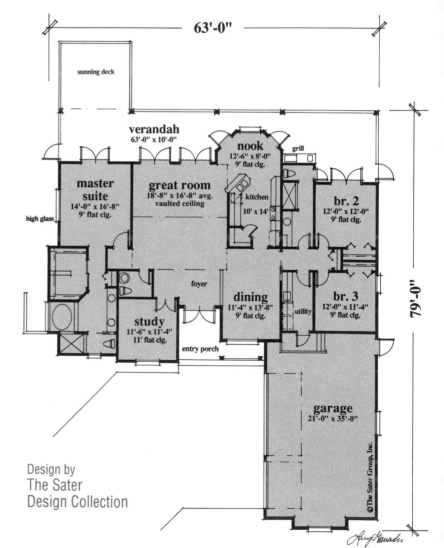

Design by
The Sater
Design Collection

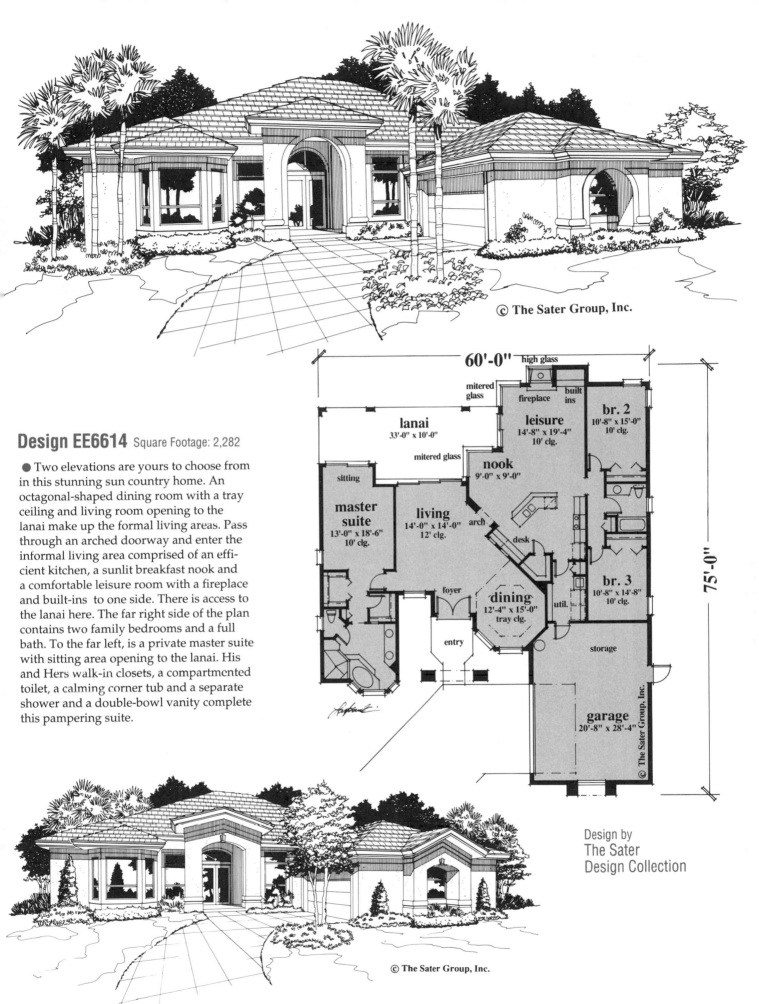

© The Sater Group, Inc.

Design EE6614 Square Footage: 2,282

● Two elevations are yours to choose from in this stunning sun country home. An octagonal-shaped dining room with a tray ceiling and living room opening to the lanai make up the formal living areas. Pass through an arched doorway and enter the informal living area comprised of an efficient kitchen, a sunlit breakfast nook and a comfortable leisure room with a fireplace and built-ins to one side. There is access to the lanai here. The far right side of the plan contains two family bedrooms and a full bath. To the far left, is a private master suite with sitting area opening to the lanai. His and Hers walk-in closets, a compartmented toilet, a calming corner tub and a separate shower and a double-bowl vanity complete this pampering suite.

60'-0"

high glass

mitered glass

lanai
33'-0" x 10'-0"

mitered glass

fireplace

built ins

leisure
14'-8" x 19'-4"
10' clg.

br. 2
10'-8" x 15'-0"
10' clg.

sitting

nook
9'-0" x 9'-0"

master suite
13'-0" x 18'-6"
10' clg.

living
14'-0" x 14'-0"
12' clg.

arch

desk

br. 3
10'-8" x 14'-8"
10' clg.

foyer

dining
12'-4" x 15'-0"
tray clg.

util.

entry

storage

garage
20'-8" x 28'-4"

75'-0"

© The Sater Group, Inc.

Design by
The Sater
Design Collection

© The Sater Group, Inc.

Design EE3463

First Floor: 1,163 square feet
Second Floor: 1,077 square feet
Total: 2,240 square feet

● Fine family living takes off in this grand two-story plan. The tiled foyer leads to a stately living room with sliding glass doors to the back terrace and columns separating it from the dining room. Additional accents include a corner curios niche and access to a covered porch. For casual living, look no further than the family room/breakfast room combination. Even more interesting, the kitchen supplies an island counter in the midst of its accommodating, angled layout. On the second floor, the master bedroom draws attention to itself by offering a fireplace, access to a deck and a spoiling bath. A smart addition, the study niche in the hallway shares the outside deck. Two family bedrooms wrap up the sleeping facilities.

QUOTE ONE™

Cost to build? See page 232 to order complete cost estimate to build this house in your area!

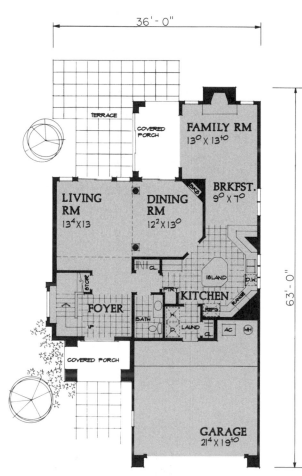

Design by
Home Planners,
Inc.

Design EE3464

First Floor: 1,776 square feet
Second Floor: 876 square feet
Total: 2,652 square feet

● If you're looking for something a little different from the rest, this dramatic home may end your search. A two-story foyer introduces an open formal area consisting of a volume living room and a dining room separated by columns. The kitchen sits to the rear of the plan and shares space with the breakfast room. Here, a curved wall adds interest—sliding glass doors take you out to a covered porch and a connecting terrace. The family room enjoys access to this terrace while maintaining great indoor livability with its see-through fireplace and volume ceiling. Also on the first floor, the master bedroom offers to its lucky occupants a pampering bath. The sleeping accommodations are complete with three upstairs bedrooms.

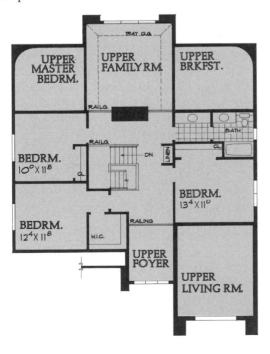

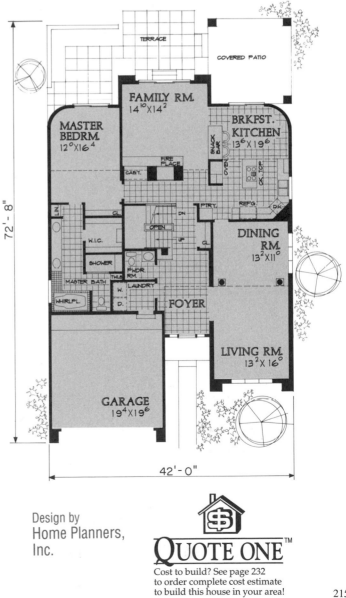

Design by
Home Planners,
Inc.

Cost to build? See page 232
to order complete cost estimate
to build this house in your area!

QUOTE ONE™

215

Design EE2947
Square Footage: 1,830

● This charming one-story story traditional home greets visitors with a covered porch. A uniquely shaped galley-style kitchen shares a snack bar with the spacious gathering room where a fireplace is the focal point. The dining room has sliding glass doors to the rear terrace as does the master suite. This bedroom area also includes a luxury bath with whirlpool tub and separate dressing room. Two additional bedrooms, one that could double as a study, are located at the front of the home. The two-car garage features a large storage area and can be reached through the service entrance to the home or from the rear terrace. For information on customizing this design, call 1-800-521-6797, ext. 800.

QUOTE ONE™

Cost to build? See page 232
to order complete cost estimate
to build this house in your area!

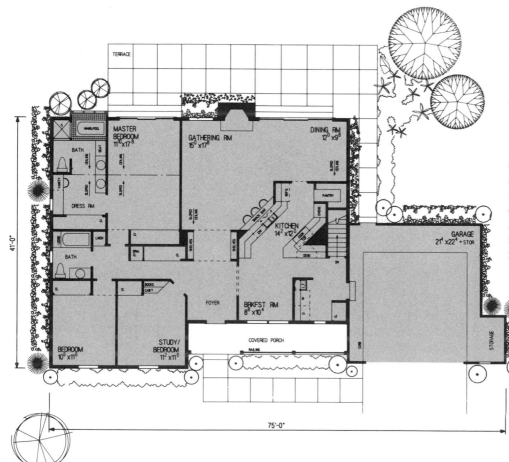

Design by
**Home Planners,
Inc.**

Design EE3460
Square Footage: 1,389

● A double dose of charm, this special farmhouse plan offers two elevations in its blueprint package. Though rooflines and porch options are different, the floor plan is basically the same and very livable. A formal living room/dining room combination features a warming fireplace and delightful bay window. The kitchen separates this area from the more casual family room. Three bedrooms include two family bedrooms served by a full, shared bath, and a lovely master suite with its own private bath. The master suite features dual vanities and a large closet. For information on customizing this design, call 1-800-521-6797, ext. 800.

Design by
Home Planners,
Inc.

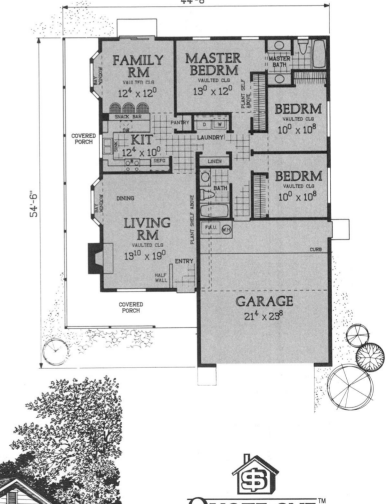

QUOTE ONE™
Cost to build? See page 232
to order complete cost estimate
to build this house in your area!

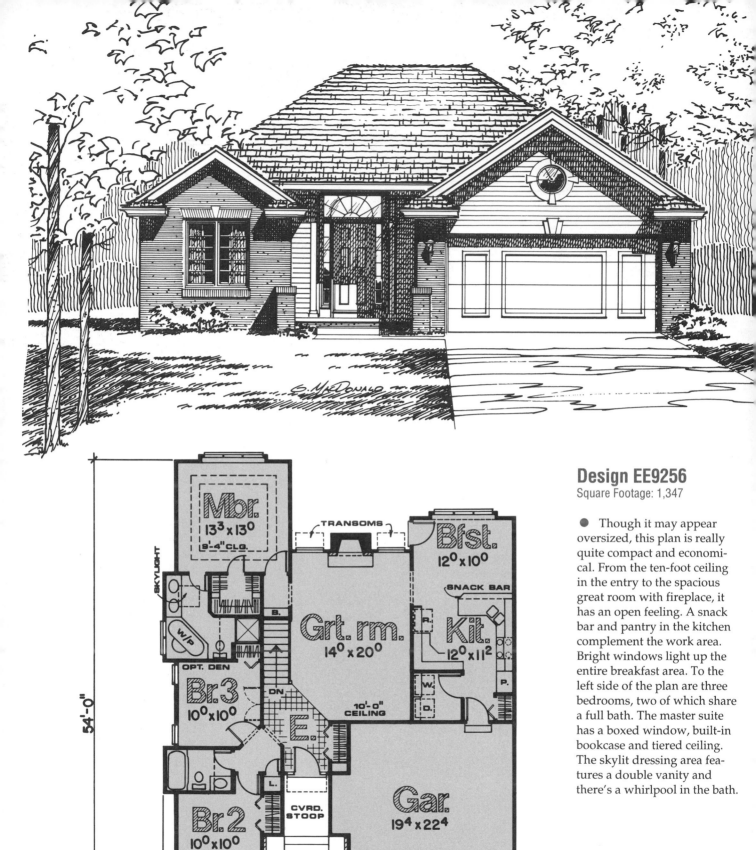

Design EE9256
Square Footage: 1,347

● Though it may appear oversized, this plan is really quite compact and economical. From the ten-foot ceiling in the entry to the spacious great room with fireplace, it has an open feeling. A snack bar and pantry in the kitchen complement the work area. Bright windows light up the entire breakfast area. To the left side of the plan are three bedrooms, two of which share a full bath. The master suite has a boxed window, built-in bookcase and tiered ceiling. The skylit dressing area features a double vanity and there's a whirlpool in the bath.

Design by
Design
Basics,
Inc.

© 1990 design basics inc.

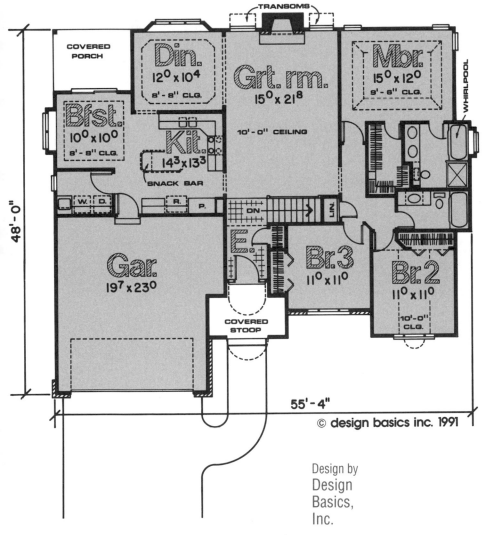

COVERED PORCH

Din.
12⁰ x 10⁴
8'- 8" CLG.

Grt. rm.
15⁰ x 21⁸
10'- 0" CEILING

Mbr.
15⁰ x 12⁰
9'- 6" CLG.

WHIRLPOOL

Bfst.
10⁰ x 10⁰
8'- 8" CLG.

Kit.
14³ x 13³
SNACK BAR

W. D.   R.   P.

DN   LIN.

Gar.
19⁷ x 23⁰

Br. 3
11⁰ x 11⁰

Br. 2
11⁰ x 11⁰
10'- 0" CLG.

COVERED STOOP

48'- 0"

55'- 4"

TRANSOMS

© design basics inc. 1991

Design by
Design
Basics,
Inc.

Design EE9361

Square Footage: 1,666

● This delightfully different plan has brick and stucco on the dramatic front elevation, showcased by sleek lines and decorative windows. An inviting entry has a view into the great room and is enhanced by an arched window and plant shelves above. The great room's fireplace is framed by sunny windows with transoms above. The bay-windowed dining room is nestled between the great room and the superb kitchen/ breakfast area. Sleeping areas are positioned to buffer noise between the master bedroom and secondary bedrooms. The master suite enjoys a vaulted ceiling, roomy walk-in closet and sunlit master bath with dual lavatories and whirlpool.

219

● This economical plan offers an impressive visual statement with its comfortable and well-proportioned appearance. The entrance foyer leads to all areas of the house. The great room, dining area and kitchen are all open to one another allowing visual interaction. The great room and dining area both have a cathedral ceiling. The fireplace is flanked by book shelves and cabinets. The master suite has a cathedral ceiling, walk-in closet and master bath with double-bowl vanity, whirlpool tub and shower. The plan is available with a crawl-space foundation.

Design by
Donald A.
Gardner,
Architects, Inc.

Design EE9664
Square Footage: 1,287

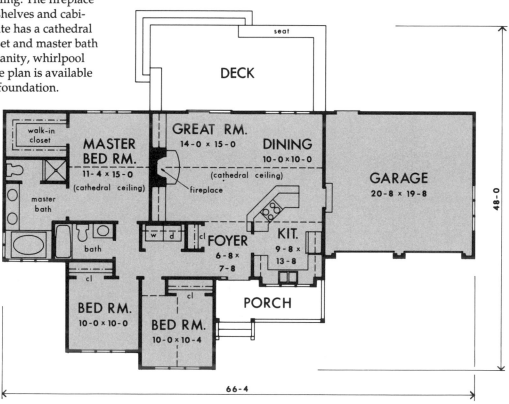

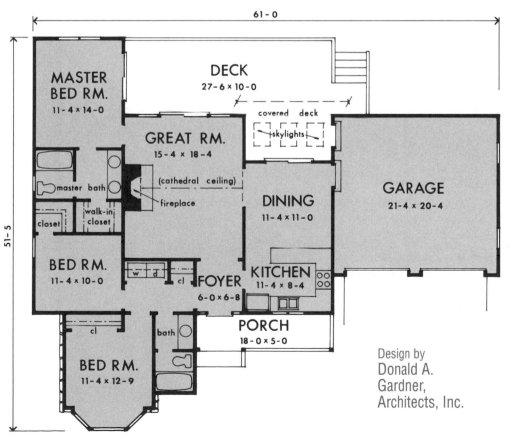

MASTER BED RM.
11-4 × 14-0

DECK
27-6 × 10-0

covered deck
skylights

GREAT RM.
15-4 × 18-4

(cathedral ceiling)

fireplace

master bath

walk-in closet

closet

BED RM.
11-4 × 10-0

w   d   cl   FOYER
6-0 × 6-8

DINING
11-4 × 11-0

KITCHEN
11-4 × 8-4

GARAGE
21-4 × 20-4

cl

bath

BED RM.
11-4 × 12-9

PORCH
18-0 × 5-0

61-0

51-5

Design by
Donald A.
Gardner,
Architects, Inc.

Design EE9620
Square Footage: 1,310

● A multi-paned bay window, dormers, a cupola, a covered porch and a variety of building materials dress up this one-story cottage. The entrance foyer leads to an impressive great room with cathedral ceiling and fireplace. The U-shaped kitchen, adjacent to the dining room, provides an ideal layout for food preparation. An expansive deck offers shelter while admitting cheery sunlight through skylights. A luxurious master bedroom located to the rear of the house takes advantage of the deck area and is assured privacy from two other bedrooms at the front of the house. These family bedrooms share a full bath.

Design EE9639

Square Footage: 1,541

● This traditional three-bedroom home projects the appearance of a much larger home. The great room features a cathedral ceiling, a fireplace and an arched window above the sliding glass door to the expansive rear deck. The master suite contains a pampering master bath and a walk-in closet. Two other bedrooms share a full bath with a double-bowl vanity. Please specify basement or crawlspace foundation when ordering.

Design by
Donald A.
Gardner,
Architects, Inc.

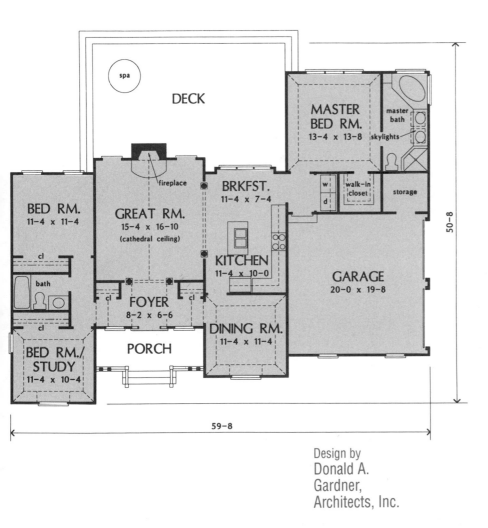

spa

DECK

MASTER
BED RM.
13-4 x 13-8

master
bath

skylights

w
d

walk-in
closet

storage

BRKFST.
11-4 x 7-4

fireplace

BED RM.
11-4 x 11-4

GREAT RM.
15-4 x 16-10
(cathedral ceiling)

cl

bath

cl

KITCHEN
11-4 x 10-0

GARAGE
20-0 x 19-8

FOYER
8-2 x 6-6

cl

cl

BED RM./
STUDY
11-4 x 10-4

PORCH

DINING RM.
11-4 x 11-4

50-8

59-8

Design by
Donald A.
Gardner,
Architects, Inc.

Design EE9726

Square Footage: 1,498

● This charming one-story home utilizes multi-pane windows, columns, dormers and a covered porch to offer a welcoming front exterior. Inside, the great room with a dramatic cathedral ceiling commands attention; the kitchen and breakfast room are just beyond a set of columns. The tiered ceilinged dining room presents a delightfully formal atmosphere for dinner parties or family gatherings. A tray ceiling in the master bedroom will please, as will a large walk-in closet and a gracious master bath with dual lavatories, a garden tub, and a separate shower. The secondary bedrooms are located at the opposite end of the house for privacy. This plan is available with a crawlspace foundation.

Design EE9666

First Floor: 1,027 square feet
Second Floor: 580 square feet
Total: 1,607 square feet

● This economical, rustic three-bedroom plan sports a relaxing country image with both front and back covered porches. The openness of the expansive great room to kitchen/dining areas and loft/study areas is reinforced with a shared cathedral ceiling for impressive space. The first level allows for two bedrooms, a full bath and a utility area. The master suite on the second level has a walk-in closet and a master bath with whirlpool tub, shower and double-bowl vanity. The plan is available with a crawl-space foundation.

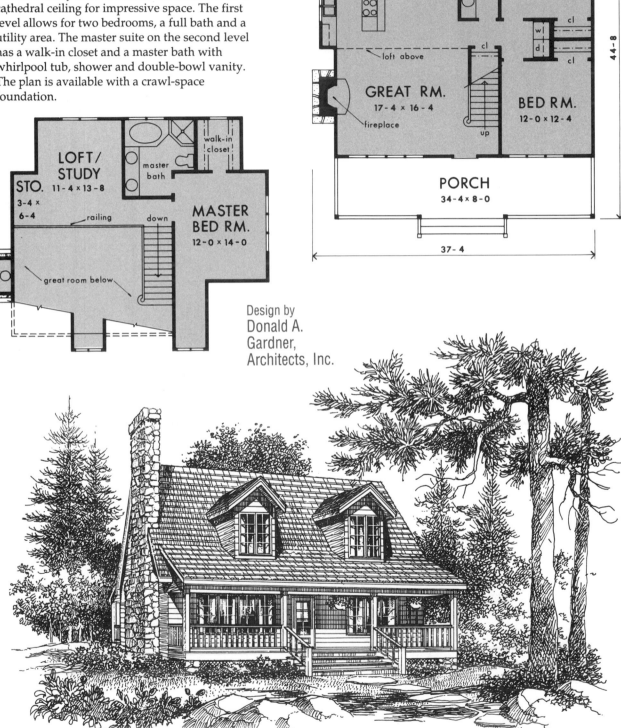

Design by
Donald A. Gardner, Architects, Inc.

Design EE4061

First Floor: 1,008 square feet
Second Floor: 323 square feet
Total: 1,331 square feet

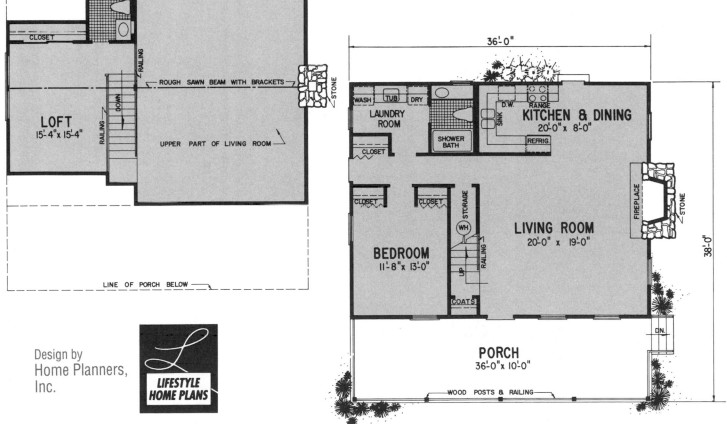

LOFT
15'-4" x 15'-4"

ROUGH SAWN BEAM WITH BRACKETS

UPPER PART OF LIVING ROOM

RAILING

DOWN

RAILING

CLOSET

STONE

LINE OF PORCH BELOW

Design by
Home Planners,
Inc.

LIFESTYLE HOME PLANS

36'-0"

38'-0"

WASH   TUB   DRY

LAUNDRY ROOM

SHOWER BATH

CLOSET

KITCHEN & DINING
20'-0" x 8'-0"

D.W.   RANGE
SINK
REFRIG.

FIREPLACE

STONE

CLOSET   CLOSET

STORAGE

WH

RAILING

UP

LIVING ROOM
20'-0" x 19'-0"

BEDROOM
11'-8" x 13'-0"

COATS

DN.

PORCH
36'-0" x 10'-0"

WOOD POSTS & RAILING

● This charming farmhouse design will be economical to build and a pleasure to occupy. Like most vacation homes, this design features an open plan. The large living area includes a living room and dining room and a massive stone fireplace. A partition separates the kitchen from the living room. Also downstairs are a bedroom, full bath, and laundry room. Upstairs is a spacious sleeping loft overlooking the living room. Don't miss the large front porch — this will be a favorite spot for relaxing.

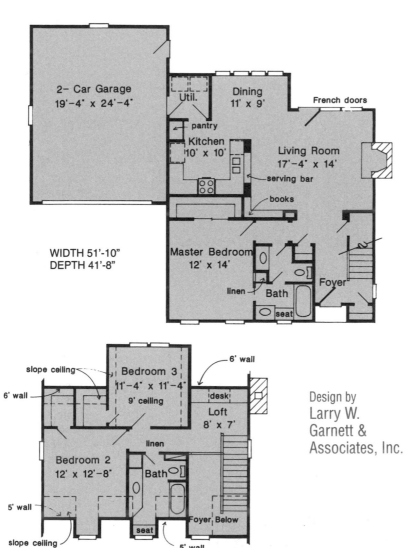

2- Car Garage
19'-4" x 24'-4"

WIDTH 51'-10"
DEPTH 41'-8"

Util.

pantry

Kitchen
10' x 10'

Dining
11' x 9'

French doors

Living Room
17'-4" x 14'

serving bar

books

Master Bedroom
12' x 14'

linen

Bath

seat

Foyer

slope ceiling

Bedroom 3
11'-4" x 11'-4"
9' ceiling

6' wall

desk

Loft
8' x 7'

6' wall

linen

Bedroom 2
12' x 12'-8"

Bath

5' wall

seat

Foyer Below

slope ceiling

5' wall

Design by
Larry W.
Garnett &
Associates, Inc.

Design EE8958

First Floor: 980 square feet
Second Floor: 546 square feet
Total: 1,526 square feet

● You'll feel right at home in this traditional-style house. A living room defined by a fireplace, French doors and built-in-book-shelves sets the tone for first-floor livability. A U-shaped kitchen benefits from such features as a pantry and a conveniently accessed dining area. A utility room supplies passage from the garage to the main house. The master bedroom enjoys first-floor frontal views and a compartmented bath. Two more bedrooms, set up-stairs, share a delightful full bath with a linen closet and a window seat. Each bedroom yields a walk-in closet. Also particularly mentionable: the loft with a built-in desk that sits atop the stairs.

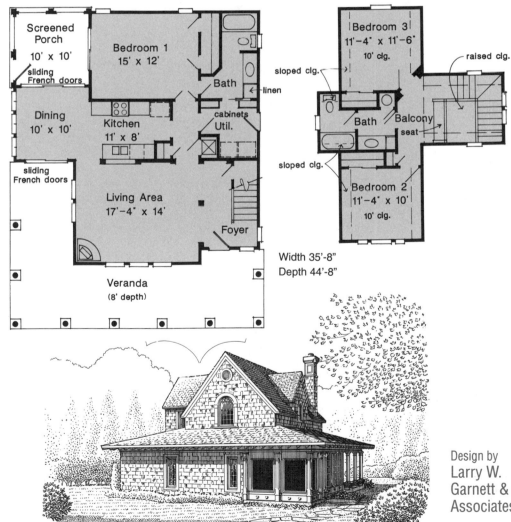

Screened Porch
10' x 10'

sliding French doors

Bedroom 1
15' x 12'

Bath

linen

Dining
10' x 10'

Kitchen
11' x 8'

cabinets

Util.

sliding French doors

Living Area
17'-4" x 14'

Foyer

Veranda
(8' depth)

Bedroom 3
11'-4" x 11'-6"
10' clg.

raised clg.

sloped clg.

Bath

Balcony

seat

sloped clg.

Bedroom 2
11'-4" x 10'
10' clg.

Width 35'-8"
Depth 44'-8"

Design EE9131

First Floor: 978 square feet
Second Floor: 464 square feet
Total: 1,442 square feet

● From the covered front veranda to the second-story Palladian window, this home exudes warmth and grace. Though smaller in square footage, the floor plan offers plenty of room. The living area is complemented by a cozy corner fireplace and is attached to a dining area with French doors to a screened porch and the front veranda. The galley-style kitchen is the central hub of the first floor. A large bedroom on this floor has an attached full bath and serves equally well as guest bedroom or master bedroom. The second floor holds two bedrooms and another full bath. An open balcony area here overlooks the foyer below.

Design by
Larry W.
Garnett &
Associates, Inc.

Design EE9008

First Floor: 1,653 square feet
Second Floor: 613 square feet
Total: 2,266 square feet

● While much less elaborate than other Victorian styles, the intersecting roof lines, arch-top windows with shutters, and detailed corner pilasters give this home a casual, yet distinctive appearance. An eight-foot-wide veranda provides plenty of room for outdoor entertaining. Inside, the large foyer opens to the formal dining area. A thirteen-foot raised ceiling with blocked panel trim and crown molding adds interest to the living room. French doors lead to a private library with built-in bookcases and a window seat. The secluded master suite offers a walk-in closet and an elegant bath with garden tub and glass-enclosed shower. Upstairs, the balcony features a built-in bookcase. Two large bedrooms each have walk-in closets and ceilings that slope from six feet to nine feet in height. Plans for a detached garage are included.

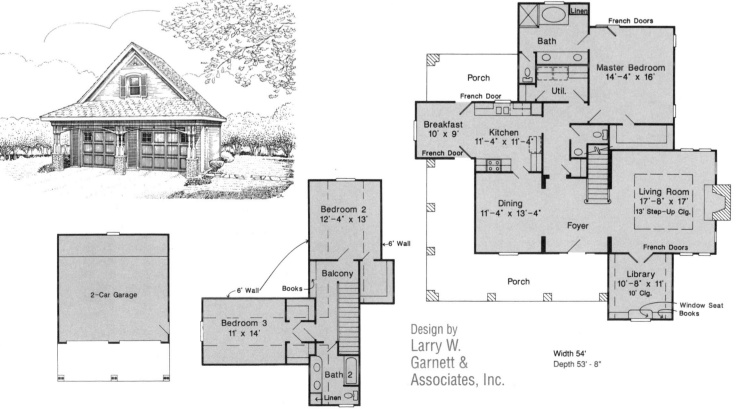

2-Car Garage

Bedroom 2
12'-4" x 13'

6' Wall

Balcony

Books

6' Wall

Bedroom 3
11' x 14'

Bath 2

Linen

Bath

Linen

French Doors

Master Bedroom
14'-4" x 16'

Porch

French Door

Util.

Breakfast
10' x 9'

Kitchen
11'-4" x 11'-4"

French Door

Dining
11'-4" x 13'-4"

Foyer

Living Room
17'-8" x 17'
13' Step-Up Clg.

French Doors

Porch

Library
10'-8" x 11'
10' Clg.

Window Seat
Books

Design by
Larry W.
Garnett &
Associates, Inc.

Width 54'
Depth 53' - 8"

228

Copyright 1992 Stephen S. Fuller

Design EE9861

First Floor: 1,960 square feet
Second Floor: 965 square feet
Total: 2,925 square feet

● The facade of this charming home is Americana at its best, with a rocking-chair porch, bay window and dormers above, finished in stone and wood siding and faithfully detailed. A convenient outdoor entrance to the two-car garage is located to the right of the front porch. The main level features an easy flow, beginning with the dining room to the right of the foyer. A hallway between the foyer and main staircase helps to promote a sense of openness. The great room features a large hearth and French doors to the patio, and leads directly to the breakfast area and kitchen. Left of the foyer is an attractive study with a large bay window. The master suite, featuring a bay-windowed sitting area and a large master bath completes the main level. On the upper level, Bedroom 2 features a full bath and has three dormer windows overlooking the front lawn. This home is designed with a basement foundation.

Design by
Design Traditions

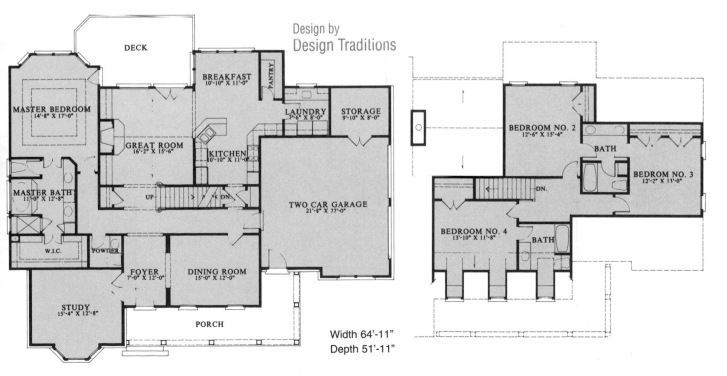

Width 64'-11"
Depth 51'-11"

When You're Ready To Order . . .

Let Us Show You Our Home Blueprint Package.

Building a home? Planning a home? Our Blueprint Package has nearly everything you need to get the job done right, whether you're working on your own or with help from an architect, designer, builder or subcontractors. Each Blueprint Package is the result of many hours of work by licensed architects or professional designers.

QUALITY

Hundreds of hours of painstaking effort have gone into the development of your blueprint set. Each home has been quality-checked by professionals to insure accuracy and buildability.

VALUE

Because we sell in volume, you can buy professional-quality blueprints at a fraction of their development cost. With our plans, your dream home design costs only a few hundred dollars, not the thousands of dollars that custom architects charge.

SERVICE

Once you've chosen your favorite home plan, you'll receive fast, efficient service whether you choose to mail or fax your order to us or call us toll free at 1-800-521-6797.

SATISFACTION

Our years of service to satisfied home plan buyers provide us the experience and knowledge that guarantee your satisfaction with our product and performance.

ORDER TOLL FREE 1-800-521-6797

After you've looked over our Blueprint Package and Important Extras on the following pages, simply mail the order form on page 237 or call toll free on our Blueprint Hotline: 1-800-521-6797. We're ready and eager to serve you.

Each set of blueprints is an interrelated collection of detail sheets which includes components such as floor plans, interior and exterior elevations, dimensions, cross-sections, diagrams and notations. These sheets show exactly how your house is to be built.

Among the sheets included may be:

Frontal Sheet
This artist's sketch of the exterior of the house gives you an idea of how the house will look when built and landscaped. Large ink-line floor plans show all levels of the house and provide an overview of your new home's livability, as well as a handy reference for deciding on furniture placement.

Foundation Plan
This sheet shows the foundation layout includ-

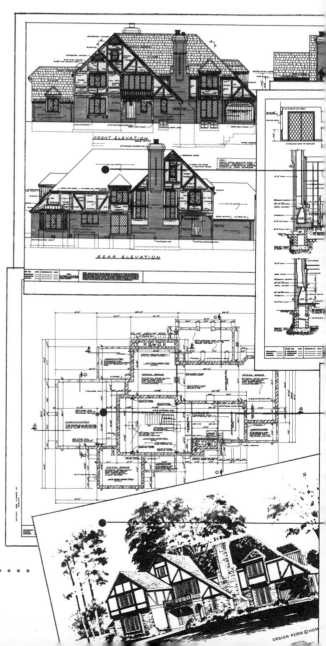

ing support walls, excavated and unexcavated areas, if any, and foundation notes. If slab construction rather the basement, the plan shows footings and details for a monolithic slab. This page, or another in the set, may include a sample plot plan for locating your house on a building site.

Detailed Floor Plans

These plans show the layout of each floor of the house. Rooms and interior spaces are carefully dimensioned and keys are given for cross-section details provided later in the plans. The positions of electrical outlets and switches are shown.

House Cross-Sections

Large-scale views show sections or cut-aways of the foundation, interior walls, exterior walls, floors, stairways and roof details. Additional cross-sections may show important changes in

floor, ceiling or roof heights or the relationship of one level to another. Extremely valuable for construction, these sections show exactly how the various parts of the house fit together.

Interior Elevations

These large-scale drawings show the design and placement of kitchen and bathroom cabinets, laundry areas, fireplaces, bookcases and other built-ins. Little "extras," such as mantelpiece and wainscoting drawings, plus moulding sections, provide details that give your home that custom touch.

Exterior Elevations

These drawings show the front, rear and sides of your house and give necessary notes on exterior materials and finishes. Particular attention is given to cornice detail, brick and stone accents or other finish items that make your home unique.

Sample Package

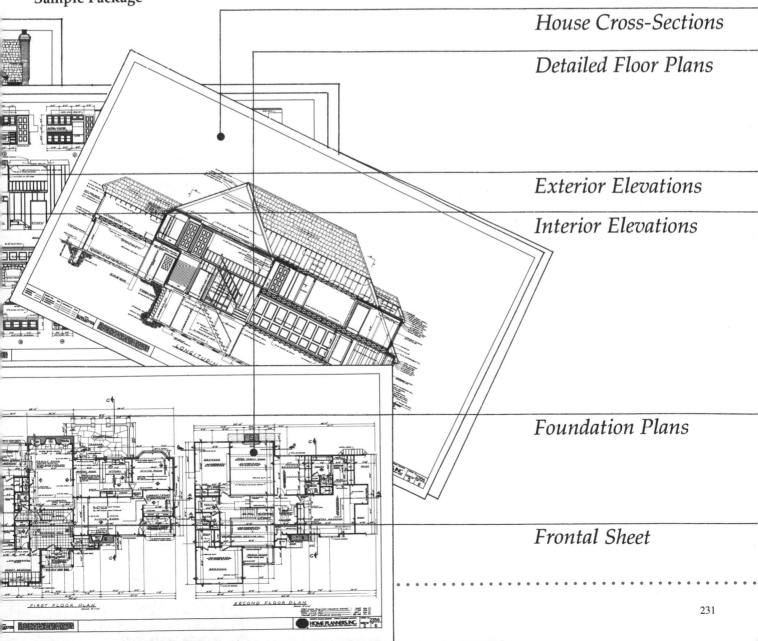

House Cross-Sections

Detailed Floor Plans

Exterior Elevations

Interior Elevations

Foundation Plans

Frontal Sheet

Important Extras To Do The Job Right!

Introducing eight important planning and construction aids developed by our professionals to help you succeed in your home-building project.

MATERIALS LIST

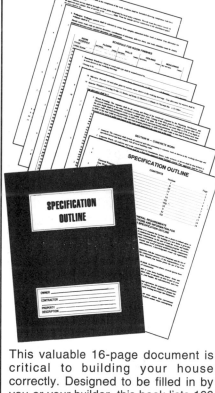

For many of the designs in our portfolio, we offer a customized materials take-off that is invaluable in planning and estimating the cost of your new home. This comprehensive list outlines the quantity, type and size of materials needed to build your house (with the exception of mechanical system items). Included are:

- framing lumber
- roofing and sheet metal
- windows and doors
- exterior sheathing material and trim
- masonry, veneer and fireplace materials
- tile and flooring materials
- kitchen and bath cabinetry
- interior drywall and trim
- rough and finish hardware
- many more items

(Note: Because of differing local codes, building methods, and availability of materials, our Materials Lists do not include mechanical materials. To obtain necessary take-offs and recommendations, consult heating, plumbing and electrical contractors. Materials Lists are not sold separately from the Blueprint Package.)

This handy list helps you or your builder cost out materials and serves as a ready reference sheet when you're compiling bids. It also provides a cross-check against the materials specified by your builder and helps coordinate the substitution of items you may need to meet local codes.

SPECIFICATION OUTLINE

This valuable 16-page document is critical to building your house correctly. Designed to be filled in by you or your builder, this book lists 166 stages or items crucial to the building process. It provides a comprehensive review of the construction process and helps in making choices of materials. When combined with the blueprints, a signed contract, and a schedule, it becomes a legal document and record for the building of your home.

QUOTE ONE™

A new service for estimating the cost of building select Home Planners designs, the Quote One™ system is available in two separate stages: The Summary Cost Report and the Detailed Cost Estimate. The Summary Cost Report shows the total cost per square foot for your chosen home in your zip-code area and then breaks that cost down into ten categories showing the costs for building materials, labor and installation. The total cost for the report (including three grades: Budget, Standard and Custom) is just $15 for one home; $25 for two and additionals are only $5. These reports allow you to evaluate your building budget and compare the costs of building a variety of homes in your area.

The Detailed Cost Estimate furnishes an even more detailed report. The material and installation (labor + equipment) cost is shown for each of

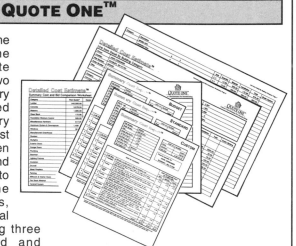

over 1,000 line items provided in the Standard grade. Space is allowed for additional estimates from contractors and subcontractors. This invaluable tool is available for a price of $100 ($110 for a Schedule E plan) which includes the price of a materials list which must be purchased at the same time.

To order these invaluable reports, use the order form on page 237 or call **1-800-521-6797**.

CONSTRUCTION INFORMATION

If you want to know more about techniques—and deal more confidently with subcontractors—we offer these useful sheets. Each set is an excellent tool that will add to your understanding of these technical subjects.

Plan-A-Home®

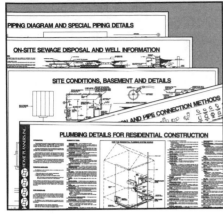

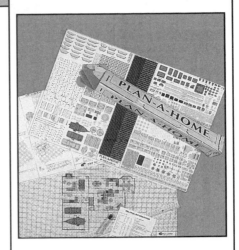

PLUMBING

The Blueprint Package includes locations for all the plumbing fixtures in your new house, including sinks, lavatories, tubs, showers, toilets, laundry trays and water heaters. However, if you want to know more about the complete plumbing system, these 24x36-inch detail sheets will prove very useful. Prepared to meet requirements of the National Plumbing Code, these six fact-filled sheets give general information on pipe schedules, fittings, sump-pump details, water-softener hookups, septic system details and much more. Color-coded sheets include a glossary of terms.

ELECTRICAL

The locations for every electrical switch, plug and outlet are shown in your Blueprint Package. However, these Electrical Details go further to take the mystery out of household electrical systems. Prepared to meet requirements of the National Electrical Code, these comprehensive 24x36-inch drawings come packed with helpful information, including wire sizing, switch-installation schematics, cable-routing details, appliance wattage, door-bell hookups, typical service panel circuitry and much more. Six sheets are bound together and color-coded for easy reference. A glossary of terms is also included.

Plan-A-Home® is an easy-to-use tool that helps you design a new home, arrange furniture in a new or existing home, or plan a remodeling project. Each package contains:

• **More than 700 reusable peel-off planning symbols** on a self-stick vinyl sheet, including walls, windows, doors, all types of furniture, kitchen components, bath fixtures and many more.

• **A reusable, transparent, 1/4-inch scale planning grid** that matches the scale of actual working drawings (1/4-inch equals 1 foot). This grid provides the basis for house layouts of up to 140x92 feet.

• **Tracing paper** and a protective sheet for copying or transferring your completed plan.

• **A felt-tip pen**, with water-soluble ink that wipes away quickly.

Plan-A-Home® lets you lay out areas as large as a 7,500 square foot, six-bedroom, seven-bath house.

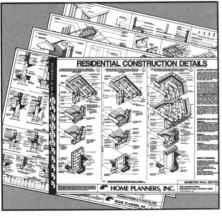

CONSTRUCTION

The Blueprint Package contains everything an experienced builder needs to construct a particular house. However, it doesn't show all the ways that houses can be built, nor does it explain alternate construction methods. To help you understand how your house will be built—and offer additional techniques—this set of drawings depicts the materials and methods used to build foundations, fireplaces, walls, floors and roofs. Where appropriate, the drawings show acceptable alternatives. These six sheets will answer questions for the advanced do-it-yourselfer or home planner.

MECHANICAL

This package contains fundamental principles and useful data that will help you make informed decisions and communicate with subcontractors about heating and cooling systems. The 24x36-inch drawings contain instructions and samples that allow you to make simple load calculations and preliminary sizing and costing analysis. Covered are today's most commonly used systems from heat pumps to solar fuel systems. The package is packed full of illustrations and diagrams to help you visualize components and how they relate to one another.

To Order, Call Toll Free
1-800-521-6797

To add these important extras to your Blueprint Package, simply indicate your choices on the order form on page 237 or call us Toll Free 1-800-521-6797 and we'll tell you more about these exciting products.

. . . . .

House Blueprint Price Schedule and Plans Index

These pages contain all the information you need to price your blueprints. In general the larger and more complicated the house, the more it costs to design and thus the higher the price we must charge for the blueprints. Remember, however, that these prices are far less than you would normally pay for the services of a licensed architect or professional designer. Custom home designs and related architectural services often cost thousands of dollars, ranging from 5% to 15% of the cost of construction. By ordering our blueprints you are potentially saving enough money to afford a larger house, or to add those "extra" amenities such as a patio, deck, swimming pool or even an upgraded kitchen or luxurious master suite.

To use the Index below, refer to the design number listed in numerical order (a helpful page reference is also given). Note the price index letter and refer to the House Blueprint Price Schedule at right for the cost of one, four or eight sets of blueprints or the cost of a reproducible sepia. Additional prices are shown for identical and reverse blueprint sets, as well as a very useful Materials List for some of the plans.

DESIGN	PRICE	PAGE	CUSTOMIZABLE	QUOTE ONE™	CALIFORNIA PLANS
▲EE2668	B	86		✓	
▲EE2683	D	87		✓	
▲EE2693	D	82		✓	✓
▲EE2694	C	24		✓	✓
▲EE2774	B	22	✓	✓	✓
▲EE2776	B	17	✓	✓	
▲EE2889	D	88		✓	✓
▲EE2908	B	23	✓	✓	
▲EE2922	D	185		✓	✓
▲EE2946	C	25	✓	✓	
▲EE2947	B	216	✓	✓	✓
▲EE2953	E	80		✓	✓
▲EE2969	C	78			
▲EE2970	D	76		✓	
▲EE2974	A	77		✓	✓
▲EE2977	D	83			
▲EE2981	D	84			
▲EE2984	E	89			
▲EE2993	D	106		✓	
▲EE3303	D	103		✓	
▲EE3309	B	79		✓	✓
▲EE3317	C	104			
▲EE3327	C	135	✓	✓	
▲EE3332	B	39		✓	✓
▲EE3337	D	102		✓	
▲EE3344	D	178		✓	
▲EE3348	C	38		✓	✓
▲EE3375	A	195		✓	
▲EE3396	C	16		✓	
▲EE3397	D	15			
▲EE3399	D	14		✓	
▲EE3429	C	190	✓	✓	
▲EE3436	C	184	✓	✓	
▲EE3460	A	217	✓	✓	
▲EE3461	B	41		✓	
▲EE3462	B	42		✓	
▲EE3463	C	214		✓	
▲EE3464	C	215		✓	
▲EE3475	D	181	✓	✓	
▲EE3480	B	179	✓	✓	
▲EE3505	E	85			
▲EE3508	C	105			
▲EE3509	E	107			
▲EE3558	C	117		✓	
▲EE3559	C	116	✓	✓	
▲EE3565	C	115			
▲EE3569	B	114		✓	
▲EE3600	C	134	✓	✓	
▲EE3602	C	180	✓		
▲EE4061	A	225			
EE6600	B	40			
EE6601	C	43			
EE6602	D	176			
EE6603	C	209			
EE6606	E	173			
EE6607	D	212			
EE6608	E	189			
EE6609	E	187			
EE6610	D	175			
EE6612	B	208			
EE6613	D	188			
EE6614	C	213			
EE6615	D	202			
EE6616	D	197			
EE6617	D	196			
EE6618	E	200			
EE6619	E	204			
EE6620	E	205			
EE6621	D	206			
EE6622	C	201			
EE6625	D	186			
EE6626	C	171			
EE6627	C	172			
EE6628	D	170			
EE6630	B	211			
EE6632	D	210			
EE6633	D	174			
EE6634	E	203			
† EE7208	E	92			
EE8001	C	198			
EE8002	C	199			
EE8003	C	149			
EE8004	D	161			
EE8005	D	147			
EE8008	C	140			
EE8011	C	141			
EE8012	C	144			
EE8013	D	127			
EE8018	D	57			
EE8024	D	125			
EE8028	D	100			
EE8029	D	160			
EE8031	E	126			
EE8036	E	101			
EE8037	D	146			
EE8038	D	163			
EE8039	D	56			
EE8041	D	124			
EE8044	D	123			
EE8045	D	123			
≠ EE8057	E	55			
EE8060	E	54			
EE8063	B	130			
EE8067	C	150			
≠ EE8070	C	131			
EE8072	C	132			
EE8074	D	133			
EE8075	D	148			
EE8077	D	128			
EE8078	E	162			
EE8910	C	136			

Before You Order . . .

Before filling out the coupon at right or calling us on our Toll-Free Blueprint Hotline, you may want to learn more about our services and products. Here's some information you will find helpful.

Quick Turnaround
We process and ship every blueprint order from our office within 48 hours. Because of this quick turnaround, we won't send a formal notice acknowledging receipt of your order.

Our Exchange Policy
Since blueprints are printed in response to your order, we cannot honor requests for refunds. However, we will exchange your entire first order for an equal number of blueprints at a price of $50 for the first set and $10 for each additional set; $70 total exchange fee for 4 sets: $100 total exchange fee for 8 sets. . . *plus* the difference in cost if exchanging for a design in a higher price bracket or *less* the difference in cost if exchanging for a design in a lower price bracket. One exchange is allowed within a year of purchase date. **(Sepias are not exchangeable. No exchanges can be made for the California Engineered Plans since they are tailored to your specific building site.)** All sets from the first order must be returned before the exchange can take place. Please add $10 for postage and handling via ground service; $20 via 2nd Day Air.

About Reverse Blueprints
If you want to build in reverse of the plan as shown, we will include an extra set of reverse blueprints (mirror image) for an additional fee of $50. Lettering and dimensions will appear backward. Right-reading reverses of Home Customizer® plans are available. Call 1-800-521-6797, ext. 800 for more details.

Modifying or Customizing Our Plans
With such a great selection of homes, you are bound to find the one that suits you. However, if you need to make alterations to a design that is customizable, you need only order our Customizer® kit or call our Customization representative at 1-800-521-6797, ext. 800 to get you started. We strongly suggest you order sepias if you decide to revise non-Customizable plans significantly.

Architectural and Engineering Seals
Some cities and states are now requiring that a licensed architect or engineer review and "seal" your blueprints prior to building due to local or regional concerns over energy consumption, safety codes, seismic ratings or other factors. For this reason, it may be necessary to talk to a local professional to have your plans reviewed. In some cases, Home Planners can seal your plans through our Customization Service. Call 1-800-521-6797, ext. 800 for more details.

Compliance with Local Codes and Regulations
At the time of creation, our plans are drawn to specifications published by the Building Officials and Code Administrators (BOCA) International, Inc.; the Southern Building Code Congress (SBCCI) International, Inc.; the International Conference of Building Officials; or the Council of American Building Officials (CABO). Our plans are designed to meet or exceed national building standards. Some states, counties and municipalities have their own codes, zoning requirements and building regulations. Before building, contact your local building authorities to make sure you comply with local ordinances and codes, including obtaining any necessary permits or inspections as building progresses. In some cases, minor modifications to your plans by your builder, architect or designer may be required to meet local conditions and requirements. Home Planners may be able to make these changes to Home Customizer® plans providing you supply all pertinent information from your local building authorities.

Foundation and Exterior Wall Changes
Most of our plans are drawn with either a full or partial basement foundation. Depending on your specific climate or regional building practices, you may wish to change this basement to a slab or crawlspace. Most professional contractors and builders can easily adapt your plans to alternate foundation types. Likewise, most can easily change 2x4 wall construction to 2x6, or vice versa. For Home Customizer® plans, Home Planners can easily make the changes for you.

How Many Blueprints Do You Need?
A single set of blueprints is sufficient to study a home in greater detail. However, if you are planning to obtain cost estimates from a contractor or subcontractors—or if you are planning to build immediately—you will need more sets. Because additional sets are cheaper when ordered in quantity with the original order, make sure you order enough blueprints to satisfy all requirements. The following checklist will help you determine how many you need:

_____ Owner

_____ Builder (generally requires at least three sets; one as a legal document, one to use during inspections, and at least one to give to subcontractors)

_____ Local Building Department (often requires two sets)

_____ Mortgage Lender (usually one set for a conventional loan; three sets for FHA or VA loans)

_____ TOTAL NUMBER OF SETS

Have You Seen Our Newest Designs?

Home Planners is one of the country's most active home design firms, creating nearly 100 new plans each year. At least 50 of our latest creations are featured in each edition of our New Design Portfolio. You may have received a copy with your latest purchase by mail. If not, or if you purchased this book from a local retailer, just return the coupon below for your FREE copy. Make sure you consider the very latest of what Home Planners has to offer.

Yes! Please send my FREE copy of your latest New Design Portfolio.

Name _____

Address _____

City _____ State _____ Zip _____

HOME PLANNERS, INC.
3275 West Ina Road, Suite 110,
Tucson, Arizona 85741

Order Form Key

TB36NDP

Canadian Customers
Order Toll-Free 1-800-561-4169
For faster service and plans that are modified for building in Canada, customers may now call in orders directly to our Canadian supplier of plans and charge the purchase to a charge card. Or, you may complete the order form at right, adding 30% to all prices and mail in Canadian funds to:

The Plan Centre 20 Cedar Street North
Kitchener, Ontario N2H 2W8

By FAX: Copy the Order Form at right and send it via our Canadian FAX line: 1-519-743-1282.

The Home Customizer®

Many of the plans in this book are customizable through our Home Customizer® service. Look for this symbol 🏠 on the pages of home designs. It indicates that the plan on that page is part of The Home Customizer® service.

Some changes to customizable plans that can be made include:

- exterior elevation changes
- kitchen and bath modifications
- roof, wall and foundation changes
- room additions
- and much more!

If the plan you have chosen to build is one of our customizable homes, you can easily order the Home Customizer® kit to start on the path to making your alterations. The kit, priced at only $29.95, may be ordered at the same time you order your blueprint package by calling our toll-free number or using the order blank at right. Or you can wait until you receive your blueprints, spend some time studying them and then order the kit by phone, FAX or mail. If you then decide to proceed with the customizing service, the $29.95 price of the kit will be refunded to you after your customization order is received. The Home Customizer® kit includes:

- instruction book with examples
- architectural scale
- clear acetate work film
- erasable red marker
- removable correction tape
- ¼" scale furniture cutouts
- 1 set of Customizable Drawings with floor plans and elevations

The service is easy, fast and *affordable*. Because we know and work with our plans and have them available on state-of-the-art computer systems, we can make the changes efficiently at prices much lower than those charged by normal architectural or drafting services. In addition, you'll be getting custom changes directly from Home Planners—the company whose dedication to excellence and long-standing professional experience are well recognized in the industry.

Call now to learn more about how simple it can be to have the *custom home* you've always wanted.

California Customers!!

For our customers in California, we now offer California Engineered Plans (CEP) and California Stock Plans (CSP) to help in meeting the strict California building codes. Check Plan Index for homes that are available through this new service or call 1-800-521-6797 for more information about the availability of the service and prices.

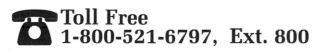

☎ **Toll Free**
1-800-521-6797, Ext. 800

BLUEPRINTS ARE NOT RETURNABLE

ORDER FORM

HOME PLANNERS, INC., 3275 WEST INA ROAD
SUITE 110, TUCSON, ARIZONA 85741

THE BASIC BLUEPRINT PACKAGE

Rush me the following (please refer to the Plans Index and Price Schedule in this section):

_____ Set(s) of blueprints for plan number(s) _____. $_____

_____ Set(s) of sepias for plan number(s) _____. $_____

_____ Additional identical blueprints in same order @ $50 per set. $_____

_____ Reverse blueprints @ $50 per set. $_____

_____ Home Customizer® Kit(s) for Plan(s)_____
@ $29.95 per kit. $_____

IMPORTANT EXTRAS

Rush me the following:

_____ Materials List: Home Planners' Designs (Not available for CEP service)
@ $40 Schedule A-D; $50 Schedule E; $50 Larry Belk's Designs;
$75 Design Basics' Designs; $40 Donald Gardner's Designs. $_____

_____ Quote One™ Summary Cost Report @ $15 for 1, $25 for 2,
$5 for each additional, for plans _____. $_____

_____ Quote One™ Detailed Cost Estimate @ $100 Schedule A-D;
$110 Schedule E for plan_____. $_____
(must be purchased with Materials List and Blueprints set)

_____ Specification Outlines @ $10 each. $_____

_____ Detail Sets @ $14.95 each; any two for $22.95; any three
for $29.95; all four for $39.95 (save $19.85). $_____
❏ Plumbing ❏ Electrical ❏ Construction ❏ Mechanical
(These helpful details provide general construction
advice and are not specific to any single plan.)

_____ Plan-A-Home® @ $29.95 each. $_____

SUB-TOTAL $_____

POSTAGE AND HANDLING	1-3 sets	4+ sets
DELIVERY (Requires street address - No P.O. Boxes)		
•Regular Service (Allow 4-6 days delivery)	❏ $8.00	❏ $10.00
•2nd Day Air (Allow 2-3 days delivery)	❏ $12.00	❏ $20.00
•Next Day Air (Allow 1 day delivery)	❏ $22.00	❏ $30.00
POST OFFICE DELIVERY	❏ $10.00	❏ $14.00
If no street address available. (Allow 4-6 days delivery)		
OVERSEAS DELIVERY		
Note: All delivery times are from date Blueprint Package is shipped.	fax, phone or mail for quote	

POSTAGE (From shaded box above) $_____

SALES TAX (Arizona residents add 5% sales tax; Michigan residents add 6% sales tax.) $_____

TOTAL (Sub-total, postage, and tax) $_____

YOUR ADDRESS (please print)

Name _____

Street _____

City _____State_____Zip _____

Daytime telephone number (_____) _____

FOR CREDIT CARD ORDERS ONLY

Please fill in the information below:

Credit card number _____

Exp. Date: Month/Year _____

Check one ❏ Visa ❏ MasterCard ❏ Discover Card

Signature _____

Please check appropriate box: ❏ Licensed Builder-Contractor
❏ Home Owner

☎ **ORDER TOLL FREE**
1-800-521-6797 or
602-297-8200

Order Form Key

TB36BP

Additional Plans Books

1. ENCYCLOPEDIA OF HOME DESIGNS (EN) Our best collection of plans is now bigger and better than ever! Over 500 plans organized by architectural category. Includes all types and styles. The most comprehensive plan book ever. 352 pages. $9.95 ($12.95 Can.)

2. THE ESSENTIAL GUIDE TO TRADITIONAL HOMES (ET) Over 400 traditional homes in one special volume. American and European styles from Farmhouses to Norman French. Best sellers shown in color photographs and renderings. 304 pages. $9.95 ($12.95 Can.)

3. THE ESSENTIAL GUIDE TO CONTEMPORARY HOMES (EC) More than 340 contemporary designs from Northwest Contemporary to Post-Modern Victorian. Color section of best sellers; two-color illustrations throughout. 304 pages. $9.95 ($12.95 Can.)

4. AFFORDABLE HOME PLANS (AH) For the prospective home builder with a modest or medium budget. Features 430 one-, 1½-, two-story and multi-level homes in a wealth of styles. Cost-saving ideas for the budget-conscious included. 320 pages. $8.95 ($11.95 Can.)

5. LUXURY DREAM HOMES (LD2) New Edition! Completely updated with 50% new designs, this exciting collection of 154 designs now contains the home you've been waiting for! 192 pages. $14.95 ($18.95 Can.)

6. ONE-STORY HOMES (V1) A collection of 470 homes to suit a range of budgets in one-story living. All popular styles, including Cape Cod, Southwestern, Tudor and French. 384 pages. $9.95 ($12.95 Can.)

7. TWO-STORY HOMES (V2) 478 plans for all budgets in a wealth of styles: Tudors, Salt-boxes, Farmhouses, Victorians, Georgians, Contemporaries and more. 416 pages. $9.95 ($12.95 Can.)

8. MULTI-LEVEL AND HILLSIDE HOMES (V3) 312 distinctive styles for both flat and sloping sites. Includes exposed lower levels, open staircases, balconies, decks and terraces. 320 pages. $6.95 ($9.95 Can.)

9. VACATION AND SECOND HOMES (V4) 258 ideal plans for a favorite vacation spot, perfect retirement or starter home. Includes cottages, chalets and one-, 1½-, two-story, and multi-level homes. 256 pages. $5.95 ($7.95 Can.)

10. STARTER HOMES (ST) 200 easy-to-build plans—from simple do-it-yourself houses to more stylish contemporary designs. Features the all-new Economy Building Series. 224 pages. $6.95 ($9.95 Can.)

11. EMPTY-NESTER HOMES (EP) Perfect for empty-nesters, retirees and couples without children. These 206 plans feature sophisticated designs and upgraded amenities. 224 pages. $6.95 ($9.95 Can.)

12. 200 FAMILY-FAVORED HOME PLANS (FF) Expanded designs for expanding families! Seven top designers present move-up homes combining beautiful styling with more living space. 224 pages. $7.95 ($10.95 Can.)

13. 200 NARROW-LOT HOME PLANS (NL) The largest collection ever of homes that meet the unique challenges of today's narrow lots. Up to 3,000 square feet at less than 60-ft. widths! 224 pages. $7.95 ($10.95 Can.)

14. 200 FARMHOUSE AND COUNTRY HOME PLANS (FH) Styles and sizes to match every taste and budget, from Classic Farmhouses to Country Capes and Cottages. Expertly drawn floor plans and renderings enhance the sections. 224 pages. $7.95 ($10.95 Can.)

15. 200 BUDGET-SMART HOME PLANS (BS) The definitive source for the home builder with a limited budget—have your home and enjoy it too! Amenity-laden homes, in many sizes and styles, can all be built from our plans. 224 pages. $7.95 ($10.95 Can.)

16. MOST POPULAR HOME DESIGNS (MP) 400 of our customers' favorites! One-story, 1½-story, two-story and multi-level homes in a variety of styles. Designs feature-laden with lounges, clutter rooms, media rooms and more. 304 pages. $9.95 ($12.95 Can.)

17. NEW ENGLAND SAMPLER (NES) New England architecture—inside and out! 264 Cape Cods, Saltboxes, Garrisons, Georgians and other Colonial classics—many developed for *Colonial Homes* magazine. 200 interior illustrations included. 384 pages. $14.95 ($18.95 Can.)

18. VICTORIAN DREAM HOMES (VDH) 160 Victorian and Farmhouse designs by three master designers. Victorian style from Second Empire homes through the Queen Anne and Folk Victorian era. Beautiful renderings with modern floor plans. 192 pages. $12.95 ($16.95 Can.)

19. WESTERN HOME PLANS (WH) Over 215 home plans from Spanish Mission and Monterey to Northwest Chateau and San Francisco Victorian. Historical notes trace the background and geographical incidence of each style. 208 pages. $8.95 ($11.95 Can.)

20. THE HOME REMODELER (HR) A revolutionary book of 31 remodeling plans backed by complete construction-ready blueprints and materials lists. Kitchens, baths, master bedrooms and much more. Ideas, advice, suggestions. 112 pages. $7.95 ($10.95 Can.)

21. DECK PLANNER (DP) 25 practical plans and details for decks the do-it-yourselfer can actually build. How-to data and project starters for a variety of decks. Construction details available separately. 112 pages. $7.95 ($10.95 Can.)

22. THE HOME LANDSCAPER (HL) 55 fabulous front and backyard plans that even the do-it-yourselfer can master. Complete construction blueprints and regionalized plant lists available for each design. 208 pages. $12.95 ($16.95 Can.)

TO ORDER BOOKS BY PHONE
1-800-322-6797

CANADIAN CUSTOMERS: Order books toll-free: 1-800-561-4169. Or, complete this form, using Canadian prices and adding postage, and mail with Canadian funds to: The Plan Centre, 20 Cedar Street North, Kitchener Ont. N2H 2W8. FAX: 1-519-743-1282.

23. THE BACKYARD LANDSCAPER (BYL) Sequel to *The Home Landscaper*, contains 40 professionally designed plans for backyards. Do yourself or contract out. Complete construction blueprints and regionalized plant lists available. 160 pages. $12.95 ($16.95 Can.)

- -

Additional Books Order Form

To order your Home Planners books, just check the box of the book numbered below and complete the coupon. We will process your order and ship it from our office within 48 hours. Send coupon and check (in U.S. funds) to: Home Planners, Inc, 3275 W. Ina Rd., Ste.110, Dept. BK, Tucson, AZ 85741

ES! Please send me the design books I've indicated:

1:	**Encyclopedia of Home Designs (EN)**	$9.95 ($12.95 Can.)
2:	**403 Traditional Home Plans (ET)**	$9.95 ($12.95 Can.)
3:	**340 Contemporary Home Plans (EC)**	$9.95 ($12.95 Can.)
4:	**Affordable Home Plans (AH)**	$8.95 ($11.95 Can.)
5:	**Luxury Dream Homes (LD2)**	$14.95 ($18.95 Can.)
6:	**One-Story Homes (V1)**	$9.95 ($12.95 Can.)
7:	**Two-Story Homes (V2)**	$9.95 ($12.95 Can.)
8:	**Multi-Level & Hillside Homes (V3)**	$6.95 ($9.95 Can.)
9:	**Vacation & Second Homes (V4)**	$5.95 ($7.95 Can.)
10:	**Starter Homes (ST)**	$6.95 ($9.95 Can.)
11:	**Empty-Nester Homes (EP)**	$6.95 ($9.95 Can.)
12:	**200 Family-Favored Home Plans (FF)**	$7.95 ($10.95 Can.)
13:	**200 Narrow-Lot Home Plans (NL)**	$7.95 ($10.95 Can.)
14:	**200 Farmhouse & Country Home Plans (FH)**	$7.95 ($10.95 Can.)
15:	**200 Budget-Smart Home Plans (BS)**	$7.95 ($10.95 Can.)
16:	**400 Most Popular Home Designs (MP)**	$9.95 ($12.95 Can.)
17:	**New England Sampler (NES)**	$14.95 ($18.95 Can.)
18:	**Victorian Dream Homes (VDH)**	$12.95 ($16.95 Can.)
19:	**Western Home Plans (WH)**	$8.95 ($11.95 Can.)
20:	**The Home Remodeler (HR)**	$7.95 ($10.95 Can.)
21:	**Deck Planner (DP)**	$7.95 ($10.95 Can.)
22:	**The Home Landscaper (HL)**	$12.95 ($16.95 Can.)
23:	**The Backyard Landscaper (BYL)**	$12.95 ($16.95 Can.)

Home Planners, Inc.
3275 W Ina Road, Suite 110, Dept. BK, Tucson, AZ 85741

Additional Books Sub-Total	$_____
ADD Postage and Handling	$ 3.00
Ariz. residents add 5% Sales Tax; Mich. residents add 6% Sales Tax	$_____
YOUR TOTAL (Sub-Total, Postage/Handling, Tax)	$_____

YOUR ADDRESS (Please print)

Name _____

Street _____

City _____ State _____ Zip _____

Phone (_____) _____—_____

YOUR PAYMENT
Check one: ☐ Check ☐ Visa ☐ MasterCard ☐ Discover Card
Required credit card information:

Credit Card Number _____

Expiration Date (Month/Year) _____ / _____

Signature Required_____

TB36BK

239

Design EE9621 p.6

OVER 3 MILLION BLUEPRINTS SOLD

"We instructed our builder to follow the plans including all of the many details which make this house so elegant... Our home is a fine example of the results one can achieve by purchasing and following the plans which you offer... Everyone who has seen it has assured us that it belongs in 'a picture book.' I truly mean it when I say that my home 'is a DREAM HOUSE.'"

S.P.
Anderson, SC

"We have had a steady stream of visitors, many of whom tell us this is the most beautiful home they've seen. Everyone is amazed at the layout and remarks on how unique it is. Our real estate attorney, who is a Chicago dweller and who deals with highly valued properties, told me this is the only suburban home he has seen that he would want to live in."

W. & P.S.
Flossmoor, IL

"Your blueprints saved us a great deal of money. I acted as the general contractor and we did a lot of the work ourselves. We probably built it for half the cost! We are thinking about more plans for another home. I purchased a competitor's book but my husband wants only your plans!"

K.M.
Grovetown, GA

"We are very happy with the product of our efforts. The neighbors and passersby appreciate what we have created. We have had many people stop by to discuss our house and kindly praise it as being the nicest house in our area of new construction. We have even had one person stop and make us an unsolicited offer to buy the house for much more than we have invested in it."

K. & L.S.
Bolingbrook, IL

"The traffic going past our house is unbelievable. On several occasions, we have heard that it is the 'prettiest house in Batvia.' Also, when meeting someone new and mentioning what street we live on, quite often we're told, 'Oh, you're the one in the yellow house with the wrap-around porch! I love it!'"

A.W.
Batvia, NY

"I have been involved in the building trades my entire life... Since building our home we have built two other homes for other families. Their plans from local professional architects were not nearly as good as yours. For that reason we are ordering additional plan books from you."

T.F.
Kingston, WA

"The blueprints we received from you were of excellent quality and provided us with exactly what we needed to get our successful home-building project underway. We appreciate your invaluable role in our home-building effort."

T.A.
Concord, TN